The Practices of Literary Translation
Constraints and Creativity

Edited by

Jean Boase-Beier and Michael Holman

ST JEROME
PUBLISHING

First published 1998 by

St. Jerome Publishing
2 Maple Road West, Brooklands
Manchester, M23 9HH, United Kingdom
Fax +44 161 905 3498
stjerome@compuserve.com
http://www.mcc.ac.uk/stjerome

ISBN 1-900650-19-3

Printed and bound in Great Britain by
Biddles Limited, Guildford, Surrey, UK

Cover design by Steve Fieldhouse, Oldham, UK (+44 161 620 2263)

British Library Cataloguing in Publication Data
A catalogue record of this book is available from the British Library.

In memory of Jon Silkin
an outstanding poet
and a true friend of translation

Acknowledgements

These essays have been developed from papers presented at the Second International Colloquium organized by the Institute of Translation and Interpreting Sub-Committee on Literary Translation in Higher Education, held at UEA, Norwich in September 1996. We would like to express our sincere thanks to our fellow members on the Committee – Peter Bush, Kirsten Malmkjær, Jenefer Coates, Nicholas Round and Terry Hale – who acted as the Editorial Board in the early stages of this publication. Our thanks also go to the Arts Council of England for their support of the Colloquium and this publication. We are also especially grateful to Kathleen Lane for the many hours she has spent typing, revising and checking the text, chasing up references and removing inconsistencies. Without her invaluable help this volume would have taken far longer to complete. It goes without saying that the editors bear full responsibility for any remaining editorial deficiencies.

Credits

The Living Torch and *Unluck* are taken from *Baudelaire: Vol I, The Complete Verse*, translated by Francis Scarfe, published by Anvil Press Poetry in 1986.

Printemps et automne and *Réveil: je sens le chu du noir* are taken from *Gerard Manley Hopkins: Poèms accompagnés de dessins et proses*, chosen and translated by Pierre Leyris, published by Éditions du Seuil in 1980; *Je m'éveille et palpe L'obscur* is taken from *Gerard Manley Hopkins: Reliquiae*, translated by Pierre Leyris, published by Éditions du Seuil in 1957.

Contents

1   Introduction
Writing, Rewriting and Translation
Through Constraint to Creativity

MICHAEL HOLMAN AND JEAN BOASE-BEIER

'Oui, l'œuvre sort plus belle
D'une forme au travail
      Rebelle,
Vers, marbre, onyx, émail.

Point de contraintes fausses!
Mais que pour marcher droit
      Tu chausses,
Muse, un cothurne étroit.

(Yes, art emerges more
Beautiful from forms that
      Resist,
Verse, marble, onyx, enamel.

No false constraints, o Muse!
But to walk straight, lace
      Tight
Your narrow shoe.)

      * * * *

Fi du rhythme commode,
Comme un soulier trop grand,
      Du mode
Que tout pied quitte et prend!'

(Fi the easy rhythm,
The roomy shoe, the sloppy fit
      Of fashion
Where every foot slips out and in.)

      (Gautier 1884:223)

1. Creativity and Writing

There are two assumptions that people commonly make when they speak of translation in contrast to original writing. One is that the translator is subject to constraints which do not apply to the original author. The other is that the act of translation is by nature less creative than the act of writing an original work.

Things are not quite so simple, however. The nature of creativity is in itself a very complex matter; it has frequently been suggested, as Pinker (1997:361) points out, that creativity simply cannot have a natural explanation, while on the other hand recent researchers such as Gibbs (1994:7) have maintained that creative thought processes are the result of conceptual constraints. In the absence of suitable tools for measuring creativity, the assumption of differences between original writing and translation is often based on little more than an intuition that translation is derivative in a way original writing is not.

But this is a very tricky assumption, for it takes for granted the supremacy of the original, as though it were in a position of unquestioned authority. Yet much recent work in both literary criticism and translation studies has challenged the notion of the authoritative original; Derrida, for example, echoing Benjamin's comment of 1923 (reprinted in Benjamin 1972), said that translation was "a moment in the growth of the original, which will complete itself *in* enlarging itself" (quoted in Venuti 1992:7). Especially in translation studies, at least two distinct reasons for this have emerged. One is the way in which all texts assimilate, borrow, imitate and rewrite other material. Thus it is not only translation which is an act of "rewriting" (Lefevere 1992b) and therefore a "political act" (Álvarez & Vidal 1996) of interpretation and transmission, but original writing, too, is rewriting. We shall return to these issues below, and many of the papers in this volume, in particular those by Jenefer Coates, Juan Zaro, Emily Salines and Kate Sturge, examine them in detail. The second main reason for questioning the notion of "original" relates to the view that art is, by its very nature, derivative. Valéry (1959:75) for example, maintained that all writing was translation, and Barnstone (1993:19), echoing Schlegel, elaborates on this view: for him, all mental activity which involves the search for meaning is translational activity. Looked at thus, as a transfer of material between media, it is possible to view painting, sculpture or writing as a translation of a mental idea into a visual, concrete image and, going back one stage further, to view the process of forming mental images as a translation from perception of external reality to conceptual knowledge. In this sense a painting or a piece of writing has already undergone several transformations before it reaches its target recipient and will undergo more before the recipient can interpret it. If the creation and appreciation of art in general are to be seen as involving so many translational transformations, does then the notion of translation in a specific sense as a transfer of literary material between languages cease to be meaningful?

The answer to this question is clearly negative. For whatever transformations the substance of a text has undergone before becoming a text, it must undergo a further one, and a much more tangible one at that, in the process of its transfer from one language to another. For this reason literary translation has been compared, for example by Tytler (in Lefevere 1992b:132), to making a copy of a painting. Though this is a useful metaphor, in that it suggests that the transfer of one already concretized meaning into another medium can be measured in terms of likeness, faithfulness or equivalence, like all such metaphors it is only partially valid, because the notions of faithfulness and equivalence are

themselves open to question. If the original is seen as something whose authority is in doubt, then equivalence to the original needs to be examined from the
point of view of multiple potential equivalences. And it is also problematic to
apply the notion of faithfulness to a translation of an original and not to the
original's representation of reality, an issue to which we return below.

An examination of the work of many writers and translators will, as the
essays in this volume show, cast doubt upon the idea that a clear distinction
between original and translation can be made, whether as process or as product, and will inevitably lead to the conclusion that terms such as "faithfulness"
or "creativity" or indeed "translation" are anything but clear-cut. A well-known
illustration of this blurring of the intuitive distinction between original writing
and translation can be seen in Edward Fitzgerald's recreation of the work of
Omar Khayyám, the eleventh-century Persian philosopher and poet (see Fitzgerald nd). In spite of the presence of several versions by Fitzgerald, as well as
extensive comment by himself and others on the process of translating Khayyám's *Rubáiyát*, these poems have often been regarded as original works by
Fitzgerald. An even more famous example is the Bible, available to the vast
majority of its readers worldwide only in translation, but rarely regarded as
anything other than an original work in the particular language of the individual reader in question. Ted Hughes' *Tales from Ovid* (1997) is another case
in point. The *Metamorphoses*, upon which Hughes' translations are based, was
itself a collection of myths and stories made by Ovid and adapted, as Hughes
points out in the introduction to the book, according to Ovid's taste and to his
purpose in showing human action transformed by passion to mythical status.
The tales, in an iconic act of metamorphosis, cut, augment and mould the ancient material into transformation stories which others, in their turn, have freely
appropriated. Both Chaucer and Shakespeare, as Hughes remarks, borrowed
freely from Ovid, often translating, transforming or adapting what Ovid had
earlier adapted. Hughes himself produced a translation of the *Metamophorses*
so compellingly Hughes-like that it won the Whitbread Award, not normally
given for translations. Nevertheless, we tend to view Hughes' version of Ovid's
Pyramus and Thisbe as a translation, but not Shakespeare's in *A Midsummer
Night's Dream.* We might well ask who were the translators here and what is
the distinction between translation and writing?

In her article on Baudelaire in this book, Salines discusses how his work
included a huge range of rewriting from close translation to free adaptation.
For Baudelaire, translation was inherent in both writing and rewriting, and
Salines, in examining these issues, invites us to question the distinction. Barnstone (1993:95) refers to *The Waste Land* (1971) as "Eliot's great contemporary
salad", composed as it was from "every element of translation". Ovid, Shakespeare, Baudelaire, Eliot; these merely provide examples of what all writers
do, namely integrate other people's writing into their own.

Allusion, too, is a process of integrating other writing, taking particular elements of another work and making explicit or implicit reference to them, building

these references into the context of the new work. It is thus different from source-borrowing or other types of reference, which are acknowledged and kept fairly separate from the text: Joyce's *Ulysses* (1960) makes reference to the hero of the *Odyssey* and the novel is intended to echo in structure that of Homer's epic. Graham Swift's *Last Orders* (1996) clearly makes allusion in structure and to some extent in content to Faulkner's *As I Lay Dying* (1930), a fact which caused it, somewhat incredibly, to be accused of plagiarism by disgruntled critics who had failed at first to recognize the allusion. Allusion, in being unacknowledged and fully integrated, would appear to differ from translation or adaptation, which nowadays almost always give sources in order to avoid the accusation of plagiarism. Yet the distinction between translation and other types of borrowing is rarely clear-cut. In Shakespeare's case, it has generally been assumed not to matter. Yet, as the example of Graham Swift shows, we have become unused to tacit reference, and questions of ownership have taken on an obsessive value, to the extent that the original often assumes paramount importance, reducing translation to an invisible, insubstantial or mechanical act, rendered merely in service to what is perceived as the original (Venuti 1995:1). Yet at the same time, as we have noted earlier, the whole notion of the stability of the original is being called into question. It is for this reason that an examination of the practices of writers and translators is essential.

Original writing and translation, so it seems, have in common that they dismantle material and re-shape it into other material, whereby that transformation may involve change of medium (reality into art, play into opera, novel into film, painting into poem) or change of language, as in translation. But what of that other aspect of writing and translation: the constraints to which they are subject? As we suggested at the beginning of this essay, translation tends to be seen as more heavily constrained than original writing. An author, it seems, can write as he or she wishes, can transform reality as seems appropriate, and create whatever worlds are desired, but a translator has to write in relation to an existing work. Yet is this entirely true? Is the writer completely free to transform reality as he or she wants? At a recent writers' round table on fiction, a discussion arose as to whether it was acceptable that William Golding, in *Lord of the Flies* (1962), included erroneous detail about the lighting of a fire with a magnifying glass. The complaint has often been made that he here fails to echo reality, as though it were a constraint on original writing that he must do so. And yet, if we accept that disbelief is suspended when we read a work of literature, that we in fact enter the world created by the author, how is it that we cannot then accept things inconsistent with real life? If, in keeping with Levin's (1977) view of metaphor, we accept metaphors such as "The man is a wolf" or "The trees wore green gloves" not as mere implicit comparisons but as descriptions of a world in which such things are possible, then why can we not accept other apparent clashes with our world knowledge?

The answer to this question is connected to the reason why translation is often perceived as "wrong" in certain elements, rather than merely as a reflection of one of a number of possible interpretations of the original work. Leaving aside straightforward errors, a translation will be perceived as "wrong" by a particular reader if it does not fit the image that the reader prefers to associate with the original text. This judgement usually comes about at a moment in the text which jars, which draws us away from our immersion in the fictional or poetic world created by the work, and makes us realize we are reading a work created of words. If an author writes something which does not reflect reality as most of us perceive it, as readers we feel jolted back to reality and the illusion is lost. Similarly in translation, the moment an element in the text draws attention to itself, it will draw the reader's attention to the fact not only that this is a translation but, consequently, that it is a piece of writing. Both original writing and translation are thus often constrained by the need to preserve illusion, though this is not a characteristic of all writing: Brecht, Joyce, Meredith, Shakespeare and many others have specifically drawn attention to the text itself and thus to its status as an instrument for creating the illusion of reality.

Original writing is also further constrained by literary tradition. The concept of unity, just to name one familiar example, has, since Plato, been an important constraint on drama, where it has often manifested itself as a set of rules about time, place and action, and on poetry, where it is often used to mean a reconciliation of meaning and form. Other constraints dictate that a particular type of poem has a certain number of lines, or stressed syllables per line, or rhymes in particular places. These rules differ from one culture to another. Thus an English or German poem will be constrained by the requirements of metre based on stressed syllables, whereas Greek or Japanese poetry uses the overall number of syllables to determine the metrical pattern. Or again, French dramatic and narrative poetry has generally used alexandrines, whereas English, with a few exceptions such as Spenser and Bridges, has not. In translation, such mismatching will give rise to some of the most difficult aspects of the translator's task; a fact which is explored in the next section.

Original writing may also be constrained by prevailing political views, or, more substantially, by censorship. As both Claudine Tourniaire and Cormac Ó Cuilleanáin show in their essays, authors may avoid certain topics, views or expressions, in order to ensure their work is published. It may also be constrained by the knowledge the author assumes its audience will have. Will they be well-read enough to pick up allusion, educated enough to understand scientific explanation, or, indeed, interested enough to engage with a complex text?

Writing is also constrained by the linguistic characteristics of its medium. These may, for example, be phonological: certain sounds appear in certain places, some words rhyme and others do not, sound can be an iconic echo of reality as it is in sound symbolism such as onomatopoeia or phonaesthesia. However, patterns formed from phonological elements are themselves subject to lexical, syntactic, semantic and stylistic conventions. Thus onomatopoeia is conventionalized: we say that an explosion makes a "bang", though from the point of view of echoing sound, we could just as well say a "beng" or a "bong", but we do not. Stylistic rules dictate that the concept of rhyme must contain an element of contrast: "bit" rhymes with "hit", but two "bits" do not rhyme. Syntactic constraints ensure that words are placed in a particular order, that sentences have a subject, that subjects and verbs agree, or that, in highly inflected languages, there are other types of agreement, such as that between adjectives and nouns.

All in all, then, original writers do not simply write what they want: they are bound by all manner of constraints: political, social, poetic and linguistic, as well as the constraints of the text itself, which creates a context potentially confining and determining the form and meaning of every utterance.

It is not sufficient, though, to see original writing as the result of creativity which is subject to constraint. For in fact creativity is often intimately tied to constraint, it is a response to it, it is enhanced by it. Indeed, it could be maintained, as Paul Valéry, for example, does in his discussion of prescription in art (1957:1305), that "rules may ... in some cases have creative qualities, suggesting ideas which would never have arisen in their absence". Constraint, in this sense, can be seen as one of the main sources of creativity.

So, for example, Tourniaire explains how the poetry of Galanaki arose out of a need to evade political censorship. Poetry, a compressed linguistic structure, which invites readers to fill gaps with their own knowledge, is an ideal vehicle for communicating what is forbidden. Ambiguity, the device by which multiple pathways to different meanings are created, is the device most appropriate to triggering personal and varied interpretations. Both Tourniaire and Ó Cuilleanáin show how, by saying what is *not* meant, an author can trigger in the reader a response to what is meant, or create space for the reader's own interpretation.

But it is not merely social and political constraints which engender a creative response; it could be argued that, especially in poetry, the art is largely the result of a response to poetic and linguistic constraint. Poetic language can thus be seen as a language marked by specific characteristics which include the stretching of standard language by creative deviation from its norms. According to this view, put forward for example by the Prague School Linguists such as Mukařovský (1964), and by many later writers, for example Boase-Beier (1987), poetic figures such as metaphor and repetition operate in creative opposition to their severely constrained and conventionalized counterparts in standard language. But poetic language, too, has norms, and strict forms, such as the sonnet, invite innovation and variation. A concept such as rhyme, which is simply the presence in two syllables, appearing in different words, of identical vowels and final consonants, is the basis for other types of phonological parallelism such as half-rhyme, slant rhyme, reverse rhyme and assonance, all of which may be used to achieve particular effects in part based on their contrast to full rhyme. Phyllis Gaffney, in her article on Leyris' translations of Hopkins, discusses his deviations, through the use of idiosyncratic compounds and violations of syntax and morphology, from both standard English and from classical forms of poetry. And iconicity, the mirroring of meaning in form, could be seen as both the essential characteristic of poetic language and its most stringent constraint. When critics, authors, or linguists such as Beckett (1976) or Ross (1980) say that a poem does what it says, they are referring to this particular characteristic. Yet in linguistic terms it is a characteristic which adds a heavy burden of constraint to what, since Saussure (1916), has generally been recognized as an arbitrary connection between meaning and form. In an arbitrary form-meaning relationship lexical choice is a matter for the author, who is constrained only by the existing inventory of lexical items, as well as morphological rules allowing for the creation of new ones. However, if words or word-patterns are actually to mimic what they denote, then some of the freedom of arbitrary association is forfeited. So, when Hopkins (1963:40) used the compound *cuckoo-echoing*, he could not simply have chosen some other form with the same meaning and still preserved the essential, non-arbitrary link between form and sense, for part of the effect of this compound is that it does what it says: [kʊ] in the first syllable is echoed by [ku] in the second, and both by [kow] in the second element of the compound. Iconicity is an extreme example of constraint forcing a poet into additional creativity, but there are many others, as discussed earlier in this section, and the ways they are perceived and interpreted vary across cultures and throughout history.

The idea that creative writing would not be possible without formal constraint is in evidence both in critical approaches, which stress formal patterns or unity of form and content, and also in the teaching of creative writing, where trainee writers are given sets of constraints within which and from which to fashion a text. Here creativity is not seen merely as a force or flow of energy which is channelled and formed by constraint but rather as something whose existence is indissolubly tied to the existence of formal constraint.

2. Translation as Constrained Activity

The relationship between the creative achievement of the writer and the creativity of the translator is one of the central concerns of literary translation studies. While the writer, as has been shown, is by no means free, being subject to a variety of constraints imposed by the chosen medium and the broad context of his or her creative activity, the translator is subject both to the ever present model of the source language (SL) text and also to the additional limitations imposed by the medium with which and the context within which the target language (TL), in turn, has to operate.

The constraints involved in the transfer between SL and TL text are legion and involve, among other things, broad cultural considerations of history, genre and linguistic convention on the one hand – both for the SL and the TL text – and on the other, considerations that also have something to do with culture, but are more narrowly, more personally defined. This is the culture of the translator, that is, the summation of the translator's overall preparation to act as an interpreter and intermediary that in turn critically determines his or her role as reader and writer. Translators first of all have to be informed, attentive readers, literary critics sensitive to the relation between the SL text and the linguistic and cultural environment in which it was exposed. They will want to know what role SL audience expectations and understanding played in the original writer's concern to earn the approval of his or her readers. Was the SL text, for example, perceived as representative of its genre or typical of its time, or did it, perhaps, without external commentary, stand out against its literary and cultural context as special? It is no bad thing for the translator to be aware, too, in so far as this is ever possible, of authorial intentions and of the particular personal constraints under which the author was operating. Was he or she concerned, like Galanaki, to communicate something to the reader whilst at the same time hiding it from the censor? And did the chosen form – again Galanaki's case may be cited, with her flight into poetic ambiguity and cryptic concision – emerge out of the impossibility of saying directly all that might have been expressed had social and political circumstances been different? The translator may further ask whether the author had any one overriding aim or, perhaps, a hierarchy of interlocking aims that needed to be observed and preserved in the translation. Or did extra-literary concerns play a part in the author's desire to release the result of his or her creative activity into the world? When, for example, Leo Tolstoy came to complete his last big novel *Resurrection* (1900), his primary concern was to raise money through its sale to make possible the emigration of a persecuted religious sect to Canada, and so he was prepared to make concessions to the censor, cutting sections in order to preserve the overall thrust of the work. The avoidance of blanket prohibition and the achievement of swift publication with maximum exposure, in Russia and worldwide, of as much of the presented text as possible, was paramount, and not the integrity of the originally conceived text. Philanthropic considerations also motivated many contemporary translators of the novel who were similarly moved by the imperative of the Tolstoyan mission. Subsequent translators, however, not driven by the same urgent philanthropic desire and working in different historical circumstances, were able to pay more attention to the integrity of Tolstoy's original text and work from an uncensored Russian version (see Holman 1997).

Having broken into the codes of the SL text and taken into account the hierarchy of political, social and personal constraints on the original writer's SL environment, translators then have to get down to the business of actually producing their version. They have to effect a transfer of as much as is appropriate of the information they have gathered into a TL text in which demands of the TL linguistic and cultural environment are given proper consideration. Here they move from being readers to being writers, and what has to be placed under scrutiny is their competence for the task as authors in their own right, for it is now that the translators' greatest skill, mastery of their own tongue, has to be effectively deployed. It is vital at this stage in the re-creative process for the individual translator to be aware of the role played by his or her own personal preparation and training in determining how the particular translating task will be approached and carried through. Upbringing, education, knowledge, sensibilities, predilections and beliefs also contribute to the formation of the individual personality of the translator, limiting, defining and also facilitating the translation process, from the initial selection of the SL text right the way through to the final release into the world of its TL progeny (see Hewson 1997:52). A translation, in other words, can never be a sheet of glass through which the original is viewed, as it were, in its pristine state, as the statement by Norman Shapiro, criticized by Venuti (1995:1) would suggest. The translator is always in the text, for the text always has to pass through the translator who is ever present as the constraining and enabling filter.

Like the original author, the translator, too, will have hierarchies of aims and agendas, some conscious, others less so, and in different ways these will all constrain and colour the re-created SL text. Two radically different approaches were adopted by Vladimir Nabokov and Boris Pasternak, both accomplished writers and translators, in their translations of Pushkin and Shakespeare respectively. In her article, Coates shows how, relatively late in his writing and translating career, Nabokov's all-pervading desire to teach, heightened by his sense of shock at the appalling ignorance in America of Russian literature and culture, led him to produce his monumental four-volume literal version of Pushkin's *Eugene Onegin* (1964) in which slightly more than 200 pages of translated text are accompanied by more than 1200 pages of commentary and notes. For Nabokov, Pushkin's masterpiece was equivalent to the Bible of Russian literature, a unique achievement against which everything that came before and after it had to be measured. Constrained, however, by his compelling desire to achieve completeness of connotation, he was obliged to sacrifice the beauty and grace of form in which so much of the appeal of the original Russian resides, and which, according to Tytler (see Lefevere 1992a:132) it is the absolute duty of the translator to preserve. Given his high aim and the disparity in awareness between SL and TL readers, this was the inevitable trade-off he had to accept. Pasternak, in his translations of Shakespeare, adopts an approach diametrically opposed to that of Nabokov. Constrained not so much by his reading public as by state control in the form of Stalin's censorship, he was for a long time unable to publish his own original writings and was forced into translation: "Mayakovsky shot himself, while I translate", he is recorded to have remarked resentfully (Friedberg 1997:115). For Pasternak, translation was second best, but as a powerful poet in his own right, like Nabokov he, too, took possession of the originals, but in a different way: he assimilated Shakespeare's originals in their totality, re-creating them as new poetry without massive externally appended exegesis. This was still Shakespeare, but Pasternak's Russian Shakespeare, Pasternak *and* Shakespeare, which "often bore greater resemblance to his *own* verse than to Shakespeare's" (Friedberg 1997:102). Moreover, whether he cared to acknowledge it or not, translation offered Pasternak, as it has many writers living under conditions of extreme external control down through history, the opportunity not only to survive in relative freedom, and with a relatively easy conscience, but also creatively to deploy his poetic gifts.

That Pasternak's firm, assimilative, directive but still deeply respectful approach to the SL text is not untypical of writer-translators with their own distinctive poetic voice is admirably demonstrated by Salines in her closely argued analysis of Baudelaire's reworkings in French of Edgar Allan Poe, as "an alchemical blending of the two".

There is, however, no agreement on the level of intervention permitted to the translator. Not all would go along with Fitzgerald's statement (quoted in Lefevere 1992b:1) in which he grants himself licence to improve on the undisciplined Persians, who needed "a little Art to shape them". And while the ideologically committed translator, as Alberto Mira demonstrates, would similarly seek to justify a high degree of corrective intervention, whether by omission, addition or other forms of active interpretation, there are those who would prefer to play down the role of the translator in the whole rewriting operation. For them, though translators may not become as sheets of glass, or even faithful reflecting mirrors, they should show more humility in their aspirations and seek no laurels for themselves. Dante Gabriel Rossetti called translation "self-denial" (see Schulte & Biguenet 1992:65) and the Soviet poet Arseny Tarkovsky is recorded as saying that "translation requires modesty. The translator must be content to remain in the background; the limelight belongs to the author of the original" (Friedberg 1997:181). How far a translator is actually able to do this is a moot point, for as we have sought to show, all translators are influenced by their own preferences and personalities. There will always be compromise between faithfulness and freedom, between the need to be true to one's own and the author's voice.

At various points in this introductory essay we have come to mention the external controls operating on the creators of written texts, and it is hardly surprising, in a volume dedicated to the constraints operating on and the creativity demonstrated in the practices of literary translation, that a substantial proportion of the essays should be concerned, in one way or another, with censorship. If one disregards the exigencies of the market, censorship, whether exercised centrally by organs of government or more locally by editors and publishers anxious not to be seen to corrupt their readers, is one of the most extreme forms of external constraint to which all writing in all cultures has been subject through the ages. Unlike the censorship of primary works, however, censorship and its effect on translation has received relatively little critical attention.

For purposes of translation one may distinguish between two contrasting situations, each demanding a different approach. On the one hand there is translating out of a more restrictive into a less restrictive environment, the situation in which Tourniaire found herself when rendering Galanaki's poems in English and French. On the other, there is translating out of a less into a more restrictive environment, the condition of translators working, for example, in Nazi Germany and examined by Sturge with particular reference to systems of control operating within the book trade. In the first situation one will further need to distinguish between preventative pre-publication censorship, and an apparently less invasive, but ultimately far more insidious system of post-publication censorship under which works may be published without any formal vetting procedures, but, if subsequently adjudged by the authorities not to have passed muster, may be confiscated, bringing considerable financial loss to all involved. The latter situation, as exemplified by Galanaki's poetry, allows the writer to decide what might or might not "get through" and demands a greater measure of self-censorship. Under the system of preventative censorship, which existed for long periods in Russia, both Tsarist and Soviet, unless a writer is so perfectly attuned to censorial sensibilities as to be able to present a text that will "pass first time", one may posit the existence of both an "original" authorial text and a post-censorial, "passed", published text. Here the translator might attempt, through archival searches or, in the case of a living author, by direct appeal to the author, to resurrect the original, pre-censorial text and work from that, thus liberating the author from the shackles of his or her native culture and releasing the translation as "unexpurgated", "authenticated" and "original". The latter system of self-censorship, however, permits of no such course of action. No "original" version is likely to have existed outside the author's thoughts and no "original" version can reliably be resurrected. Moreover, under this system of self-censorship, resistance is broken down at source, and with time the unpublishable thought itself becomes not worth thinking and therefore also not thought.

When translating from a less restrictive into a more restrictive environment, as with the writers examined by Sturge or the Spanish translation of *The Boys in the Band* analyzed by Mira, it is the translators, anxious to see their works published and, in extreme cases, also to stay out of prison, who have to decide what might or might not "get through". In fact, they have to assume the role of censor, or self-censor, for, as Ó Cuilleanáin so eloquently and humorously demonstrates, the activities of translator and censor are in many ways related. Both are gatekeepers, standing at crucial points of control, monitoring what comes in and what stays outside any given cultural or linguistic territory. And just as censors have to resolve how best to restrict access to information considered detrimental to the public in whose interests they presume to act, so too do translators have to resolve what tactics to adopt when presenting to the TL reading public new information and fresh forms coming in from the outside. Whether to play safe and preserve the status quo by domesticating the foreign, or whether to be adventurous agents of innovation by opening up to the alien and acting as a channel for the new, that is the translators' central dilemma.

As with original works, so with translations, there is no land where there are no constraints, no controls, no watchdogs, no filters, no pre-existing poetic patterns, no guardians of public morality. But perceptions of what constitutes a danger to the security of the state or the morals of the private individual rarely coincide from one environment to another; at one level or another there is always a mismatch imposing its own constraints in addition to those embodied independently in the SL texts and cultures. This particular mismatch – one

dependent on what is considered likely to deprave, corrupt or otherwise de-
stabilize – is just one of many with which the translator, operating in the space
between perceptions and attempting to reduce the tension between them, constantly has to grapple. For the constraints of mismatch are legion: cultural,
linguistic and political, as demonstrated by Ramadan Megrab, but also genre-
determined, stylistic, historical, philosophical, psychological, pragmatic.
Nevertheless, despite the supposed impossibility of translation, and even if there
exists no exact or obvious match, if there is to be a product, entities in the SL
still have to be mapped on to entities in the TL. Translating decisions will depend to a great degree on the dimension of the entities: temporal, spatial,
cultural, within which a match is sought, of what is thought of as "the text".
Translating a chapter in a novel or a whole novel, a single poem or a complete
cycle of poems will provide for different levels of compensation and therefore
present different possibilities of matching texts and realizing their different
potentials. No matter how the translator tries, no single work can stand for a
whole culture, and compromises always have to be found. These will be different at different times, and as Megrab shows, the solutions will necessarily
depend on the translator's individual estimation of the different levels of perception and preparation in SL and TL audiences.

    While it may be argued that there are original writers who create not for any
consciously conceived public, we would maintain that the translator, in spite of
Benjamin's comment (see Benjamin 1972) to the effect that readers should be
ignored, is always translating for somebody or some group of people. Even if
there is not always a client, there is always a perceived consumer, a targeted
reader within a community of readers, whose needs translators ignore at their
peril. The translator always has to calculate what will be acceptable in a political, cultural, social and moral sense to the TL reader – and to those who for one
reason or another wish to monitor and control what the TL reader reads. In
what environment will the TL text be exposed? In a book? In a journal? In a
series, perhaps, with its own internally defined norms of content, design and
presentation? What readership is envisaged? If the readership is to be children,
primarily American children, for example, in a series of simplified classics,
Hans Christian Andersen's fairy tales or the tales of the Brothers Grimm, how
will that determine the translator's proffered solutions? What should be cut,
what altered, what left? How far should the translator, or the publisher, presume to alter the content of the original in order to avoid causing offence to
potential readers? And how will titles such as *Ten Little Nigger Boys, Little
Black Quasha* or even *Three Blind Mice, Fat and Thin* and *Little and Large*
fare in the PC culture of contemporary North America? These, and many more,
are questions which translators have to ask themselves and to which they need
to find answers in the form of practical, pragmatic, manageable textual solutions. As Mona Baker (1992:250) writes: "In translation, anything that is likely
to violate the target reader's expectations must be carefully examined and, if
necessary, adjusted in order to avoid conveying the wrong implicatures or even

failing to make sense altogether". It is in finding the appropriate level of adjust-ment that so much of the translator's art resides.

3. Constraint as a Source of Creativity in Translation

Though we have said that there is in both original writing and translation an intimate connection between creativity and the constraints which both mould and engender it, there are obvious differences, both in that there are constraints such as those examined in the previous section which are peculiar to transla-tion, and in the particular type of creativity in translation to which they give rise.

As we have seen, a translator must take into consideration all the constraints, whether social and contextual, poetic and conventional, or linguistic and for-mal, which helped shape the original. In addition, he or she must carry the added burden of constraint imposed by the new target language, culture and audience, and by the need to balance freedom with faithfulness and one's own knowledge, background and beliefs with those of the author. Then, too, there are added constraints caused by cultural, linguistic or pragmatic mismatches between SL and TL.

In a purely additive sense, therefore, it is quite clear that the burden of con-straint is bound to be greater in translation than in original writing. Yet just as constraint moulded and gave rise to the creative impulse in the original, so in translation this added burden of constraint can force a translator into new ways of overcoming it and thus into new creativity. This is nowhere more in evidence in this volume than in Gaffney's article, which shows Leyris's extraordinary inventiveness in translating Hopkins into French.

So if translation is indeed more constrained than original writing, then, by virtue of the ability of constraint to engender creativity, it at least has the poten-tial to be more creative, though of course an excessive burden of constraint can be crippling. Then, also, there has often been the view that it is the translator's job to improve upon the original. Susan Bassnett (1996:10ff), quoting the Earl of Roscommon at length, remarks on the judgment which the translator must execute in doing this. Tytler, too (quoted in Lefevere 1992a:129), spoke of the need to keep faith with the original author in a particular way: by supporting him when he failed. This is indeed an idea quite familiar to us from other types of translation and adaptation. We accept almost without question that an opera may be better than the obscure story on which it was based, and we are not especially surprised when the television series *Inspector Morse* turns out far superior to Colin Dexter's dull novels. It seems unusual in translation only because the prevailing view of the translator is still as one whose role is sub-sidiary and who must be faithful even to the extent of copying weaknesses.

Just as the language of an original literary text will creatively deviate from standard language, so the translation can regard the original as a standard to deviate from, and the extent to which deviation is perceived will vary accord-ing to the cultural context in which the TT is to be embedded. Sometimes there are political or social reasons for the apparent freedom of the translation as compared to the original. Tourniaire shows us how Galanaki's poetry used ambiguity to avoid falling foul of censorship and to create multiple interpretations and, if these interpretations are realized in bilingual translation, they give rise to a vast array of meanings associated with each translation. And indeed the case for multiple translation is not only based on censorship of the ST: Ezra Pound (1934) for example, maintained that no single language was capable of expressing everything that humans could comprehend. Sophia Totzeva's article shows how different levels of meaning inherent in a dramatic text can be expressed both in performance and in translation. In this sense translation is a way of allowing both writer and text to achieve their full potential.

A translator, therefore, is a rewriter who determines the implied meanings of the TL text, and who also, in the act of rewriting, redetermines the meaning of the original (Álvarez and Vidal 1996:4). Translation as radical rewriting can thus be seen as a way of rescuing the original from unwanted constraint. Translations may rewrite originals from a feminist perspective, from a post-colonial perspective, from a gay perspective, or indeed from any other perspective (see, for example, the essays in Venuti 1992).

It could be argued that such freedom is not consistent with the role of the translator as a faithful copier. Yet it is in principle no greater than that of any translator who takes on the right to interpret, nor indeed of any author who claims the right to present material as he or she sees fit. In this view, the role of the translator has changed from that of a faithful reproducer to an inventive interventionist. And of course it is important to note here that it is those works whose creative energies appear to have been most constrained which are most often subject to translation as radical rewriting; the works which appear anti-feminist, bowdlerized or censored are the very ones which demand the release of rewriting translations, as in particular the articles by Ó Cuilleanáin and Tourniaire show. So here, too, it is the constraint itself which gives rise to a new creativity. We are all party to such radical recreative translation. Most mothers in the eighties and nineties, reading aloud to a small child, will have changed the wording of their own old children's books to suit their changing views. Most of us will have edited an elderly parent's joke in the re-telling to make it more politically correct. Such adaptations, just as much as the rewriting of major works, whether done by Eugene Nida and his colleagues (see, for example, Nida & de Waard 1986) to pass on the word of God to those lacking the background of ancient Hebrew custom, or by Ted Hughes (1997) preparing Ovid for a new readership, are acts of creative translation which recognize the constraints of the original and use them as the means to provide a version that has been freed from them.

Octavio Paz (in Schulte & Biguenet 1992) said that reading is a form of translation. So, too, translation is in turn a form of critical reading, and a concrete realization of that reading, and in this sense it has much in common with the tradition of literary and biblical exegesis, commentary and exposition. Coates shows in her discussion of Nabokov how his translation of Pushkin's

Onegin was a work of cultural and literary exegesis. We saw earlier how the particular stylistic device of ambiguity is used to circumvent censorship and to point to possible uncensored readings. But there are many other stylistic devices which specifically invite the creative participation of the reader. Compression, seen for example by Samuel Levin (1971) as the essence of poetry, is essentially a device to ensure ambiguity and thus multiple readings. A compound from a poem by Hughes (1983:56), *"dog-bark stillness"*, is compressed in that the relationship between *dog-bark* and *stillness* is not expressed, and so it is up to the reader to supply it. This relation could be a simple metaphorical one of similarity: "stillness like a dog's bark" or a more complicated metaphor: "stillness like the stillness a dog's bark reminds you of". Or it could be something like "stillness in which a dog's bark could be heard". It could be any combination of these or other possible meanings, but without the direct involvement of the reader it will remain incomplete, as will any compressed form. Even those apparently more stable stylistic devices of rhyme and alliteration invite the creative participation of the reader, for words linked by any type of sound-similarity suggest other links, semantic in nature, as our use of idioms such as "right as rain" or "good as gold" suggests. However, alliteration, rhyme and assonance are devices in their own right and the translator who links different words by such repetition of sound will create different connections. Interpretation is a creative act carried out by every reader and thus by every translator; even when stylistic devices do not provide obvious gaps to be filled or obvious patterns to be complied with or creatively subverted, the translator cannot be free from the unconscious act of creative interpretation.

But creative rewriting is not just a matter for the individual translator, exercising the reader's freedom to interpret and the writer's freedom to shape. The TL may in fact be changed, often permanently, by creative acts of translation, borrowing and adaptation. Even the most cursory glance at the inventory of words in English will show the important role of loan words in borrowings such as *divan, algebra* or, more recently, *fatwa, Wende* and *perestroika*. A TL culture can also be extended by the introduction of new ideas and styles, such as Chinese medicine, Indian philosophy, Italian cooking or English gardening. And the constraints of the translational act may give rise to new forms of the TL. "Biblical English" is nothing more than a particular form of English which results from translating the original Hebrew, Greek and Aramaic of the Bible into seventeenth-century English. This is sometimes forgotten, as though Biblical English were simply the normal English with the common lexis and familiar cultural references of 1611.

Steiner (1992:333ff.) convincingly shows how Chateaubriand's 1836 translation of Milton's *Paradise Lost* (1961) (see Chateaubriand nd) not only takes on Milton's seventeenth-century Latinate English, but also the Latin behind the English, to produce a new type of Latinate French which has echoes, too, of the 1611 English version of the Bible, and how Hölderlin's versions of Homer, Pindar and Sophocles achieve what he calls a "mid-zone between antique and modern, Greek and German" (Steiner 1992:341). Or consider Michael Hamburger's English translations of Hölderlin (1998) which, by virtue of a similar fusion, give us a new and unusual English: "Now for it words like flowers leaping alive he must find" (ibid:155).

Nabokov, too, as Coates explains in her article, wrote under the influence of his native Russian, inventing his own English when he thought it appropriate. Or take the language of the Icelandic sagas; the following is Magnus Magnusson & Herman Pálsson's translation of *Njal's Saga* (1960:84):

> Asgrim had a brother called Sigfus, the father of
> Thorgerd, the mother of Sigfus, the father of
> Saemund the Learned.
> He also had a sworn-brother called Gauk
> Trandilsson ...

It is not only the genealogy which is unusual, but the word *sworn-brother* is unknown in English outside of the sagas and is obviously a direct translation from Old Icelandic. So a style of writing arises which has its own customs and lexis and could reasonably be called a particular type of English.

This view of translation as a creative stretching of the TL goes back, according to Steiner (1992), to the Romans, who, in translating the Classics, hoped to import foreign modes of writing and thought into their own work, and it is clear that such creative stretching of the TL is not merely a purely linguistic matter: in English, we have not only gained the rhythms and lexis of Hebrew via Bible translation or of Greek via translation from the Classics, or Old Icelandic via translation from the sagas, but we have also increased access to foreign cultures, understanding of foreign ideas and perceptions of otherness. Although the creative stretching of the TL, along with the background non-linguistic knowledge of the TL reader, will be greater in a foreignizing translation than in a domesticating one, to use Venuti's (1995) terms, it is unlikely that the long-term effect on the TL is in direct proportion to the amount of foreignization. In an extreme example such as Zukofsky and Zukofsky's *Catullus* (1969), quoted by, among many others, Venuti (1995:215ff), in which the aim of translators is to reproduce as closely as possible the sounds of the Latin original, with only a minimal attempt to convey the meaning, the foreignizing effect is so great that the translation is unlikely to be perceived as English at all, and so its effects upon the language will be negligible. This applies, too, to Nabokov's *Pushkin*, as discussed by Coates. A less obviously foreignizing translation, such as Moratín's 1798 translation of *Hamlet,* discussed in the paper by Zaro, in which Moratín domesticated names and locations, while clearly seeking to balance the tradition of the TL, the language Shakespeare used, and his own judgement of the play, is far more likely to have lasting effects upon the language and literary tradition into which it is translated.

Translation, then, can act as an agent for change, altering and stretching perceptions, knowledge and language in the target culture, and threatening the status quo (see Hewson 1997:49), as it presents a challenge to the indigenous culture. What the papers in this book show is that it is the very fact that translation is so highly constrained which gives it the power to effect such change. In the world today the concept of "constraint" normally has only negative connotations, to do with compulsion, coercion, with a denial of dignity, with not being allowed to exercise free will or to express individuality, conditions under which creativity cannot thrive. The translator's art, as we have seen, is creativity guided and controlled in a whole variety of different ways, and from this it might seem to follow that the translator, engaged in the business of guided text generation and therefore not properly in control, cannot be genuinely creative. It is true that in conditions of extreme constraint creativity will be curbed but what the articles in this volume show is that merely to reason thus is to ignore those other connotations of "constraint" that have to do not so much with un-dignified submission to external pressure as with the development of inner strengths that positively demand constraint and are dependent on the exercise of discipline and self-control. To ignore the importance of such connotations would be to deny the importance in the creative act of measure, balance, pattern and form, all restrictions without which there could be no poetry, no prose, no art, no rebellion, no genuine creativity. Indeed, returning to Théophile Gautier and his statement that enduring art emerges out of the constraints imposed by "difficult" base material, the artistic achievement, and especially the achievement of translation, may often be assessed in terms of the successful struggle with and mastery over constraints, making use of them so that the full potential of medium and artists are realized together. "Fi the easy rhythm,/ the roomy shoe, the sloppy fit/ of fashion/ where every foot slips out and in" wrote Gautier in *L'art,* the programmatic poem with which this essay begins, and indeed it could be argued that what comes easily will have as art no lasting value. Tight shoes, however, do not only enable the wearer to walk straight, but according to the proverb they also make for new dances. Similarly in translation, constraint, which is one of its central characteristics, is of critical importance for its creative achievement.

2 Baudelaire and the Alchemy of Translation

EMILY SALINES

The extent of Baudelaire's translation activity and the range of methods and approaches present in his translation corpus raise questions about the status of translation in the works of author-translators in general and about the link between translation and creation. The aim of this paper is to look at Baudelaire's translation practices, to link them both to 19th century theories and practices of translation and to his "creative" works, and to reflect on the notion of creativity as applied to translation.

Baudelaire's approaches to translation were far from uniform, ranging from very close translation to free adaptations of foreign texts; one can, however, define two main strands in his translations (although variations do exist even within these strands and there is a degree of overlap in some cases; see Appendix). The first strand could be called direct translations – translations, that is, in which the source text is paramount, and the act of translating is constrained by the aim of faithfully rendering the original. The second strand consists of adaptations and transformations – texts in which the source text is appropriated, sometimes even hijacked, to suit Baudelaire's aims. In this latter case, the target text becomes paramount, the source text serving mainly as the bottom layer of the creative palimpsest. To use Genette's terminology, the relationship between the French text and the English text is then hypertextual: the end result of the textual manipulation which involves the transformation of the English hypotext is a text which exists in its own right, not just as a secondary by-product (Genette 1982).

Many 20th century definitions of translation would only consider the first type as translations. Indeed, only the first type satisfies the concerns for faithfulness and closeness to the original – predicating, as a consequence, an ancillary role for translation. That role is now strongly established in our culture thanks to what Roland Mortier (1982) calls "le terrorisme artistique" (the artistic terrorism) of originality, and to the veneration of creativity, authorship and literary property, all attitudes inherited from the Romantic Revolution. I would argue, however, that both types of approach should be looked at together, as part of a study of translation practices. The two poles of Baudelaire's treatment of the foreign text do indeed reflect a more general situation in his century, caught as it was between the tradition of *belles infidèles* and emerging concerns for closeness to the original, and this general situation must be clearly understood as a preliminary to a study of Baudelaire's translating practices. To this purpose, a translation by Amédée Pichot of Elizabeth Barrett's poem *To George Sand* which appeared in the *Revue Britannique* in December 1844 (that is to say at a time when the debate was raging), provides a good starting point, and is emblematic of the choices available to Baudelaire:

To George Sand	Traduction libre
Thou large-brained woman and large-hearted man	O femme au large front, homme à large poitrine,
Self-called George Sand, whose soul amid the lions	Si parfois de tes sens la révolte intestine
Of thy tumultuous senses, moans defiance,	Cherche à troubler ton âme, à leurs rugissements
And answers roar for roar, as spirits can:	Sa voix mâle répond et fait taire tes sens;
I would some wild miraculous thunder ran	Telle que ces martyrs que la Rome idolâtre
Above the applauded circus, in appliance	Vit dompter les lions dans son amphi-
Of thine own nobler nature's strength and science,	théâtre.
	Un ciel sombre sur toi semble s'appesantir;
Drawing two pinions, white as wings of swan,	Mais de ce même ciel un éclair doit jaillir,
	Miraculeux rayon qui des plus hautes
From thy strong shoulders, to amaze the place	sphères
	Versera sur tes yeux les divines lumières;
With holier light! that thou, to woman's claim,	Un ange en descendra: de son chaste baiser
	Il calmera les feux qui semblent t'embraser,
And man's, might join beside the angel's grace	Et soudain t'emportant dans le pli de son aile,
Of a pure genius sanctified from blame;	Te dira: Viens, ma sœur, toi qui fus grande et belle,
Till child and maiden pressed to thine embrace	Sois pure aussi, renais; je veux de mon amour
To kiss upon thy lips a stainless fame.	Imprégner ton génie et ton cœur tour à tour,
	Afin que, consacré par une sainte flamme,
Elizabeth Barrett	Ton nom ait un autel dans tous les cœurs de femme.
	A.P.

The translation and its original have little in common. Rather than a translation, what we have here is a poem inspired by Elizabeth Barrett's text, of which most elements are redistributed and developed in the French text. The first visible element of frenchification is the metre used in the French version: the alexandrines immediately impart a French poetic rhythm to the translation. Although the first line of Pichot's version may seem to follow the English text closely, the use of the metonymies ("front", literally "forehead", for "brain", "poitrine", literally "breast", for "heart"), in conjunction with the alexandrine, establish from the outset a classical – almost *précieux* – tone. The rest of Pichot's version departs even further from the original. The next three lines of his poem are loosely based on lines 2 to 5 of Barrett's, in that they refer indirectly to "tumultuous senses" and "defiance" with "de tes sens la révolte intestine" ("of your senses the internal revolt"), while "Sa voix mâle" ("her male voice") could be inspired by George Sand's masculine name. In the next few lines, Barrett's image of the lions and the circus is developed by Pichot into classical imagery: "Telle que ces martyrs que la Rome idolâtre / Vit dompter les lions dans son amphithéâtre" ("Such as the martyrs who tamed the lions in idolatrous Rome's amphitheatre"). Further down, Barrett's Christian imagery is transposed by Pichot into very direct but different references ("two pinions white as wings of swan", "holier light", "the angel's grace", "sanctified", "stainless" become "Miraculeux rayon qui des plus hautes sphères" ("miraculous ray from the highest spheres"), "divines lumières" ("divine lights"), "Un ange" ("an angel"), "sainte flamme" ("holy flame") and is further developed in the images of purification and rebirth which pervade the second half of Pichot's poem. In short, the constraints of the French form (rhymes and rhythm) force Pichot to completely redistribute and vary from the elements of Barrett's poem. But there is more: in addition to these purely formal motivations, cultural assumptions are at work and lead Pichot to change the focus of the poem – while in the source text George Sand is transfigured into an angel, in the target text she is reinvested with her purity by an angel. The fact that the word "ange" is masculine in French makes this transformation particularly revealing: both linguistically and culturally, the idealisation of George Sand into an angel is more difficult in French than in English. Interestingly, having openly followed the method of "traduction libre", Amédée Pichot nevertheless offers in a footnote a more literal, almost word-for-word rendering, pointing out as an introduction to this second translation that literal translation is "sometimes even more inexact than imitation":

> Toi femme à large cerveau et homme à large cœur, qui t'appelles George Sand! dont l'âme au milieu des lions de tes sens tumultueux mugit le défi et répond rugissement pour rugissement, comme les esprits le peuvent: je voudrais que quelque étrange et miraculeux tonnerre courut par-dessus le cirque applaudi, et s'adressant à la force et à la science de ta plus noble nature, tirât de tes fortes épaules deux ailes, blanches comme ailes de cygne, pour éblouir la terre par une plus sainte lumière, afin que toi, aux attributs de la femme et de l'homme, tu puisses joindre la grâce angélique d'un pur génie sanctifié du blâme, jusqu'à ce que enfant et jeune fille viennent se presser dans tes embrassements pour baiser sur tes lèvres une gloire sans tache.

The juxtaposition of a free translation and a literal translation of the same poem encourages a comparison of the traditions and favours openly the first type. The justification for this choice, which focuses on the question of the actual faithfulness of free translation, is typical of the advocates of this method of translation. To mention just one example, the very George Sand of Barrett's poem justified in similar terms her translation of Shakespeare's *As You Like It* as late as 1856 in her preface to the French text: according to her, literal translation kills the original, and good translations are the result of necessary adjustments of the source text to the target language and culture. In addition, she insists that such transformations are "neither profanations nor outrages", but rather an attempt to do the original justice by "giving it French clothes"

(Sand 1856: 15-16). (All translations are mine unless otherwise noted.)

On the other hand, the fact that Pichot felt he had to give a literal translation as well as a free translation of Barrett's poem reminds us that concerns for faithfulness in translation were becoming more and more important during the 19th century – Madame de Staël and Chateaubriand were in this respect amongst the first to denounce the excesses of free translation, to point out the danger of naturalization and to advocate the presence of the foreign in translation:

> When translating, one shouldn't, as the French do, give one's colour to anything one translates; even if this transformed everything one touched into gold, the result would still be that one could not find any nourishment in it; one would not find any new food for the mind, and one would see again and again the same face with barely differing adornments.
>
> (de Staël 1838 [first publication 1816]:602)

Thus de Staël wrote, using the Midas image to suggest the sterility of *belles infidèles*. Very similar views were expressed by, among others, Chateaubriand in his preface to his translation of Milton's *Paradise Lost*, first published in 1830: the debate clearly opposed defenders of close translation and free translation in equal numbers.

In parallel with the debate on translation methods, there was a growing movement to include translation in the literary property laws, and such a movement may be explained, at least partly, by growing concerns for faithfulness in translation which reduced the imaginative, creative process of the exercise. An article by Hippolite Castille, written in 1852, that is to say at the time when French literary property laws were starting to be applied to works published abroad, summarized the debate for and against the application of property rights to translations (Castille 1852). Castille's argument rested on the idea that unauthorized translation is as much of a crime as plagiarism because of its entire dependence on the original work. It is symptomatic of the period that such views should have needed to be asserted and defended in such detail; for a large part of the century, and despite the efforts of people like Castille, concerns for the copyright of translations were little more than lip-service: for many, the translating act was seen as a creative process, which meant that translations were considered original works. As W. Bandy notes: "stealing from a fellow-countryman was a crime, but stealing from a foreigner was permissible" (Bandy 1973:xi).

As already suggested, Baudelaire's varying approaches to translation are undoubtedly the fruit of his times and of the debate I have just outlined. However, it would be wrong to see his translations as mere illustrations of the situation of translation in the 19th century. The strong presence of translation in the works of such a major literary figure suggests a bridge between translation and creation. Baudelaire's translations must therefore be seen as proof of his deep interest in the creative possibilities offered by translation, and of a desire to explore and exploit these possibilities – and this is another reason for looking at all his approaches together, as they represent varying stages of his use of translation as a means of creation.

If we look at the range of methods used by Baudelaire, we soon note that it embraces all the various levels of appropriation of the source-text. The approach which is the most respectful of the original can be found in his translations of Edgar Allan Poe's works, in which the source text is always fully acknowledged and respected as an original to be reproduced as faithfully as possible. In a note published in 1848 with his translation of *Mesmeric Revelation*, Baudelaire clearly subscribes to the same views as de Staël and Chateaubriand:

> One must first and foremost attempt to follow the literal text. Some things would have become far more obscure if I had tried to paraphrase my author, instead of servilely following the letter ("au lieu de me tenir servilement attaché à la lettre"). I chose to write in difficult and sometimes baroque French ("français pénible et parfois baroque") in order to express fully Edgar Allan Poe's philosophical art ("donner dans toute sa vérité la technie philosophique d'Edgar Poe").
>
> (Poe 1951:1105)

This "français pénible et parfois baroque" chosen in opposition to paraphrase, that is, the approach of *belles infidèles*, seems to announce Antoine Berman's "étrangeté" of translation, the necessary foreignness which is one of the specific features of the language of translation (Berman 1984). At the same time, Baudelaire's statement denies the translator any sort of autonomy: his role is that of an intermediary, his aim is to reproduce the original, to make Poe known in France. Translation thus has an ancillary function, and the constraints of the target language are overlooked in favour of those of the source text and culture. The reality of Baudelaire's Poe translations is not as clear as presented in the above quotation, however. As Marilyn Gaddis Rose (1997:32) has recently noted, Poe's style "allowed Baudelaire full expression of desperation, morbidity, excess; full expression, in short, of the extravagance of feelings beyond the strictures of high bourgeois taste exemplified by his mother and stepfather". In other words, whereas Baudelaire's strategy is clearly source-orientated, and follows concerns of closeness to the original (Gaddis Rose calls this "translation in the usual sense" (p. 31), implicitly contrasting this approach with the adaptations), the source text also unleashes his poetic creativity. The case of *Le Jeune Enchanteur* (see Appendix) confirms Baudelaire's ambivalence towards close translation. Although this text is a very close translation of an 1836 English story by the Reverend Croly, its original was not disclosed by Baudelaire, so that the story passed as an original story from its publication in 1846 until W.T. Bandy's discovery of the truth in 1950. So Baudelaire's very first published translation both submits to the original by staying close to it and yet denies the secondary function of translation, by claiming the target text as original, that is to say as independent from its source.

This tendency is naturally more developed in texts where the approach towards the foreign text is more free, suggesting a more complex mechanism of appropriation. *Le Guignon* (see Appendix), which was first published in 1855, for instance, is a blend of Baudelairean aesthetics (the title describes the bad luck and lack of success which is the fate of the artist) and extracts from Gray's *Elegy Written in a Country Church-Yard* and Longfellow's *A Psalm of Life*. The very juxtaposition of the two extracts within the same poem transforms their meanings, as do the first two opening lines, the only two lines which are not translated from the English.

Le Guignon	*A Psalm of Life*
Pour soulever un poids si lourd	Art is long, and Time is fleeting,
Sisyphe, il faudrait ton courage!	And our hearts, though stout and brave,
Bien qu'on ait du cœur à l'ouvrage	Still, like muffled drums, are beating
L'Art est long et le temps est court.	Funeral marches to the grave.
Loin des sépultures célèbres,	
Vers un cimetière isolé,	*Elegy Written in a Country Church-Yard*
Mon cœur, comme un tambour voilé,	
Va battant des marches funèbres.	Full many a gem of purest ray serene,
	The dark unfathom'd caves of ocean bear:
– Maint joyau dort enseveli	Full many a flower is born to blush unseen,
Dans les ténèbres et l'oubli,	And waste its sweetness on the desert air.
Bien loin des pioches et des sondes;	
Mainte fleur épanche à regret	
Son parfum doux comme un secret	
Dans les solitudes profondes.	

Francis Scarfe's close translation of Baudelaire's poem is as follows:

Unluck

To lift such a burden the courage of Sisyphus would be needed. However eagerly one labours, Art is long and Time is short.
Far from the graves of the renowned my heart, like a muffled drum, beats its dead-march towards some desolate graveyard.
Many a gem sleeps buried in darkness and oblivion, far beyond the reach of spade or sounding-rod;
Many a flower squanders its perfume with regret, its scent sweet as a secret, in the depths of solitude.

(Scarfe 1986:70)

The two quatrains of this sonnet develop what is expressed in the corresponding quatrain from Longfellow's *A Psalm of Life*, while the two tercets are based on a quatrain from Gray's *Elegy Written in a Country Church-Yard*. The title and the first two lines of the sonnet, which are the only elements *not* borrowed from Longfellow or Gray, set the tone of the poem and influence our reading of the rest of it. Taken out of context, Longfellow's and Gray's verses take on the meaning intended by Baudelaire: Longfellow's poem does not have in general a negative tone, but is rather an encouragement to action, while Baudelaire focuses on the difficulties of artistic creation and recognition. By cutting and pasting the two poems, Baudelaire links them together and to his title, and creates a fusion between them and his own poetry. Translation here is first and foremost a form of creation, the foreign text being used to the poet's purpose. The mechanism of appropriation at work in *Le Guignon* is clearly the result of views of translation as a creative process, a form of authorship making concerns of plagiarism irrelevant to its aesthetics.

Le Flambeau vivant (see Appendix) is very close in approach to *Le Guignon*, based this time on a poem by Poe, *To Helen*:

Le Flambeau vivant

Ils marchent devant moi, ces Yeux pleins de lumières,
Qu'un Ange très savant a sans doute aimantés;
Ils marchent, ces divins frères qui sont mes frères,
Secouant dans mes yeux leur feux diamantés.

Me sauvant de tout piège et de tout péché grave,
Ils conduisent mes pas dans la route du Beau;
Ils sont mes serviteurs et je suis leur esclave;
Tout mon être obéit à ce vivant flambeau.

Charmants Yeux, vous brillez de la clarté mystique
Qu'ont les cierges brûlant en plein jour; le soleil
Rougit, mais n'éteint pas leur flamme fantastique;

Ils célèbrent la Mort, vous chantez le Réveil;
Vous marchez en chantant le réveil de mon âme,
Astres dont nul soleil ne peut flétrir la flamme!

To Helen [48-66]

But now, at length, dear Dian sank from sight,
Into a western couch of thunder-cloud;
And thou, a ghost, amid the entombing trees
Didst glide away. *Only thine eyes remained.*
They *would not* go – they never yet have gone.
Lighting my lonely pathway home that night,
They have not left me (as my hopes have) since.
They follow me – they lead me through the years.
They are my ministers – yet I their slave.
Their office is to illumine and enkindle –
My duty, to be saved by their bright light,
And purified in their electric fire,
And sanctified in their elysian fire.
They fill my soul with Beauty (which is Hope),
And are far up in Heaven – the stars I kneel to
In the sad, silent watches of my night;
While even in the meridian glare of day
I see them still – two sweetly scintillant Venuses,
unextinguished by the sun!

Here again, Francis Scarfe's close translation is useful:

The Living Torch

They go before me, those eyes full of many lights, which some angel's craft must have made magnetic; they advance, those divine brothers, my own brothers, flashing into my eyes their diamond-lustred flames.

Preserving me from every snare and every grievous sin, they guide my

steps along the paths of Beauty: although they serve me I am their bonds-
man; my entire being obeys this living torch.

Entrancing eyes, you glitter with the mysterious radiance of candles lit
in the broad light of day; the sun glows red but cannot douse their eerie
flame.

The candles honour Death, but you hymn the Resurrection: as you
advance you sing the awakening of my soul, O stars whose fire no Sun has
power to dim.

(Scarfe 1986:111)

The two poems have much in common both thematically and stylistically.
The Petrarquist image of the eyes of the beloved as a flame guiding the poet is
present in both poems, and so is the aspiration to Beauty. A close look at the
two poems leaves little doubt about the identity of the hypotext of *Le Flambeau
vivant*. What Baudelaire has done here is focus onto the last 19 lines of *To
Helen* and adapt their imagery and themes to his poetry and style. The most
obvious use of Poe's poem by Baudelaire is in his direct translations from the
English text: "Ils sont mes serviteurs et je suis leur esclave" [7] and "Astres
dont nul soleil ne peut flétrir la flamme" [14] are merely renderings of Poe's
"They are my ministers – yet I their slave" [56] and "Venuses, unextinguished
by the sun" [66]; there is no doubt that *To Helen* is the hypotext of *Le Flambeau*
vivant. Yet *Le Flambeau vivant* is much more than a mere translation. A frequent feature of Baudelaire's use of Poe's material is the way he combines
several lines from Poe's poem into a single line of his own poem: in the first
line of *Le Flambeau vivant*, "Ils marchent devant moi" ("they walk in front of
me") recalls "Lighting my lonely pathway home that night" [53] and "they lead
me through the years" [55], while "ces Yeux pleins de lumières" (literally,
"these Eyes full of lights") concentrates the many references to light which
pervade Poe's poem (for instance, "their bright light" [58], "their electric fire"
[59], "their elysian fire" [60], "two sweetly scintillant Venuses" [65-6]). Another way in which he uses Poe's text is through adaptations of particular lines
to his own themes: "Ils conduisent mes pas dans la route du Beau" [6] ("they
lead my steps in the path to Beauty") is loosely based on "They fill my soul
with Beauty (which is Hope)" [61] but also recalls "they lead me through the
years"; however, Baudelaire's reference to Beauty has a slightly different meaning from Poe's, as it refers more directly to poetic inspiration. He also often
summarizes chunks of *To Helen* into a single line, as in "Me sauvant de tout
piège et de tout péché grave" [5] ("saving me from any trap and deep sin")
which is based on Poe's

Their office is to illumine and enkindle –
My duty, *to be saved* by their bright light,
And purified in their electric fire,
And sanctified in their elysian fire. [57-60]

Conversely, Baudelaire sometimes develops Poe's imagery instead of concentrating it: Poe's generally Christian imagery ("to be saved", "purified",
"sanctified", "Heaven"), is more specific and extended throughout *Le Flambeau
vivant* ("Ange", "divins", "sauvant", "péché", "cierges"). Similarly, the third
stanza of Baudelaire's poem [9-11], which develops further the Christian imagery of the previous stanza, is itself an expansion of Poe's

> While even in the meridian glare of day
> I see them still [64-5]

The comparison of *Le Flambeau vivant* and *To Helen* shows the close relationship between the texts, but also reveals some fundamental differences. By
discarding the beginning of *To Helen*, Baudelaire chooses to omit the general
setting of the poem and to concentrate on its climax: where Poe took 47 lines to
create the atmosphere necessary to his poetic effect (through a melancholic description of the circumstances of the encounter with the woman inspiring the
poem – a "July midnight" [1.3], "a full-orbed moon" [1.4], an enchanted garden,
the supernatural apparition of a woman, the vision of her eyes), Baudelaire
launches directly into the theme of the eyes of the Muse as guides to the poet.
While the general tense of *To Helen* is the past, in accordance with Poe's poetic
principle that Melancholy is the most appropriate poetic tone, Baudelaire's
poem is anchored in the present. The absence of supernatural context, together
with the sonnet form and the distinctly Petrarquist tone make *Le Flambeau
vivant* quite separate from *To Helen*. Here again, translation is but a stage in the
creative process, the translator keeping control of the meaning of the words he
translates. Translation erases the original meaning; the translator becomes
author.

Perhaps unsurprisingly given the long-lasting influence of Romantic concerns for originality and authorship in our culture, such appropriation through
translation has prompted critics to accuse Baudelaire of plagiarism and to talk
about his "creative incapacity", thus implying that translation is a stopgap activity inferior to creation (see for instance Pichois 1967). It is clear that Baudelaire,
who struggled all his life to make a living out of literature, found translation a
good way to make money (Baudelaire claims in his correspondence that translations are very easy to sell) but it is a mistake to see the time and effort he
spent on translation as only a stopgap, and replacing "creative work". Translation and poetry were not separate activities – in fact poetry **was** translation:

> What is a poet (...) if not a translator, a decipherer?
>
> (Baudelaire 1976:133)

Based on the theory of *correspondances* explored in the sonnet of the same
title, this statement stresses the infinite translatability of the world and the role
of the poetry as interpreter of the world. Clearly, the term "translation" is taken
as a metaphor. But apart from this, translation from English created poetry for
Baudelaire, and was part of poetic creation. So is the source text only a tool for

poetic creation? *Un Mangeur d'opium* (See Appendix) suggests a more complex situation.

Based on Thomas De Quincey's *Confessions of an English Opium Eater* and its sequel, *Suspiria de Profundis*, Baudelaire's text openly reworks its hypotexts through a blend of close translations (in the large number of quotations from the original), free translations, paraphrases, summaries, omissions, and additions, thereby achieving a double transplantation: first into the French cultural system and second into the *Paradis artificiels*, of which it constitutes the second part. The genesis of *Un Mangeur d'opium* was far from simple: initially wishing to write an article on opium, Baudelaire than started a translation of De Quincey's text, but had to rework his text and shorten it to suit his publisher. First published in periodical form as *Enchantements et tortures d'un mangeur d'opium*, with a subtitle which made full bibliographical reference to the original, the text was subsequently renamed to form part of the *Paradis artificiels*, the new title making no reference to the hypotext.

Baudelaire's changing projects explain the complex structure of *Un Mangeur d'opium*: the blend of analysis, reflection, summaries, paraphrases and quotations it offers is in fact a combination of initially separate intentions. The numerous quotations from the original are a consequence of Baudelaire's project to publish a full translation of the text, and the approach in those quotations is close to the Poe translations; on the other hand, the analyses and personal commentaries by Baudelaire are a result of his initial project (an article), while the numerous summaries, paraphrases and omissions respond to a need for brevity imposed on Baudelaire. Baudelaire himself frequently referred to the hybrid nature of the text – on 16 February 1860 he wrote to Auguste Poulet Malassis:

> I wanted to blend my own sensations with the original author's ideas in order to produce a complete amalgam (un amalgame dont les parties fussent indiscernables),

an idea which was repeated in almost exactly the same terms in his project for his Belgian lectures:

> I made such an amalgam that I could not say which part comes from me.

This notion of amalgam, that is to say, blending of the two authors' sensitivities, is a very accurate description of the transformations achieved in the text. Although the professed aim of *Un Mangeur d'opium* is to present De Quincey's experience, De Quincey's autobiography acts as a springboard for the release of Baudelaire's imagery. De Quincey's account of his experience in London, for instance, finds an echo in Baudelaire's aesthetics of the city; similarly, the young prostitute De Quincey befriends in London becomes a Baudelairean female in Baudelaire's version (Salines 1996). *Un Mangeur d'opium* is a meeting point between two compatible sensitivities – Baudelaire writes about the "fraternel" charm of De Quincey's text for him, an affinity which recalls his experience with the texts of Edgar Allan Poe, in whom he saw a poetic brother.

It is as if for Baudelaire translation could not occur unless author and translator could mirror each other, unless their sensitivities could meet, to such an extent that the question of authorship could not interfere in the encounter.

Even more importantly, the alchemical meaning of the term "amalgam" can provide a further key to the relationship between De Quincey's and Baudelaire's texts and by extension the function of translation for Baudelaire. The image of the alchemist is often present in his works, most notably in "Alchimie de la douleur" or "Au lecteur" in the *Fleurs du mal*, and in particular in a preface for the 1861 edition of *Les Fleurs du mal* on which he was working when *Les Paradis artificiels* was published, and which, addressed to the city, describes the poetic experience in alchemical terms:

> Car j'ai de chaque chose extrait la quintessence,
> Tu m'as donné ta boue et j'en ai fait de l'or.

> (I have extracted the quintessential of all things/you gave me your mud and I turned it into gold.)

The fact that the alchemical metaphor should be used by Baudelaire to describe both his poetic work and his approach to the foreign text, in the same way as the term "translation" for him refers both to the interpretation of the world which is the privilege of the poet and to interlingual translation, points to a unity in his literary activity and is a proof of the fallacy of a distinction between translation and creation in his corpus.

The case of Charles Baudelaire, extreme as it may be, reminds us that there is more to translation than subservience and faithfulness to the original. The issues frequently raised about Baudelaire's treatment of the foreign text – his lack of creativity and his tendency towards plagiarism – stem from the application of romantic ideals of originality and authorship that cannot be applied to the act of translation, which by nature is an encounter between two sensitivities and cultures and, if we follow Baudelaire, an alchemical blending of the two.

Appendix: Baudelaire's translation corpus

Direct translations

Le Jeune Enchanteur, published in *L'Esprit Public* (20-22 February 1846) and translated from *The Young Enchanter* by Rev. Croly

The Poe translations, from 1848 to 1865, and published in book form as:
Histoires extraordinaires (12 March 1856)
Nouvelles Histoires extraordinaires (8 March 1857)
Histoires grotesques et sérieuses, published by Michel Lévy (16 March 1865)

Translation of two English songs published in *Paris* (29 January 1853)

Thomas Hood's *Bridge of Sighs* (1865)

Adaptations and transformations

Edgar Allan Poe, sa vie et ses ouvrages, published in *La Revue de Paris* (March and April 1852) – parts of this article were directly translated from articles found in American newspapers

Le Guignon, first published on 1 June 1855 in *Revue des Deux Mondes*, and which includes passages translated from Longfellow and Gray (N.B.: manuscript dates from 1851 or 1852)

Le Flambeau vivant, published on 20 April 1857 in *Revue Française*, and which includes a passage translated from Poe (N.B.: manuscript sent to Mme Sabatier on 7 February 1854)

Enchantements et tortures d'un mangeur d'opium, in the *Revue Contemporaine* (15 and 31 January 1860), and adapted from De Quincey

Les Paradis artificiels, published by Poulet-Malassis (end of May 1860), including *Un Mangeur d'opium*, adapted from De Quincey

Le Calumet de paix, published in the *Revue Contemporaine* (28 February 1961), and loosely translated from Longfellow's *Hiawatha*

3 Not in Front of the Servants
Forms of Bowdlerism and Censorship in Translation

CORMAC Ó CUILLEANÁIN

Writers, students and translators of literature know that language is more than a transparent medium for conveying information, and that gaps between languages cannot always be bridged.

These axioms are most obviously true when words are used creatively, and the present essay will look at literary examples which illustrate the ambiguous role of the translator caught between languages, between cultures, between text and audience. The special case to be examined is one where social constraints impose creative constraints, and the translator's role is not to create understanding but to preserve a pious fiction of misunderstanding.

It is well to be aware at the outset, however, that similar anomalies affecting intelligibility occur in non-literary contexts. We live in a world of overlapping language-communities, where, as Meir Sternberg points out, "the profusion and confusion of tongues" is "not only a verbal but also an existential fact" (Sternberg 1981:221). Each language, says Sternberg, carries "the burden of reporting messages originally encoded in other languages. This forms of course the common source of all translational problems (ibid)". As we shall see, that burden can be discharged in a number of interesting ways, ranging from simple quotation in a foreign language to full translation into a target language. And the choice of reporting strategy is constrained by the social fact that many speech communities enjoy some level of understanding of other languages – an understanding which may be determined by social as well as purely linguistic factors.

Some complications in the smooth flow of reciprocal understanding between languages were explored in an article by Hans Wolff concerning the Nembe and the Kalabari, two groups occupying contiguous geographical areas in the Eastern Niger Delta and speaking two closely related dialects within the linguistically very homogeneous group of Ijaw languages. The Nembe freely acknowledged the linguistic closeness and claimed to be able to understand speakers of Kalabari. The Kalabari, however, claimed that Nembe is a very different language, "unintelligible except for scattered word recognition" (Wolff 1959:442). The Kalabari, being the largest and most prosperous group in the region, tended to look down on the Nembe as poor country cousins. From this and other evidence, Wolff (442-43) advanced the view that "intelligibility, or interlingual communication, is a function of intercultural or interethnic trends and relationships". And although any pair of neighbouring languages may have undergone asymmetrical phonetic changes which would cause one to be articulated less intelligibly than the other, it is hard to disagree with S. Pit-Corder's comment on Wolff's article: "We must conclude that there is some *subjective* social-psychological dimension in mutual intelligibility" (Pit-Corder 1973:53).

One can imagine that an inability to understand an utterance in a neighbour's dialect may serve among other things to confirm the superior status of our own mother tongue. Within the language professions in today's polylingual world one can point to a somewhat analogous situation: an interpreter may be required to tell an audience in their own language what they have already understood in another, or even to help them pretend that they have not understood.

An example of this last variant: Bob Geldof, interviewed through an interpreter on an Italian television talk-show in 1995, said of a certain football team in the USA 94 World Cup that "they were shite". The studio audience howled with laughter, whereupon the interpreter explained that in Geldof's opinion the players "non sono stati proprio brillanti" [haven't exactly been brilliant]. In telling this transparent lie, she was preserving a number of things: the social normality of the talk-show, the non-transgressive function of the interpreter – and also, I suggest, the prestige of her mother tongue as a civilised language. Her audience added to the pleasure of understanding Mr Geldof the equally important pleasure of not understanding him.

This is of course a more complex case than the Nembe-Kalabari example, as English is a language with a high functional value, and a knowledge of it yields notable economic and cultural dividends. Wolff (1959:444) argues that such "practical" languages are "likely to command far greater intelligibility than others, regardless of the degree of lexical or morphemic similarity which may be involved". Hence the audience's ready reaction to Geldof's remark. In mistranslating it into Italian, the interpreter was not denying its intelligibility in its source language, merely the appropriateness of translating it immediately into the receptor language.

These introductory points – Sternberg's observations on polylingualism, Wolff's view on non-reciprocal intelligibility, the Geldof example of comprehensibility without translatability – serve to provide a broad communicative framework for the narrower examples of constrained creativity which will take up the remainder of the present essay.

Given that translation – whether oral or written, literary or non-literary – involves the appropriation of a text as part of a new culture with its own values and sensitivities, it is not surprising that translation and censorship are related activities. Indeed, there are contrary impulses at work in the very act of translation, which reveals a text by concealing it in a new language. In a sense, it preserves by destroying. And (as will be seen in the case of Boccaccio's *Decameron*) a similar tension between concealment and revelation often operates in original writing. The principle of misunderstanding is constantly at work.

Translation, in fact, is both a linguistic and a social process. From a purely literary standpoint, it can provide a useful key to some underlying questions. In an article on English versions of the *Agamemnon*, a Greek text from the fifth century BC, Reuben Brower (1959:175) suggested "that the study of translations, especially from a literature produced by a civilization very different from our own, was one of the simplest ways of showing what is expected at various times in answer to the question of 'What is poetry?'". Looking more closely at social constraints, modern re-translations of the ruder classics could be studied as indices of changing conditions of acceptability in literature.

The present essay will focus on seemingly anomalous cases where full translation is refused at certain points within a translated or pseudo-translated literary text. In my chosen examples of fragmentary "non-translation", the ultimate aim is to produce imperfect understanding in the target language while sometimes allowing for the possibility of full understanding in a source or intermediate language to those who can avail of it. And if the preservation of decency in our mother tongue compels us to leave gaps in it, confining indecencies to other people's languages, the status of our own dear language may actually be enhanced by a perception of other languages as low and louche.

As we shall see, the "other language" need not always be a foreign one. The desired result can sometimes be achieved by rewording the offending text within the same language – the process defined by Jakobson (1959:233) as intralingual (as opposed to interlingual or intersemiotic) translation – or even by confining a text to one of the two official languages in a supposedly bilingual nation state.

1. Voltaire's Panglossia – A Refusal to Translate

Our first literary example comes from Voltaire. In Chapter XI of *Candide* (1759) an old woman recalls how, many years ago, as a beautiful fifteen-year-old princess and the daughter of a Pope, she was captured by pirates and carried off to Morocco. Following one of the book's many bloody massacres, she awoke to hear an exclamation in her native Italian: "*O che sciagura d'essere senza coglioni!*" ["Oh what a misfortune to be without testicles!"]. These untranslated words are spoken by a eunuch, who, regretting his inability to take advantage of her, sells her as a white slave in Algiers. (O.R. Taylor, editing this text for an English student readership in 1942, leaves the phrase un-annotated; this omission is an example of a scholar's "refusal to translate", and examples will be given later of more virulent forms of scholarly concealment.)

Was it through modesty that Voltaire "failed" to translate this single phrase from Italian? The whole of *Candide* is, after all, fictionally presented as a translation from a German original, and characters within the story who speak Dutch, Portuguese, Spanish, English, Turkish and indeed Italian regularly have their speech "reported" in French. Some other rude bits of this same narrative by the old woman are also relayed in that language, as when, describing how she was body-searched for hidden diamonds by the pirates, she finds a delicate circumlocution: "ils nous mirent à tous le doigt dans un endroit où nous autres femmes ne nous laissons mettre d'ordinaire que les canules" ["they put their fingers in a place where we women normally admit nothing but a syringe-tube" (Butt 1947:51)]. Circumlocution in French saves the author from mentioning the unmentionable; outright obscenity in Italian achieves much the same end. Or perhaps the brief foray into Italian is a signal that the book's "inner" readership is restricted to erudite polyglots, people so sophisticated that they can appreciate the lowest things in life so long as they are presented in an exotic context.

One such erudite reader, a Trinity graduate in French and Italian, Samuel Beckett, took Voltaire's Italian exclamation as the starting-point for an early dialogue sketch, published in *TCD: A College Miscellany* on 14 November 1929 (vol. 36, no. 629, 42). Even when assured (Bair 1990:92-93; Knowlson 1996:51) that "Che Sciagura" is a satirical attack against the ban on contraception in Ireland, the text remains largely unintelligible. It opens as follows:

> Che Sciagura

> "Frequently."
> "In this country?"
> "Strictly speaking – never in this country."
> "Permit me to protest against the double-barrelled qualification. Am I to reduce the coefficient of spatial, or that of qualitative elasticity?"

The editorial subcommittee of the magazine, in their report for Michaelmas Term 1929, categorize Beckett's contribution as "extremely clever, though *fortunately* [emphasis added] a trifle obscure for those who do not know their JOYCE and their VOLTAIRE" (vol. 36, 137). Under his allusive title, Beckett is writing English so dense that it baffles not only the censor but the reader.

2. Boccaccio's Translators – Not in Front of the Servants

The same practice of printing frank obscenities in a foreign or second language, thereby preserving the purity of one's first language, was sometimes resorted to by translators of Boccaccio's *Decameron* – an expedient described in Professor Harry McWilliam's entertaining survey of previous versions in the first (1972) edition of his Penguin Classics translation of the book. English translators were particularly careful of their readers' sensibilities; one described his method as "so to manage the Expression, and conceal the Matter, that the fair sex may read it without blushing" (McWilliam 1972:26), while another translator, in 1741, allowed that "Boccace is so licentious in many places, that it requires some management to preserve his wit and humour, and render him tolerably decent. This I have attempted with the loss of two novels, which I judged incapable of such treatment " (ibid:27).

Boccaccio's two most indecent *novelle* are, as every schoolboy knows, day 3 story 10, and day 9 story 10. In the first, a hermit shows a pious young girl how to put the devil into hell, while in the second, a country priest transforms a woman into a horse, but sticks the tail on a little too low. The editor of the 1872 translation boasts that whereas previous English versions lacked these two stories, "the present edition will be found to be COMPLETE, although a few passages are in French or Italian" (McWilliam 1972:28). A further refinement, practised in the English versions of 1822 and 1855, was to leave part of the tenth story of the third day in Italian, but with a French translation at the foot of the page (McWilliam 1972:32) – thereby offering the reader a choice between two depraved foreign languages.

McWilliam records (1972:28-29) that "in 1886, more than 500 years after

Boccaccio's death, the English reader was finally enabled to read the whole of the *Decameron* in the splendidly scrupulous but curiously archaic translation of John Payne ... printed for the Villon Society by private subscription and for private circulation only ... The two missing stories are accurately translated in English for the first time ...". But private subscription, scholarly scrupulousness and curious archaism are, in social terms, the continuation of French by other means: distancing devices to conceal the text not from the actual reader, a person of unshakable morality, but from other inferior members of the speech community. And even within this exalted social sphere, archaic English may not be a strong enough defence.

A lavish 1893 reprint (one thousand copies for England and America) of Payne's *Decameron* translation, although sporting mildly pornographic Pre-Raphaelite illustrations by Louis Chalon, resiles somewhat from the boldness of the 1886 edition. The tenth story of the third day carries a footnote (Vol. 1, 247): "It being usual, for obvious reasons, to omit this story, it has been thought well, for sake of completeness, to substitute the French version from the fine sixteenth-century translation of Antoine Le Maçon, secretary to Marguerite de Navarre, authoress of the *Heptameron*."

The seamless switch from archaic English into sixteenth-century French comes just as the hermit Rustico is outlining his proposition to the pious young girl (p. 249):

> Accordingly, having sounded her with sundry questions, he found that she had never known man and was in truth as simple as she seemed; wherefore he bethought him how, under colour of the service of God, he might bring her to his pleasures. Et premierement lui monstra auec plusieurs parolles combien le diable estoit ennemy de nostre Seigneur: & apres lui donna à entedre que le seruice qui plus plaisoit à Dieu, estoit de remettre le diable en enfer, auquel nostre Seigneur l'auoit condemné.

The McWilliam translation (1972:316) of the passage runs as follows: "He began by delivering a long speech in which he showed her how powerful an enemy the devil was to the Lord God, and followed this up by impressing upon her that of all the ways of serving God, the one that He most appreciated consisted in putting the devil back into Hell, to which the Almighty had consigned him in the first place." McWilliam records (1972:29) another edition in 1895 which reproduced the 1741 English translation with Le Maçon's sixteenth-century French supplying "part of one novel".

Outdated French spellings have been scrupulously retained, and there is even a manuscript abbreviation in the word "entendre". This is French of a kind that can only be understood by the erudite but (for some reason) non-Italian-speaking gentleman who has purchased this fine edition. If the scholarly reader's monoglot chambermaid comes to dust his study while his *Decameron* lies open on the desk, she will not understand a word. Even his daughters with their contemporary school French will be baffled.

The first line of defence in the Victorians' rearguard action against dangerous literature was economic. In his fascinating study, *Dr Bowdler's Legacy: A History of expurgated books in England and America* (1969), Noel Perrin notes that the nineteenth century saw a great increase in literacy, especially among what were called the lower orders. A writer in the *Edinburgh Review* "guessed in 1812 that there were 20,000 upper-class readers in Great Britain, and 200,000 of the common sort" (Perrin 1969:13). The readership of one periodical publication was estimated in 1832 at one million. Given this alarming situation, "even people who did not see the need of expurgation for themselves began to think they had better protect all those new readers. ... the gentleman, moved by *noblesse oblige*, kindly sets out to save his inferiors from temptation. *He* can be trusted to read *Hamlet*, but a newly educated grocer will pick up bad ideas."

One way of protecting the common herd, and avoiding the full democratization of literature, was by simple price differentiation. "As late as 1800, most books came out in editions of 250 or 500 copies; and a common price was one guinea – a week's income even for many curates and beginning lawyers. By 1850, with incomes no lower, one-shilling books and first editions of 5,000 were common" (Perrin 1969:14). Hence, "Victorian publishers tended to expurgate large editions, even while continuing to print small unexpurgated editions of the same authors at higher prices for the old upper-class audience."

Behind the economic barrier lay a linguistic barrier. In the case of foreign books, incomplete translation underscored the point that full understanding is not for everyone, even at the top end of the market. The macaronic approach extended far beyond the *Decameron*. Perrin notes (1969:162) that "Augustine's *City of God*, for example, was regularly expurgated in England after about 1870. Some editions, such as one done in London in 1890, do not actually omit any of Augustine's words, to be sure; they just leave a certain number in Latin."

This double distancing strategy now seems ridiculous. But perhaps we should recall that concealment is not just at work in translation; it was also a principle, for example of Boccaccio's original *Decameron*, where gross details are euphemistically conveyed – "translated", one might say – through metaphors to the respectable ladies constituting the fictional audience of Boccaccio's *Hundred Tales*.

At the end of day 3 story 10, with its veiled jokes about "the resurrection of the flesh" and "taming the devil", Boccaccio records: "So aptly and cleverly worded did Dioneo's tale appear to the virtuous ladies, that they shook with mirth a thousand times or more" (McWilliam 1972:319). At the end of day 9 story 10 we also learn that "the ladies laughed to hear this tale, whose meaning they had grasped more readily than Dioneo had intended" (McWilliam 1972: 730). In short, part of the pleasure of storytelling in the original *Decameron* lies in describing very rude things, in acceptable language, to a polite audience. There is the pleasure of understanding the speaker (or the writer), and the equally important pleasure of ostensibly not understanding him.

A *double-entendre* works on two contradictory levels: creative tension arises precisely from the contradiction. Socially-determined verbal constraints become a creative force: metaphorical words render unspeakable things; language integrates outrageous acts into the social sphere. At the risk of overstretching the concept, one might argue that the principle of translation, with all its contradictions, is at work in the original. As already remarked, the "other language" in which the unspeakable is veiled need not always be a foreign language.

3. Shakespeare's Editors – Intralingual Translation and Sins of Omission
The next example illustrates this last observation in an Irish setting. At secondary school in Dublin in the 1960s, we read *Hamlet* in an edition prepared by the Professor of English at University College Dublin. J.J. Hogan's "Malone Shakespeare" edition of 1948 was called after Edmund Malone, an eighteenth-century scholar born in Dublin. It is perhaps ironic in view of what follows that Malone had himself exposed as fraudulent an expurgated "original Shakespeare manuscript" forged by an eighteen-year-old contemporary and published in 1795 (Perrin 1969:71).

For the "Malone" *Hamlet*, Professor Hogan furnished copious notes and an intelligent introduction revealing a genuine love of Shakespeare. A prefatory note pointed out that the play contains "several peculiar modes of expression – Hamlet's wilful obscurities, the crabbed rhetoric sometimes used by Claudius and Polonius, the euphuistic affectation of Osric, the antiquated style of the Player's speech and the Gonzago Play. Thus there is much to be explained ..." (Hogan 1948:5). And in many instances, Hogan's edition succeeded in its explanatory mission. However, he also added, without acknowledgment, some "wilful obscurities" of his own, by careful editing and intralingual translation designed to conceal some of the author's excesses.

A striking example comes from Act Two, Scene Two, where Hamlet is indulging in characteristic self-abasement. Our school text was plausible:

> Why, what an ass am I! This is most brave.
> That I, the son of a dear father murder'd,
> Prompted to my revenge by heaven and hell,
> Must, like a jade, unpack my heart with words,
> And fall a-cursing, like a very drab,
> A scullion!

> II.ii, 575ff.

But one of our classmates, who came from a bookselling family, had a complete Shakespeare in his schoolbag, and read out with gusto a somewhat different version:

> ... Prompted to my revenge by heaven and hell,
> Must like a **whore** unpack my heart with words
> And fall a-cursing, like a very drab,
> **A stallion!**

The "whore", in particular, produced something of a *coup de théâtre*. What we had been studying was a bowdlerized Shakespeare, and we were unaware of this because Hogan had not admitted it. Such reticence was traditional; the Bard had attracted many bowdlerists, and in his chapter on "Shakespeare in Shreds" Perrin (1969:82) explains why the two "distinguished college professors" who edited the "New Hudson Shakespeare" in 1909 also concealed what they had been up to:

> They do not admit that they are producing an expurgation at all. ... Presumably they were afraid that if the high-school and college students who read the New Hudson Shakespeare knew what they were missing, some of them might go look in the attic for pre-Civil War editions. It seems a reasonable fear. But bowdlerism now involves not merely tampering with one's author but lying to one's readers.

It must be said that Hogan's 1948 emendation comes nowhere near the radical surgery practised on these same lines by the eponymous Thomas Bowdler MD, editor of "The Family Shakespeare" (1818):

> ... Prompted to my revenge by heaven and hell,
> Must like a drab unpack my heart with words
> And fall a-cursing!
>
> > II,ii, 575 ff. (Bowdler)

Bowdler excises a whole line, reassigns "drab" to the position of "whore" and eliminates all talk of stallions, or scullions.

If we consider Professor Hogan's two variants, *scullion* and *jade*, and the word he leaves untouched, *drab*, we see that his more modest strategy is one of minimal intervention consistent with decency. And to be fair, there is some doubt about the *stallion*. The First Quarto (1603) had "scalion", the Second Quarto (1605) "stallyon", and the First Folio (1623) "scullion". The OED has some surprising definitions of *stallion*: not only "a male horse not castrated" but also "a man of lascivious life" and "a courtesan". Even if these aspects were unknown to a class of Irish schoolchildren, its primary meaning is dangerous enough. Far better if the textual tradition can allow Hamlet to call himself a hermaphrodite prostitute only twice – *whore* and *drab* – climaxing his self-denunciation by calling himself a housemaid.

The word *whore* also has overtones relevant to the general tenor of Hamlet's speech: the OED defines it, with examples dating from 1100 to 1976, as "A woman who prostitutes herself for hire ... More generally: An unchaste or lewd woman ... A male prostitute; any promiscuous or unprincipled person." Those hermaphrodite tendencies are shared by Professor Hogan's preferred *jade*, which the OED defines, with examples dating from 1386 to 1819, as "1. A contemptuous name for a horse; a horse of inferior breed, e.g. a cart- or draught-horse ... A term of reprobation applied to a woman. Also used playfully, like *hussy* or *minx* ... Rarely applied to a man; usually in some figure drawn from sense 1."

The great advantage of *jade* over *whore*, from a bowdlerist's point of view, is that its sexual connotations have been lost; indeed the word itself has fallen into disuse, making it sound plausibly Shakespearean. Despite his promise to clarify, rather than add to, Shakespeare's "wilful obscurities" and "antiquated style', Professor Hogan offers no gloss of *jade* in his notes, nor does he acknowledge the change. This monosyllable is an act of intralingual translation designed purely to shield his readers from the still current term *whore* – although it does at least restore the horsy element which he lost by excising the stallion.

Why, then, does Hogan leave that filthy *drab*? The OED comments: "Not known before 16th c.; derivation uncertain. 1. A dirty and untidy woman ... 2. A harlot, prostitute, strumpet." One of the examples for the second meaning, dated 1589, is "he-drab", which again offers hermaphrodite overtones.

In the modern schoolroom *drab* has one supreme advantage: nobody has the slightest idea what it means. Hogan's notes do not gloss it. If *jade* is censorship by commission in the text, *drab* is censorship by omission in the footnotes. Both are perverse variants of translation, in the sense used by George Steiner when he says that literature "has no chance of life outside constant translation within its own language", and that "we possess civilisation because we have learnt to translate out of time" (Steiner 1992:31).

4. Brian Merriman's Censors – Not in Front of the Neighbours

Shakespeare, then, had to be rendered *senza coglioni* – the rude Voltairean metaphor is not inappropriate, as Perrin (1969:31) records "castrate", "geld" and "mutilate" as eighteenth-century English verbs for expurgation, with "purge", "prune" and "chasten" appearing around 1800 and "Bowdlerise" in 1836 – because of two conflicting impulses felt by twentieth-century Irish educators: a desire to connect with the classics of English literature, coupled with an anxiety to preserve simple piety among the young. A similar cultural ambivalence affected the relationship between the English and Irish languages, and led to some interesting quirks of translation policy in Ireland.

The Irish-speaking community had declined disastrously during the nineteenth-century. The Irish Free State, founded in 1922, set itself the hopeless task of restoring Irish to a dominant position. The Republic of Ireland is today a bilingual state, with Irish as the first national language and English, as the main vernacular language, recognised as having equal status, but in fact the position of Irish has declined still further over seven decades of political independence. One method of nurturing Irish, starting in the 1920s, was a government-sponsored translation programme to increase the range of writing in Irish by producing Irish-language versions of many books, including such English authors as Emily Brontë, Dickens and George Eliot. Ernest Blythe, the Free State minister in charge of the translation scheme, saw a need for "great masses of reading matter in Irish and reading matter to suit all tastes", including "English novels and detective stories" (Cronin 1996:156).

A recent framework which may help in understanding Blythe's policy of omnivorous translation comes from an article by Itamar Even-Zohar on "The Position of Translated Literature Within the Literary Polysystem" (1978). Even-Zohar suggests that translation may take on a primary role in a literature which is still becoming established, or is peripheral or weak, or contains vacuums within its literature.

But if vacuums had to be filled on the Irish-language side of our national culture, the creation of a state-sponsored "polysystem" also demanded that certain vacuums be created on the English-language side. For fifty years, censorship was a cornerstone of Irish cultural policy, and when it came to literature in translation the censors excluded not only undesirable aliens like Proust, Sartre, Moravia, Graham Greene and Thomas Mann (Adams 1968:240-253), but also, in the 1940s, two English versions of Brian Merriman's earthy poem, *Cúirt an Mheán-Oíche* (*The Midnight Court*), written in Irish in County Clare in the eighteenth-century.

The banning, in 1946 and 1949, of translations of this poem by Frank O'Connor and Lord Longford (Adams 1968:249; Merriman 1971:12) may represent an extreme moment of national prudery; a translation from 1926 had been allowed to stand and later translations have circulated without difficulty. In an introductory essay to the 1912 edition of the Irish text, the Gaelic Leaguer and Catholic revolutionary Piaras Béaslaí had celebrated Merriman's "sense of proportion and sense of humour ... his love of nature, his frank animalism, his healthy sanity ... his entire absence of *a sense of the spiritual*" (Merryman [sic] 1912:5). But there was a more anxious attitude at mid-century. The spiritual superiority of the Gaelic tradition had to be constantly asserted, particularly to those who did not know Irish. A link was drawn between the Roman Catholic religion, nationalism and the Irish language, and the current supremacy of the Catholic clergy was justified by, among other things, carefully nurtured memories of the appalling discrimination against Catholics under the Penal Laws in the eighteenth-century. Yet *Cúirt an Mheán-Oíche*, a major Irish poem from the penal days, embarrassingly suggested that women have sexual requirements, made jokes about impotence among elderly husbands, and questioned clerical celibacy in theory and in practice.

The really significant point, for the purposes of the present essay, is that the ban on *The Midnight Court* extended only to the English text. In 1949 a new edition of the poem in Irish was published in Dublin by subscription: the distinguished list of subscribers included such respectable names as Séan T. O'Kelly, President of Ireland, Eamon de Valera, former Taoiseach and future President of Ireland, and Cearbhall Ó Dálaigh, also a future President of Ireland (Merriman 1949:47). And the poem was well-known in the oral Gaelic tradition; one of its recent translators notes (Merriman 1971:8) that it "became exceedingly popular in Munster and many of the old Gaelic speakers could quote long passages by heart and very often the whole poem" – which was more than a thousand lines long.

The Midnight Court was acceptable in Irish, then, but embarrassing if

Anglophones gained access to it. "Not in front of the neighbours!" Like the Victorian gentleman with his limited editions, Irish speakers were deemed capable of handling material which would be dangerous to their weaker-minded Anglophone fellow-citizens. The refusal of translation, in this case, must be read in the context of Ireland's overlapping linguistic and cultural identities. Translation between the two national languages was perhaps too explicit an intrusion into their delicate and sometimes contradictory relationship.

5. O'Faolain, Vizinczey, e.e. cummings – Transgression not Translation

The article by Meir Sternberg on "Polylingualism as Reality and Translation as Mimesis", quoted at the start of the present essay, charts a number of strategies which a writer can use to represent the diversity of speech types found in the real world (Sternberg 1981:232). At one extreme, following the "homogenizing convention" the author may blend all non-standard speech, including foreign expressions, into one standard unilingual form. At the other end of the spectrum, "untranslated heterolingual" forms may be left as they stand, by a process of what Sternberg calls "vehicular matching".

In popular fiction, those heterolingual forms may be confined to "mimetic clichés" which are felt to be characteristic of the foreign speech community involved, as with exclamations of "Parbleu!" or "Donnerwetter!" by French or German characters (Sternberg 1981:226). Sometimes there is a hint of malice in this: manuscripts of the original Gaelic *Cúirt an Mheán-Oíche* occasionally included untranslated or borrowed English words which happened to have lewd connotations: "pimp" (Merriman 1971: line 128), "stays" (line 396), "brush" (line 764). Such selective reporting of foreign languages may recall Voltaire's *coglioni*. Turning to modern examples of "vehicular matching", I want to reflect on the cultural significance of some examples of the "refusal to translate" in three twentieth-century writers: Irish, Hungarian and American.

Julia O'Faolain's first novel, *Godded and Codded*, has a heroine who undergoes a number of formative experiences as a postgraduate student in Paris, and the text is liberally peppered with French expressions, as well as fragments of Latin, Italian, Spanish, Arabic and Irish. A character is *épris* (O'Faolain 1970:149) rather than smitten, and reflects that "I've always made it a point to be kind to women but comes a day when ... sauve qui peut" (70). The heroine is *coincée* (176) which the author glosses as "cornered".

These expressions may be erudite versions of the "mimetic cliché" but they also function at other levels. They are spoken by non-French characters, they carry important elements of meaning in the story, and they are intermittently translated. The heroine's Algerian boyfriend berates himself (rather Hamletically) for neglecting his revolutionary duties and turning into "a lazy, sensual *couillon* who hides in women's bedrooms and weeps on their shoulders!" (98) And when he is being unsupportive about the heroine's pregnancy, he correctly accuses himself (205) of being "a selfish bastard ... *Un con*."

The effect of intermittent translation here is one neither of censorship nor of modest concealment, but serves instead as a veiled compliment to the reader's erudite knowledge of *gros mots* in French, their valency and their degrees of translatability. Translation has given way to transgression. We are in overseas territory, where they order these things differently, and rude foreign words can be used with a sense of diminished responsibility.

In his sixties bestseller, *In Praise of Older Women*, the Hungarian émigré writer Stephen Vizinczey (1965:35) teaches the reader "the most obscene word in the Hungarian language" [*pina*, which he glosses as "a synonym for vagina"] and then recalls a classroom of boys shouting it in unison. And when his protagonist describes his first unsatisfactory sexual encounter, the woman says "Mach' schnell!" This German phrase, once again translated for us in advance "she told me *to hurry up*" (28), has the effect of making the narrative more vivid and more distanced at the same time.

A last example of vehicular matching (replacing an unacceptable piece of homogenizing convention) comes from Noel Perrin's book on bowdlerism (1969:191):

> When E.E. Cummings published his war memoir, *The Enormous Room*, in 1922, he had a character named Jean Le Nègre exclaim, "My father is dead! Shit. Oh well. The war is over." This greatly upset John S. Sumner, the Secretary of the New York Society for the Suppression of Vice; and in order to calm him, a girl in the publisher's office inked out the word "shit" in every copy left in stock. When the second edition came along in 1927, Cummings found a typically cummingsesque solution, and put Jean's remark into French. He now says, "*Mon père est mort. Merde! Eh b'en! La guerre est finie.*" (In America, even French provides the decent obscurity of a learned language, and Sumner was still satisfied.)

6. Ó Cuilleanáin's Rodari – Not in Front of the Parents

Having mocked the reticence of bowdlerists, translators and heterolinguists generally, I should mention some extenuating circumstances.

Dr Bowdler promised in his 1818 Shakespeare that "those words and expressions are omitted which cannot with propriety be read in a family". Even Noel Perrin, a hostile historian of Bowdlerism, tells how his own young daughters taught him that "some bowdlerism of the parental, reading-aloud sort is almost inevitable" (1969:xii). Nowadays, in our literate times, children still have books read aloud to them, but in the past, works of adult literature were also consumed by hearers as well as readers. To what extent were earlier inhibitions exacerbated by this practise? Are our ideas of acceptable literature today based on the convention of silent reading? To what extent is our contemporary verbal tolerance based on the cultural primacy of writing over speech? These are large questions that may merit further considerations but fall outside our present scope.

My last-minute backtracking is self-interested, as I have to end this essay with a confession. I too have been guilty of wilful distortion and deliberate censorship, designed (in the best paternalistic tradition) to protect a target readership. Some years ago, in connection with a schools' colouring competition, I was asked to translate some poems by the Italian children's writer Gianni Rodari (1920-1980). The Italian text of "I colori dei mestieri" from *Filastrocche in cielo e in terra* [*Rigmaroles up and down*] is as follows:

I colori dei mestieri[1]

Io so i colori dei mestieri
sono bianchi i panettieri
s'alzano prima degli uccelli
e han la farina nei capelli;
sono neri gli spazzacamini,
di sette colori sono gli imbianchini;
gli operai dell'officina
hanno una bella tuta azzurrina,
hanno le mani sporche di grasso;
i fannulloni vanno a spasso
non si sporcano nemmeno un dito,
ma il loro mestiere non è pulito.

Here is my English version:

The colours of the trades

I know the colours of the different trades.
White is the colour the bakers wear;
they're up with the birds in the early light
and there's flour all over their hair.
The chimney-sweeps are black as night;
painters are seven different shades;
workmen behind their factory walls
dress up in dark-blue overalls,
and their hands are covered with grease and grime.
The idle rich have an easy time
keeping their fingers all clean and pink
but that's not an honest trade, I think.

My problem arose with the line "I fannulloni vanno a spasso". Poems for a colouring competition may be taken home by children, some of whose parents may be unemployed. A literal, uninflected translation of the last three lines would read: "The idlers hang around, don't even get one finger dirty, but their trade is not clean." To insult an unemployed parent would in my view be obscene, and also contrary to the socially progressive and humane views which emerge from Gianni Rodari's works generally. With this in mind, and without

---

[1] 'I colori dei mestieri' by Gianni Rodari is reproduced by kind permission of Edizioni EL S.r. l., Trieste.

any proper textual authority from within the poem itself, I abused my position as translator to narrow the term "fannulloni" – "idlers" – to mean only "the idle rich" – always a legitimate target of resentment, as we can all think of people richer and less deserving than ourselves.

Conclusion

This essay has looked at the interplay of words within languages and between languages, in a dual perspective of translation and censorship – two activities which have much in common.

Brower (1959:173) rightly asserts that "translations are the most obvious examples of works which, in Valéry's words, are 'as it were created by their public'". The role of the reader is widely recognized in literary studies. More generally, all completed acts of communication must involve understanding by particular people, and therefore must respect their capacity for understanding and their need to negotiate the acceptability of what they are prepared to understand, especially in their own mother tongue. As we saw in the case of the *Decameron*, such constraints on communication can also be found in original literary works, and by posing challenges to the author's ingenuity, social constraints may indeed stimulate linguistic creativity. This is presumably one reason why Boccaccio went to the trouble of simulating a socially constrained and decorous milieu in which to tell his risqué tales, playing on the ambiguities of understanding, misunderstanding and pretended misunderstanding to add extra layers of enjoyment to his text.

If the aim of rudeness in literature is to explore hidden recesses, one way of doing this is to pretend to keep them hidden. This may not be a valid procedure at a level of surface description, but at a deeper subconscious level the principle of concealment may create an icon of a reality not so much described as recreated or suggested. To avoid the risk of disappearing into the elusive realms of what Professor Morris Zapp calls "textuality as striptease" (Lodge 1984:24-27), we may safely conclude that literary translation, like many other forms of social communication, shows that the principle of concealment as well as the desire for revelation is central to the languages we use.

4 "The achieve of, the mastery of the thing!" Pierre Leyris's Verse Translations of Gerard Manley Hopkins

PHYLLIS GAFFNEY

1. Introduction: A Unique Set of Constraints

The art of translating the strongly ideolectal verse of the English Jesuit, Gerard Manley Hopkins (1844-1889; the above quotation is from 1963:30), has been compared to the art of taming a wild beast, coaxing it down unaccustomed paths while appearing to give it full rein (Jacquin 1994:93).

His poetry is a particularly strange beast to French eyes. In attempting to cope with it, French commentators have compared Hopkins to a curious range of French writers, from Mallarmé and Ponge to the sixteenth-century Jean-Antoine de Baïf, not to mention Claudel, Péguy and Proust (Leyris 1948:551; De Magny 1958:252, 254; Cattaui 1947:30-1, 38-9). An *agonie pascalienne* has been detected in the so-called "terrible sonnets" of his later period; he has even been likened to Rimbaud, in order to convey to a French readership the revolutionary effect of Hopkins's *The Wreck of the Deutschland* (De Grunne 1953:582). And Georges Cattaui characterized the Jesuit Hopkins as a baroque poet, with all that the term implies of Jesuitical extravaganza and disregard for classical proportion (Cattaui 1947:7-44).

Hopkins presents his French-language translators with enormous lexical, morphosyntactic and rhythmical difficulties. Apart from the poet's fondness for using words of Saxon or dialect origin and his deliberate avoidance of Romance words, there is a further difficulty in his delight in coining new compound words and his inventive use of parts of speech. The search for plausible French equivalences for lines such as "Cloud-puffball, torn tufts, tossed pillows flaunt forth, then chevy on an airbuilt thoroughfare", "heaven-roysterers, in gay-gangs they throng", "Squadroned masks and manmarks treadmire toil there / Footfretted in it" – (to quote from just one poem, *That Nature is a Heraclitean Fire*, Hopkins (1963:65f) – clearly challenges the translator to the limits of creative inventiveness within the constraints of the target language.

Violations of syntax and morphology pose an even greater challenge. Hopkins breaks all the rules, substituting a verb for a noun, an adjective for an adverb, or vice versa, choosing to omit those parts of speech which would dilute the intensity of his poetic expression: subordinating conjunctions, articles, auxiliary verbs, relative pronouns. The resulting compressed diction can be a major logical problem for a translator into French. Even if a semantic equivalent for lines like the following examples were to be found in French, there would still be the constraints imposed by standard French syntax, and so the original yet again calls for a creative response if it is to be echoed in the translation:

Not, I'll not, carrion comfort, Despair, not feast on thee
                              (*Carrion Comfort*, p. 60);

This is hoard unheard,
Heard unheeded, leaves me a lonely began
                              (*To seem the stranger lies my lot*, p. 62);

Let him easter in us, be a dayspring to the dimness of us, be a
crimson-cresseted east,
More brightening her, rare-dear Britain, as his reign rolls,
Pride, rose, prince, hero of us, high-priest,
Our heart's charity's hearth's fire, our thought's chivalry's throng's
Lord
                              (*The Wreck of the Deutschland*, XXXV, p. 24)

The third difficulty is acoustic. Hopkins wanted to restore to English poetry
the prosody of earlier times, trying to combine in his verse the metre of ancient
Greece, of early Welsh poetry and of traditional English ballads and nursery
rhymes. Eminently oral, his poetry is measured by stress rather than syllabic
count. But these rhythms of spoken English are alien to those of spoken French;
at best, a translator into French can try to achieve an equivalent effect, particularly by introducing into the target version an abundance of internal rhymes,
assonances and alliterations.

Such a unique set of challenges needs to be matched by an equal degree of
creativity in his translator – indeed, by a degree of poetic intuition – if the translation is to succeed as poetry, and if the constraints of Hopkins's peculiar diction
are to lead to an equivalent liberation in the target tongue.

Several French translators have grappled with Hopkins since the 1930's.
Isolated poems have been published in French, for example, by Edouard Roditi,
Robert Marteau and Georges Cattaui, who included a few translations in the
Appendix to his volume *Trois poètes: Hopkins, Yeats, Eliot* (Roditi 1935; Marteau 1990; Cattaui 1947). As far as collections are concerned, that of Pierre
Leyris, one of the first to make Gerard Manley Hopkins accessible to a French
readership, appeared in the autumn of 1957, under the title *Reliquiae*, contain-
ing nineteen poems and a selection of letters, diary entries and sermons. Seuil
re-issued the volume in 1980, as *Poèmes accompagnés de proses et de dessins*,
this time expanding it to include Leyris's rendering of *The Wreck of the
Deutschland*. Two other collections also came out in 1980: a selection of twenty-
two poems translated by the Jesuit poet, Jean Mambrino (Mambrino 1980), and
Jean-Georges Ritz's complete edition, ambitiously presenting in French the entire
poetic output (Ritz 1980). Then the volume published by Jean-Pierre Audigier
and René Gallet, coinciding with the centenary of Hopkins's death, offers a
further selection of verse and prose pieces (Audigier/Gallet 1989; for further
details of French translations, see Gallet 1980; Gallet 1993).[1]

---

[1] I am grateful to Professor Gallet for this last reference.

Space does not permit a detailed comparison of these translators, but among all of them, two are of outstanding merit, because of the way they manage to import into their own language not just the sense of the English original, but also its poetry. Indeed, it is no accident that Jean Mambrino and Pierre Leyris shared the *Prix du Meilleur Livre Étranger* for their translations of Hopkins.[2] The present essay will focus on the work of Leyris.

Leyris's talents as a translator are widely acknowledged, both inside and outside his native country (Brion 1958; de Grunne 1953; de Magny 1958; Jacquin 1994; Mambrino 1958; Thomas 1958). In France, during his long career, he has won the *Prix Valery Larbaud* and the *Grand Prix National de Traduction*. The *Times Literary Supplement* gave his Hopkins collection an ecstatic review in April 1958 (TLS 1958). George Steiner, in *After Babel* (1992:430-5), cites as a near-ideal translation Leyris's version of the curtal sonnet *Pied Beauty*. His renderings of two other Hopkins poems are praised by Danielle Jacquin (1994: 84-91), and his translations of T.S. Eliot likewise testify to his particular genius and disciplined professionalism (Hooker 1983). Translations have been his life's work: he has been publishing them, in both prose and verse, since 1931, when he was aged twenty-four. Writers he has translated include Blake, Crane, Dickens, Dickinson, Edgeworth, Eliot, Hawthorne, James, Lawrence, McGahern, Melville, Shakespeare, Synge and Yeats.

In exploring Leyris's response to the crushing constraints of Hopkins's poetry, one may characterize his achievements as both lexical and aural, as his finely-tuned sensitivity to words and their resonances echoes both the sense and the sounds of his source by producing equivalent effects in French. Some sample translations of isolated phrases will first be presented, before a close examination of two individual poems in translation – a model translation and a revised translation – leading to some concluding remarks on the creative processes involved in Leyris's work. While the resulting close focus will lack speculative breadth, it may claim some value as belonging to that part of Translation Studies which involves a detailed appraisal of cases where the translator is successful and faithful to the original, despite the difficulties it presents.

2. Leyris's Lexical Range and Aural Sensitivity

In the matter of lexical range, Leyris, like Hopkins, draws on a huge vocabulary, not bounded by modern French, often veering to the archaic in his translations. Thus, for example, in the third line of his version of *That Nature is a Heraclitean Fire ...*, *Que la nature est un feu héraclitéen ...*: "Ils s'ameutent, cohuent en joie, ils vont scintillant en arroi" (Leyris 1980:145), the word "cohuent" and the Old French construction *aller + present participle* give a medieval flavour to "in gay-gangs they throng; they glitter in marches"; in *Tom's Garland*, *La guirlande de Tom* (p. 139), we also find echoes of medieval

---

[2] Mambrino's translations were brought to my attention by Professor Roger Little of Trinity College Dublin. Their qualities are highlighted by Jacquin (1994).

dialogue: "peu me chaut" (line 9) for "Little I reck", "non pas" (line 14) for "O no"; or in *Duns Scotus's Oxford, L'Oxford de Duns Scot*, his last line omits the definite article, as would Old French: "Et qui France enflamma" ("Who fired France"; p. 101). A glance through his translations yields an abundant use of archaic verbs: verbs like *ardre*, to burn; *chaloir*, to matter; *clore*, to close; *octroyer*, to grant; *œuvrer*, to work; *ouïr*, to hear; *quérir*, to seek; and there are others.

While many such archaic turns of phrase are inevitably Latinate, they constitute a proper response, from a Romance language translator, to the rich repertory of indigenous non-Latin word-stock in English, the Saxon and dialect veins so consciously mined by Hopkins. The obsolete helps to convey in French that "vital strangeness and 'otherness'" which Steiner (1992:67) believes essential for a successful translation, all the more essential for successfully translating Hopkins, a poet who, as Pick put it, almost created a new language without providing a dictionary (Leyris 1980:9).

Leyris's response to Hopkins's famous coined compounds displays an equivalent inventiveness and use of archaisms. To match the opening of *Duns Scotus's Oxford*, he gives almost as good as he gets:

> Cité tourée, cité branchue entre tes tours;
> Coucou-sonnante, embourdonnée, d'aloues charmée, de freux rouée,
> de rus cernée   (p. 101)

succeeds in emulating Hopkins:

> Towery city and branchy between towers;
> Cuckoo-echoing, bell-swarmèd, lark-charmèd, rook-racked, river-
> rounded.   (p. 40)

The "towery" and "towers" of the original are carried over in the first line of the French, which repeats "cité" to give it the emphasis which "city" has in the rhythm of the English line. In the following line, the coined "embourdonnée" connotes both resonating bells and buzzing bees filling the air with vibrating sounds, suggested by the compound "bell-swarmèd", while "rook-racked" is echoed, both in alliteration and in sense, by "de freux rouée", with the latter term suggesting the wheel of torture ("roue") connoted by the English "racked" as well as the circular path of rooks in flight. The word "ru[s]" for "river" is a particularly good choice of an archaic or regional term, as it suggests the rustic calm of the university town being evoked, and "de rus", followed by "cernée" ("surrounded"), allows the French version to capture the four syllables and something of the alliteration of the English "river-rounded".

In *Tom's Garland, La guirlande de Tom* (p. 139), line 2, his rendering of the compound "fallowbootfellow" is ingenious: "pote-ès-brodequins" combines assonance and an archaism ("ès") with the familiar ("pote" = "mate, pal") and the curious ("brodequins") to yield a French expression which, like the English, juxtaposes incongruous elements. The term "brodequin" seems particularly apt in the context. Apart from its modern designation of rough military boot, it used to denote quite the reverse kind of footwear: in the 17th century, and later in the early 19th century, it apparently meant an ornate and delicate shoe made of cloth, worn by women and children (Rey et al 1993, vol. 1, p. 296). Similarly, Leyris's translation of the "dapple-dawn-drawn Falcon" from the opening of *The Windhover* (p. 30) (*Le faucon*) by "le Faucon-phaéton de l'aube miroitée" (p. 97), is a rendering which combines alliteration, assonance and mythological reference, as well as being semantically very faithful to its source. And, to take just one out of a range of comparable examples from his *Le Naufrage du Deutschland* (*The Wreck of the Deutschland*): "la douce-comme-phalène Voie lactée" (p. 85) echoes about as well as French can "the moth-soft Milky Way" of stanza XXVI, line 6 (p. 21). With its alliteration ([l], [k]) and soft fricatives ([s], [f]) it echoes the sounds of the original while retaining its meaning and transgressive syntax.

Leyris's finely-tuned sense of the cultural resonance of individual words can be seen again and again, especially when one compares his choices with those of other translators. Take for example his title for *Pied Beauty*: *Beauté Piolée*. Ritz translates it as *Beauté Bigarrée* and Audigier/Gallet use *Beauté Diaprée*. Which is the most appropriate French title? All three adjectives – *piolée, bigarrée, diaprée* – mean "multicoloured". Leyris's choice of the term *piolé(e)* is perhaps explained by a search in Littré (1971,vol. 5,p. 1905), which gives as a probable derivation for the term the noun *pie*, which in one of its meanings relates to land divisions due to crop rotation (ibid. p. 1850). Thus, Leyris's title, at least to some readers, will suggest the varied texture of the landscape that inspires the poem, as well as the "couple-coloured" qualities of the other two denotations of *pie*, "magpie" and "piebald horse".

The translator's real *trouvaille*, as others have noticed before, is to be found in line 7 of *As Kingfishers Catch Fire*, *Le martin-pêcheur flambe*. In his attempt to express the individuality of things around him, Hopkins coined a new verb out of the noun "the self": "to self", which is here conjugated in the present indicative: "Selves – goes itself; *myself* it speaks and spells" (p. 51). Like his model, Leyris is equally creative with the French language in his translation of this line: "S'avère, per-*se*-vère, incante et dit *moi-même*" (p. 127). The verb "s'avère", expresses several notions at once: the ontological certainty, the integrity of phenomena in the world about us, and the coined "per-*se*-vère" – with its hyphenated italicized reflexive pronoun and its echoes of the Latin *per se*, and of Old French or Latin words for "true" (*voir, verus*) – renders with subtlety the English "goes itself", as well as denoting perseverance and continuity of purpose (see Leyris 1980:16).

Further in the same line, the translator opts for the less prosaic reading of the English verb "spells" ("myself it speaks and spells") by translating it as *incante*. There is nothing wrong with using the verb *épeler*, "to spell": *épelle* has the right number of syllables, it is a correct translation, and indeed, it is the word Leyris used in an earlier draft of this poem (Leyris 1948:553). His later choice of the verb *incanter* is, however, an improvement, because this slightly archaic verb, with its overtones of the supernatural, brings to the translation an almost liturgical connotation, in keeping with the spirit of the original poem. If preserving ambiguities is the mark of a skilled translator, it is also important to know (as in this case) when not to preserve them. As will be seen in Section 4 below, this is by no means the only instance of the painstaking approach of a translator who sees his work as never quite finished.

The same attentiveness to tone can be detected in his version of line 8 of the same poem, where the phrase "for that I came" is lengthened by Audigier/ Gallet to "pour cela je suis née" and by Ritz to "je suis venu pour cela". Leyris simply keeps the four syllables of the English intact, translating them accurately and concisely by a phrase which smacks of Old French: "pour ce je vins" (p. 127). With his dramatic monosyllables, he can place the caesura of the French line before the last four syllables, echoing the rhythm of the English line. More strikingly, his choice of the *passé simple* ("je vins") enhances the tone of solemnity in which this poetic celebration of the mystery of creation bathes. The anecdotal "je suis venu" or "je suis née" are comparatively off the mark.

By and large, Leyris is extremely faithful to the overall sound patterns of the original poems. Where he cannot reproduce in French the rhythms of Hopkins's English, he compensates by introducing internal rhymes, assonances and alliterations; he achieves very plausible rhyme schemes; and he frequently translates Hopkins into alexandrine verse, the preferred metre of classical French poetry.

His response to the assonance in the following lines from *The Wreck of the Deutschland* (V, lines 7-8):

> His mystery must be instressed, stressed;
> For I greet him the days I meet him, and bless when I understand   (p. 14)

exploits the target language to produce an equivalent cluster of alliterations and assonances with no loss of meaning:

> Son mystère doit s'imprimer, doit s'intimer;
> Aussi je Le salue aussitôt que perçu, et je bénis quand je saisis.   (p. 63)

In the same poem (VIII, ls. 3-5), he is undeterred by the internal rhymes and thoroughly Anglo-Saxon derivations and sounds of:

> How a lush-kept plush-capped sloe
> Will, mouthed to flesh-burst,
> Gush!
>   (p. 15)

but, taking the opportunity to hyphenate where French permits, he renders the syntax, assonance and sense while yielding an end-rhyme into the bargain:

Lestée de suc, coiffée-de-peluche, la prunelle,
L'embouche-t-on à craque-chair, comme elle
Jute!   (p. 67)

Or one can note how, in the second quatrain of *To seem the stranger* ... (*Paraître l'étranger* ...), Hopkins's convoluted word order is carried over in the translation, sense for sense, sound for sound, break for break, with the French alexandrines one syllable shorter in the third line in response to the enjambment of the English. Thus:

L'Angleterre ô mon cœur en quiert l'honneur! épouse
De mon penser créant, ne m'écouterait pas
Si je plaidais, ni ne plaidé-je: combien las-
sé d'être là, oisif, où les guerres abondent   (p. 141)

strikingly conveys the meaning and tone of Hopkins's original:

England, whose honour O all my heart woos, wife
To my creating thought, would neither hear
Me, were I pleading, plead nor do I: I wear-
y of idle a being but by where wars are rife.   (p. 62)

3. *Spring and Fall*: a Model Translation

Having catalogued some of the strengths which Pierre Leyris brings to the unique challenge of Gerard Manley Hopkins, it is time to consider a specific poem in its entirety: Leyris's translation of *Spring and Fall*, where near perfect equiva-lence is achieved, on every level – rhyme, rhythm and sense. First, the original poem and Leyris's rendering:

SPRING AND FALL
To a young child

    Margaret, are you grieving
    Over Goldengrove unleaving?
    Leaves, like the things of man, you
4   With your fresh thoughts care for, can you?
    Ah! as the heart grows older
    It will come to such sights colder
    By and by, nor spare a sigh
8   Though worlds of wanwood leafmeal lie;
    And yet you will weep and know why.
    Now no matter, child, the name:
    Sorrow's springs are the same.
12 Nor mouth had, no nor mind, expressed
    What heart heard of, ghost guessed:
    It is the blight man was born for,
    It is Margaret you mourn for.   (p. 50)

PRINTEMPS ET AUTOMNE
A une jeune enfant

      Marguerite, mènes-tu deuil
      Sur le Bois-Doré qui s'effeuille?
      Ainsi, de feuilles, comme humaines,
4   Voici tes frais pensers en peine?
      Ah! quand le cœur vient à vieillir
      C'est, peu à peu, pour s'endurcir
      Sans plus gratifier d'un soupir
8   Un monde effeuillé de bois mort;
      Alors pourtant tu pleureras
      Sans laisser de savoir pourquoi.
      Mais quelque nom qu'on donne aux peines,
12   Enfant, leurs sources sont les mêmes.
      L'âme a deviné, le cœur ouï
      Ce qu'esprit ni lèvres n'ont dit:
      Si l'homme naît, c'est pour qu'il meure,
16   C'est Marguerite que tu pleures.   (p. 109)

The translation is particularly successful in conveying the rhythm of the original, through its masterful control of the octosyllable, which is maintained throughout. The translator also approximates the original rhyme pattern: only four of the French lines are not rhyming couplets (lines 7-8 and lines 11-12). But as the latter pair of lines are assonanced instead (the vowel sound of *peines* echoes that of *mêmes*), and as line 7 actually continues the rhyme of the preceding couplet (with *soupir* picking up *vieillir* and *s'endurcir*), there is really only one exception to the flow of octosyllabic rhyming couplets. And, significantly, this one exception (lines 7-8) is faithful to the English rhyme pattern, which also changes at a similar point in the poem: Hopkins's rhyming couplets change at lines 7, 8 and 9 to form a rhyming triplet, while Leyris rhymes lines 5, 6 and 7.

One of the more untranslatable lines, "Though worlds of wanwood leafmeal lie", occurs in the centre of the three rhymed lines, and at the mid-point of the poem, being the eighth line out of fifteen lines of verse. Leyris does not perhaps fully do justice to the import of those Hopkinsian compounds, "wanwood" and "leafmeal" – suggesting the piecemeal falling of leaves, one by one, to rot down into a lifeless heap – by his "Un monde effeuillé de bois mort". But he compensates for this semantic loss by a gain in terms of rhythm, by rhyming the three lines leading up to his exceptional line 8, and by adding an extra line at this moment in the French poem: line 9 of the English ("And yet you will weep and know why") is expanded to two lines in the French ("Alors pourtant tu pleureras / Sans laisser de savoir pourquoi"). This lengthening of one line into two arrests the rhythm, matching the ponderous monosyllables of the English line 9, and making the recipient of the poem dwell on the emotion being expressed.

The opening couplet, with its alliterations and long rhyme sound [œj], offers suitable French equivalents for the alliteration and long sounds of the English: "Marguerite, mènes-tu deuil" / "Sur le Bois-Doré qui s'effeuille?" Leyris exploits the fact that both languages contain rhyme possibilities for the same linguistic signs – *grief/leaf*, *grieving/leaving* are echoed by the French *deuil/feuille, deuil/s'effeuille*. And further associations are brought out by the translation. There is the expression to depict a wintry landscape, *la nature en deuil*. Moreover, in French, as in English, *marguerite* is a type of daisy; the verb *s'effeuiller* means to shed petals or to shed leaves. Thus, behind the autumnal image of falling leaves, there is also the image of the flower losing its petals, just as the young child's (Margaret's) youth will pass. This links in a potent way with the final "It is Margaret you mourn for". Then the phrase *effeuiller la marguerite* (denoting the rustic game of picking off petals, one by one, while chanting "S/he loves me, s/he loves me not") will perhaps strike a chord in a French audience. Whether this is a conscious or unconscious association on Leyris's part is beside the point; what matters is his creative ability to exploit the resources of his target language to add to the source language text, changing neither its meaning nor its tone, but rather enhancing both.

Not every translator would render the second couplet in the way Leyris does, rhyming "humaines" (= "things of man") with "en peine" (= "care for"). His approach succeeds both in rhyming the lines and in catching some of the flavour of the curious syntax of Hopkins's lines 3 and 4. By conveying the almost conversational tone of the question posed in line 4 ("Voici ...") he also introduces into French the elliptical compression of the original.

The translation contains a wealth of alliteration in response to the English. A particularly successful example can be seen in the [s], [p], [w] and [r] sounds of lines 9 and 10:

> Alors pourtant tu pleureras
> Sans laisser de savoir pourquoi...
> (= And yet you will weep and know why).

On the level of sense, too, the translation succeeds in rendering all the semantic units of the original. This is achieved almost line for line, with the exception of the expanded line 9 already mentioned, and the last four lines. Lines 12 and 13 of the original are changed syntactically. The order of the negative main statement introducing a positive subordinate in the proposition:

> Nor mouth had, no nor mind, expressed
> What heart heard of, ghost guessed

is reversed, so that the French opens with a positive statement introducing a negative one:

> L'âme a deviné, le cœur ouï
> Ce qu'esprit ni lèvres n'ont dit.

But this shift in emphasis is compensated by Leyris's use of the archaic verb *ouïr* and the archaic negative form, which together help to render the evocative biblical solemnity of these lines (cf. 1 Cor 2.9).

A more striking departure from the original is found in the last couplet. Although the poem is about decay and human mortality, Hopkins does not mention death openly; he alludes to our common lot by his concluding:

> It is the blight man was born for,
> It is Margaret you mourn for.

Leyris opts for the rather obvious French rhyme of *meure* and *pleures*:

> Si l'homme naît, c'est pour qu'il meure,
> C'est Marguerite que tu pleures.

The French poem ends, then, on an aphorism, with a more explicit reference to death than the allusive English conclusion. Does it render the translated poem "more French"? One may be reminded of the moral tradition of La Fontaine, of La Rochefoucauld. It certainly clarifies any doubts, in case we were wondering what the poem was about. A different light is cast on the poem, not any additional sense. And, because it is done for the sake of the rhyme and the rhythm, this instance of "creative transposition" (Jakobson 1959) is eminently defensible.

In contrast to Leyris's, Jean-Georges Ritz's translation of *Spring and Fall* is prosaic; it retains little or no sense of the sounds of the original English, its line lengths vary from eight syllables (line 2) to seventeen syllables (line 13), and it is more than once semantically suspect. A reading of the two versions helps to highlight the difference between a truly *literary* translation, with all the creativity that the term implies, and a rendering that cannot lay claim to much poetic merit.

4. *I wake and feel the fell of dark, not day* ...: A Translation Revisited
The translator's meticulous attention to his craft prompts him to go back to his translations and revise them, making apparently very minor adjustments. For example, Leyris's early translation of *I wake and feel the fell of dark, not day* – one of the poet's so-called "terrible sonnets" dating from his Dublin days – has been slightly but significantly modified by the 1980 edition. (Italics have been used to indicate the alterations in the revised translation.)

> I wake and feel the fell of dark, not day.
> What hours, O what black hours we have spent
> This night! what sights you, heart, saw; ways you went!
> 4   And more must, in yet longer light's delay.
> With witness I speak this. But where I say
> Hours I mean years, mean life. And my lament
> Is cries countless, cries like dead letters sent
> 8   To dearest him that lives alas! away.

> I am gall, I am heartburn. God's most deep decree
> Bitter would have me taste: my taste was me;
> Bones built in me, flesh filled, blood brimmed the curse.
> 12   Selfyeast of spirit a dull dough sours. I see
> The lost are like this, and their scourge to be
> As I am mine, their sweating selves; but worse.   (p. 62)

Leyris's early rendering is in itself very good. The French is composed of alexandrines; meticulous attention is paid to the rhythms of the English; the second quatrain is cross-rhymed (*-is/-ainte*); and the sestet, while not achieving end-rhymes, uses nasals (*-onde/ sang*) or assonance (*maléfice/pire, aigre/être*).

> *Je m'éveille et palpe l'obscur, non la lumière.*
> Quelles, *déjà pour nous*, ô quelles noires heures
> De nuit! *Quelles visions tu vis, cœur; voies allas!*
> 4   *Et davantage encore t'incombe d'ici l'aube.*
> J'ai témoin pour ce que j'avance. Or quand je dis
> Heures, j'entends années, j'entends vie. Et ma plainte
> Est cris sans nombre, cris lancés comme des plis
> 8   Perdus vers le très cher qui vit las! hors d'atteinte.
> Je suis fiel, aigreurs. Dieu selon sa loi profonde,
> M'a fait goûter l'amer: mon goût propre: os, chair, sang
> Ont *armé, étoffé*, comblé le maléfice.
> 12   Self-levain de l'esprit sûrit une pâte aigre.
> C'est le lot des damnés et leur fléau doit être
> Comme je suis le mien, leur moi suant, mais pire.
>   (de Grunne 1953:590f)

In the 1980 version of the translation, most of the changes occur in the first quatrain; otherwise, two words in line 11 have been altered; a plural has become a singular (line 9); and there are a few changes in punctuation.

> *Réveil: je sens le chu du noir, non pas le jour.*
> Quelles *heures, déjà*, ô quelles noires heures
> De nuit! *Mon cœur, quelles visions! Par quelles voies!*
> 4   *Et quelles à subir tant que tarde encor l'aube!*
> J'ai témoin pour ce que j'avance. Or, quand je dis
> Heures, j'entends années, j'entends vie. Et ma plainte
> Est cris sans nombre, cris lancés comme des plis
> 8   Perdus vers le très cher qui vit las! hors d'atteinte.
> Je suis fiel, *aigreur*. Dieu, selon sa loi profonde,
> M'a fait goûter l'amer: mon goût propre: os, chair, sang
> Ont *charpenté, rempli*, comblé le maléfice.
> 12   Self-levain de l'esprit sûrit une pâte aigre.
> C'est le lot des damnés et leur fléau doit être
> Comme je suis le mien, leur moi suant; mais pire.   (1980:143)

Presumably the punctuation changes, involving additional commas or one substitution of a semi-colon for a comma, are intended to match more closely the
rhythm of the English lines.

Each change of wording involves an improvement. Take the first line: "I
wake and feel the fell of dark, not day"; instead of: "Je m'éveille et palpe
l'obscur, non la lumière" Leyris eventually opted for: "Réveil: je sens le chu du
noir, non pas le jour." This is both aurally and semantically more successful.
Aurally, because the translator goes for as many monosyllables as possible, to
echo the cadence of the English, and because the only word that is not a monosyllable, the first word, the noun *Réveil*, gives the poem a stronger, more direct
opening than "Je m'éveille", as well as the fact that its sound imitates the two
opening syllables of the original: "I wake". The line is semantically more successful, as "feel the fell of dark" is rendered more closely by "sens le chu du
noir" than by "palpe l'obscur"; "le chu" for "the fell" suggests the felling of
trees, connoting even perhaps the downward motion of a cruel blow that is
implied in one of its English meanings. "Chu du" suggests *chute*, the noun for
"a fall". Then, using "jour" instead of "lumière" to translate "day" is also a
change for the better, as the French word "jour" often denotes "daylight" as
opposed to "darkness", and so connects with "réveil" in the same way as "I
wake" connects with "day".

The second line of the poem, too, is improved in the 1980 version. For "What
hours, O what black hours we have spent", the earlier "Quelles, déjà pour nous,
ô quelles noires heures" has been changed to "Quelles heures, déjà, ô quelles
noires heures". Both French versions are more concise than the English line, as
both omit the direct translation of "we have spent". Presumably the speaker's
personal experience is contained by implication in the adverb "déjà". The earlier French version, although its syntax is Hopkinsian, reads awkwardly; and
the substitution of "heures" for "pour nous" allows the repetition of the word
"heures" just as the English line repeats the word "hours".

It is less evident why the translator changed line three: "what sights you,
heart, saw; ways you went!" is more literally rendered by the earlier "Quelles
visions tu vis, cœur; voies allas!" than by the later version, which runs " ... Mon
cœur, quelles visions! Par quelles voies!" Why does Leyris move from a more
to a less literal translation, omitting two verb forms? On reflection, one can
propose several possible reasons. His 1980 version is more elliptical than the
previous version; it is also more intimate ("Mon cœur"), suggesting a heart-to-
heart between the poet and his inner self, which is present in the English – "we
have spent" (line 2) – but not yet present in the translation. The choice is in
favour of words that matter; the verbs in "quelles visions *tu vis*" and in "[quelles]
voies *allas*", although mirroring the English line, are perhaps unnecessary, as
tautologous, and therefore done away with, in favour of a (highly Hopkinsian)
set of nouns and exclamation marks. The economy of the line is sufficient to
impart the sense without the verbs. And, apart from the fact that "voies allas" is
not a very harmonious phrase, it is also potentially ambiguous, given all the

homonyms in French of the phoneme [vwa]. Finally, the deletion of the two verbs in the *passé simple* makes sense in terms of the overall impact of the poem. All the other verbs in this poem are in the present or *passé composé*, in order to convey the immediacy of the depressed state being described.

The fourth line involves a gain, too, in the newer version. "Et davantage encore t'incombe d'ici l'aube" is less successful than "Et quelles à subir tant que tarde encor l'aube". "D'ici l'aube" is too concise for "in yet longer light's delay"; "tant que tarde encor l'aube", which alliterates the [t] sound, echoes the English more faithfully.

The translator is rightly happy with the next four lines (only a comma to be inserted), and with most of the remainder of the poem. With the exception of two more word changes in line 11: "Bones built in me, flesh filled, bloom brimmed the curse". The French starts the translation of this line at the end of line 10 which runs into line 11: "os, chair, sang / Ont armé, étoffé, comblé le maléfice". Leyris later altered "armé, étoffé" to "charpenté, rempli". Apart from being semantically more precise, as their connotations are more directly associated with "built" and "filled", these two active past participles also improve the sound pattern of the translation. The assonanced nasals and alliterations of "Charpenté, rempli, comblé", following "os, chair, sang", suggest a French equivalent for the assonance and alliteration in the English verb sequence "built ... filled ... brimmed".

The end result is a superb example of a poem where the translation not only says what the original poem says, but does what the original poem does.

5. Conclusion: Creative Processes

Having scrutinized the end-product of some of Pierre Leyris's translations of Gerard Manley Hopkins, it may be appropriate to conclude by offering a word on the processes involved. In the Preface to his collection, Leyris discusses syntax and lexis as constituting the main challenges for a French translator of Hopkins (Leyris 1980:9-23). On what is arguably an even greater challenge, that of achieving equivalence in sound, he is more reticent. And yet it is precisely in this area where his own work can often be outstanding.

The importance of reading Hopkins's verse aloud has always been recognized, even by the poet himself. Paul Valéry, on discovering the poet's work, contrasted in his *Cahiers* the French attitude to poetry with the English. The former, Valéry claimed, was characterized by a "négligence totale de l'élément musical"; and he remarked, just as Hopkins himself had indicated to Robert Bridges, that Hopkins's poetry was written for the ear, and that "tel poème d'Hopkins qui est «obscur» et étrange (et donc à rejeter) pour l'œil devient tout autre si on le lit avec l'oreille" (Valéry 1974:1123-24).[3]

---

[3] Thus Hopkins, in a letter to Robert Bridges: "(...) above all remember what applies to all my verse, that it is, as living art should be, made for performance and that its performance is not reading with the eye but loud, leisurely, poetical (not rhetorical) recitation..." (Colleer Abbott 1955:246).

Monsieur Leyris very kindly replied by letter to some questions put by the present writer, outlining the processes whereby he moves from Hopkins to French. He explained that he first translates the impression that the poem leaves in his ear and his heart. The receptivity is simultaneously aural and semantic; it yields a formless rough mass, over which the translator gradually works very consciously, over months at a time, using all available dictionaries and never losing sight of his original. He proceeds by stages, but his approach is by no means systematic.

The sense that he operates in an impressionistic, unsystematic way is further reinforced in a postscript to the same letter, where, to illustrate the importance of the subconscious in the translation process, he relates how he had once arrived at an impasse in translating a short piece by Stephen Crane. In the line "The dull fall of dirt on wood" he could not come up with a word for "dirt". The following night, half asleep, but aware of a drift of trivial unconscious thoughts completely unrelated to his translation, the word *fange* suddenly presented itself, perfectly appropriate for the problematic line in question. He leapt from his bed to note it down.[4]

That Proustian view of the translator in touch with his subconscious echoes an image found in Leyris's Preface, where he compares the French language to a smooth stone wall, against which the battering ram of Hopkins's poem vainly struggles, only suddenly to yield a hidden breach (Leyris 1980:16). Sudden flashes of insight, sudden ways forward, are part of the process of translating a difficult original. There is much that is intuitive, creative and unconscious at play, and the *mémoire involontaire* (or should we call it the *dictionnaire involontaire*?) will do more than all the treatises on semantics or rules of versification.

In a lecture delivered in 1969, Cecil Day-Lewis compared the process of translating poetry with the process of writing original verse: "A translation, like an original poem, is partly a search for truth: the translator uses the impressions his original makes upon him, both as guides to that poem's meaning, and as motives towards finding an equivalent for it in his own tongue" (Day-Lewis 1970:20). As with Leyris, the *impressions* are the starting-point.

In order to convey in translation the flavour of Gerard Manley Hopkins, one must achieve a similarly idiosyncratic poetic voice in the target language. This is exactly what Pierre Leyris achieves by the exploitation of the resources of French and by his natural talents: a highly receptive ear, an exceptional sensitivity to words, their origins, connotations and contexts, and finally an intuitive sixth sense which leaves the creative mind open to the subconscious. To quote the English reviewer of Leyris's first edition: "Hopkins's music and cadence, transmuted through his interpreter's ear, have created a striking new poetical language of which the influence in France (if it is listened to) might be incalculable" (*TLS*, April 4, 1958:184).

---

[4] Leyris, personal letter to Phyllis Gaffney, 26/7/1994

5   Ideological Shifts in Cross-Cultural Translation

R. A. MEGRAB

Rendering foreign texts raises questions not only about universals but about the equally significant dissimilarities between human languages. English and Arabic are two distinct languages with vastly different characteristics: they share no common linguistic or cultural ancestry, have few lexical cognates and, above all, have no exact correspondences or grammar and rhetoric.

Translation means rewriting the source text (ST) in the form of the target text (TT), and this involves both interpretation of the ST and transformation of the target language (TL). In interpretation, the translator attempts to analyze the text and identify the ideologies – intended or unintended – which have constrained the use of linguistic signs. The process, however, is often accompanied by a set of language shifts, especially when the ideology of the translator differs widely from that of the original author. This is because, as Hodge and Kress (1993:5) point out, "we all interpret the flux of experience through means of interpretive schemata, initial expectations about the world, and priorities of interests".

It is on the basis of this interaction between what is in the text and what is in the translator's mind that the transformation procedure is decided. Two ideological shifts can be clearly observed during the process of transformation: the first involves a shift away from the source culture; the second is a shift in the direction of the target culture, usually resulting in an identification based more or less in ideology.

1. Interpretation

The interpretation of texts has long been the subject of controversy and debate among linguists and philosophers. Positivists have considered interpretation as the product of a single, unique act, namely the intention of one person (the author), which the reader has to seek out and respect regardless of any other discourse agents. Others have seen it as a constantly varying product of an infinite and incomplete act of reading (Steiner, 1992). In fact, interpretation already differs from one individual to another within the same linguistic community let alone between individuals from different cultures. Interpretation, as the product of a delicate interaction between what is in the text and what is in the interpreter's mind, involves a combination of knowledge inherent in the ST and knowledge in the mind of the interpreter/translator. Thus the interpretation process is determined by the nature of the relationship that binds the translator to the ST, which is in turn bound up with the identity of the translator.

Although the process of interpretation cannot be totally free of ideology – for it inherently presupposes subjective involvement – the translator has to maximize objectivity at this stage because of the importance of being objective at subsequent stages. Interpretation should be made with the intentions of the original author always uppermost in mind, by recourse in the first place to the

ST and thereafter to contextual cues if and when these are accessible and available. The following extract taken from an advertisement by Nordic Sport for skiing illustrates this:

(1) Your secret to lasting weight loss is a faster metabolism with Nordic Sport Ski.
  • Scientific tests prove Nordic Sport burns more fat - up to 1,000 calories per hour.
  • Nordic Sport Ski is for everyone - no experience necessary.
  • Nordic Sport Ski, your High-Tech approach to weight loss.
  • Nordic Sport by Nordic Track, America's fitness leader for over 18 years.

                                      (*The Independent*, 23 April 1994)

The text consists of a set of what Fairclough (1989:15) calls classification schemes, that is, particular ways of structuring or organizing the words of a text following the particular ideological organisation of the information expressed in the text. In the above example the claim made is that "Nordic Sport Ski" will help people achieve physical fitness; nevertheless, material gain for the company remains the undisclosed primary objective, and the various schemes in the text work towards this end. The first scheme is psychologically orientated, being built upon people's desire for efficient and rapid weight loss. Reference to scientific tests gives the claim greater authority for people who are prepared to accept scientific evidence. Another scheme draws upon the belief that high technology improves things or means progress. Yet another refers to America as the country where the equipment has long been used, thus seeking to profit from the status of America as a world power in terms of politics, economics, and scientific developments.

Classification schemes operate and are organized in accordance with the message they are intended to convey as well as the conception of reality that activates them. This is well illustrated by the following example from an article about Hassan II (King of Morocco) in the Arabic magazine *Al-Majalla*.

(2) al-Hassan al-thaanii waqt li-dawla wa waqt
     lil-aSdiqaa'wa waqt li-naffs

A close translation of (2) above into English might read as:

    Hassan II: A time for the state, a time for friends, and a time for himself.

The classification schemes referred to earlier reflect here a certain ideological reality. It is important to understand that the slightest alteration in the phrasal order − (i) time for the state; (ii) time for friends; (iii) time for himself − will drastically affect the pragmatic meaning. The significance of this positioning stems from its being symbolic of behaviour and a set of values that give absolute priority to the public interest, followed next by friends and finally oneself.

Interpretation of a text, therefore, not only relates the semantic value of words to their grammatical forms but also depends on pragmatic knowledge, such as that evidenced in classification schemes, which ultimately determines the meaning. In this respect, the cultural context, which includes ideological and moral values, remains paramount for the analysis and translation of the ideologies embedded in the text. The cultural context is, as defined by Goldman (1964), a world vision that links together the members of a social group and distinguishes them from others. In other words, it is a set of cultural predispositions (conventions, beliefs, values and assumptions) internalized in the mind of the individual but socially determined. The interpretation of a text therefore becomes the product of a social (or inter-subjective) practice. For instance, the expression:

(3) `amaliyya istishhaadiyya (act of martyrdom)

which remains a controversial issue in international politics, can enjoy two ideologically conflicting meanings depending on the contexts of their production. The use of the religious term "martyrdom" has two functions in the Arab cultural context. It serves as an instrument which legitimates the act of martyrdom against the "unjust", "the evil one", "the enemy", and so forth, a function which conforms with Aptor's suggestion that the sacred can be employed to develop a system of legitimacy (in Hudson 1977:11). Another function of the term derives from its use during the Islamic conquests. This confers on the cause of the performer of the same act some sort of sacredness and impels a positive response from the receiver.

In the Western world, however, there is no equivalence for this expression. It is usually represented in the English media by expressions such as:

(3a) a suicide bomb
(3b) a terrorist/suicide attack

The terms used in the translation have the effect of stigmatizing by associating the act of martyrdom with violence and crime and even fanaticism. The Whorfian principle that words and structures create as well as reflecting social behaviour holds good. They do indeed provide legitimating or stigmatizing vocabularies of motive to influence, conceal, or reveal structures of power (Brown 1993:44).

The major point here is that in seeking to retrieve from a whole range of possible meanings what actually is meant in the text, differences are bound to occur depending on the associations made by readers between what they read and their own experience. Interpretation thus involves an ideological relationship between the translator's experience and the text as a set of signs with plural meanings going far beyond what they actually seem to say if not processed critically.

In the following example:

(4) umm al-ma`aarik (the mother of battles)

"the mother of battles" is a name given to the Gulf War by Iraqi president Saddam Hussein and has been adopted by the Iraqi media. The choice of words in the above example was not random for there is here a high degree of ideological motivation. If interpreted within its context, the expression *umm al-ma`aarik* can open up a variety of associated meanings: (i) the decisive war, that is, the war which will decide the faith of the whole nation, (ii) the sacred war, that is, a war named after the battle where two nephews of the Prophet Muhammad died fighting the Umayyah illegitimate seizure of power after the death of the fourth Caliph (successor of the Prophet Muhammad) – an association which addresses not only the emotions of the Iraqi people but also the concerns of Muslims all over the world – and (iii) the vast war, a meaning arising from the large number of participating allied countries.

When translating such a text into English, the translator will have to decide which of these ST meanings (i), (ii) and/or (iii) are to be kept in the TT. Obviously, the translator bases a decision upon a number of other factors, the most important of which are the pragmatic function of the text and the ideological inclination of the audience. For instance, if the event of the war itself is more important to the meaning of the text than its associated meanings, it can simply be translated as:

(4a) the Gulf War

No matter how important some aspects of meaning might be in the ST context, the translator might have to represent them according to the ideological expectations of the target audience. The Arabic daily *al-Hayaat* in January 1995 used the following expression:

(5)   al-qanaabil al-'irnaldiyya `aadat 'ilaa landan (the Irish bombs have
      returned to London)

The text seems to imply that there is a conflict or war between Ireland and England, the latter symbolized by London in the text. This translation is, however, most inappropriate in a British context. Example 5 was part of a text translated into English by English native-speakers at the University of Leeds:

(5a) IRA bombs have returned to London

The rendering of (5a) is not merely a product of the students' creativity; it is also an outcome of ideological constraints imposed by the target language culture and audience. Discussion of interpretation as a part of translation involves such matters as the writer of the source language (SL) text, the translator, and the socio-political conditions of the production, as well as those of its translation. Readers apply various patterns of selection, retrospection, anticipation, and formulation of their own expectations in the process of making sense of a text.

Certainly, interpretation offers a free-play signification system of meanings which allows the translator to remove the veil on concealed ideologies and identify areas of cross-ideological variation that can be problematic in the translation. Yet it does not solve the problem of when to stop the process of multiplication of meanings since, as Silverman (1983:31) points out, one single lexeme can lead into the same amount of meaning as a 500-page novel.

Interpretation also cannot offer a way to deal with ideological variations between the SL and the TL during the translation process. Translators are, therefore, faced with two other main tasks: they should constrain the plurality of meanings and create a way to bridge the ideological gap between the two languages throughout the process of transformation from the SL into the TL.

2. Transformation

Transformation is a decision-making process. It represents the ultimate stage that precedes the reception of the text in the TL. At this stage the translator, who acts as the agent of a cultural practice, will have already assimilated and interpreted the ST, either consciously or unconsciously, under specific motivations from a specific perspective. It is often the case that the bigger the ideological gap between the source and target languages, the more interference there will be from the translator's own ideologies. Indeed, it is my contention that the major problem faced when translating from one language into another is more ideological than linguistic.

It is in the nature of things that people have specific and different deep-seated perceptions of the world built upon social institutionalization. Because of the expected familiarity and predictability of others, people are often eager to relate what they read to their immediate level of experience. The following is an extract from an Arabic text which both Libyan and English students of translation were asked to render into English:

(6) rafD al-niZaam al-liibii tasliim muttahamayh fii Haadith tafjiir Taa'irat baan am fawq iscotlanda

(the refusal of the Libyan regime to extradite its two suspects in the Pan Am bombing accident over Scotland)

The SL author used *Haadith* (accident) with *tafjiir* (bombing) where it would have been possible for him to use *tafjiir* alone. Here, the author's semantic choice is potent with ideological meaning. The word *Haadith* is used to play down the seriousness of the bombing. The following are the translations by the English students (6a) and Libyan students (6b):

(6a) ...Libya's continued refusal to extradite the two suspects in the bombing of the Pan Am jet over Scotland

(6b) ...the Libyan refusal to extradite its two suspects in the explosion of the Pan Am plane over Scotland

Comparing the two translations, the conflict of ideologies is quite obvious. English trainees transferred *haadith tafjiir* (accident of bombing) into a single

word "bombing'" in (6a). Likewise, Libyans opted for a single-word translation
but with a different meaning: explosion (6b). Obviously, "bombing" is stigma-
tising while "explosion" is neutral. This shows that translators can be driven,
consciously or unconsciously, by the dominant ideologies in their native language and culture. They need, therefore, to develop more than linguistic skills.
Acute sensitivity towards the ideological subtleties of the text they are translating must take precedence over all other prerequisite skills. But will an analysis
and interpretation of the ideological load at the ST level suffice for a successful
translation?

Part of the translators' task is also to be aware of the ideological impact of
their translation on the TL reader, since ideological conflict often operates cross-
culturally. Ideological conflict in language can be best illustrated in times of
war for it is in such situations that the boundaries between true and false are
most easily blurred, giving rise to massive stereotypes. In effect, stereotyping
accrues mainly from ideological struggles that are waged in words through
texts in various forms of language. An example cited by Hodge and Kress
(1993:162) illustrates this fact. It is a list of vocabulary used in The British
media in its coverage of the Gulf war and published by *The Guardian* newspa-
per. It goes without saying that the vocabulary describing the enemy in the list
below is charged with negative connotations which in turn structure the thought
of its audience. The translator, being part of this audience, is often prone to
being influenced by such social values and stereotypes.

Mad Dogs and Englishmen

We have	*They have*
Army, Navy and Air Force	A war machine
Reporting guidelines	Censorship
Press briefings	Propaganda

Our boys are	*Theirs are*
Professional	Brain washed
Lion-hearts	Paper tigers
Cautious	Cowardly
Confident	Desperate
Heroes	Cornered
Dare-devils	Cannon fodder
Young knights of the skies	Bastards of Baghdad
Loyal	Blindly obedient
Desert rats	Mad dogs
Resolute	Ruthless
Brave	Fanatical

Our missiles are	*Their missiles are*
Like Luke Skywalker	Ageing duds
Darth Vader	(rhymes with zapping with Scuds)

Our POWs are	**Their POWs are**
Gallant boys	Overgrown school children

George Bush is	**Saddam Hussain is**
At peace with himself	Demented
Resolute	Defiant
Statesmanlike	An evil tyrant
Assured	A crackpot monster

Our Planes	**Their Planes**
Suffer a high rate of attrition	Are shot out of the sky
Fail to return from mission	Are zapped

As mentioned before, this categorization is bound to ferment in the reader's mind in such a way as to become a kind of natural or standard image the reader will recall when thinking, hearing, or reading about the same thing. In circumstances like these, translation, given the social impact it makes as a socio-cultural practice, turns into an agency reinforcing or de-emphasizing a set of ideologies already ingrained in the mind of the TL reader (Karama 1996). For this purpose, the translator needs also, as Dryden points out, to be "a nice critic in his mother tongue before he attempts to translate a foreign language" (in Shulte & Biguenet 1992:1). This statement finds justification in the view that translators are privileged readers whose interpretation of the text is the version of reality that will reach the masses. It is essential that they should be very careful in handling matters such as the meaning of the text both propositionally and expressively, and the conditions of its production in the SL and subsequently in the TL. But most important of all is the extent to which they indulge in the modification of the informational structure of the ST. Generally, the translator is faced with two alternatives: alienation or foreignization (cf. Venuti 1995).

As to the alienation method, the translator attempts to manage or steer the text in a manner favourable to the TL and target culture in respect of the receiver's ideologies and expectations. In this case, the role of the translator is defined by commitment and loyalty to the socio-cultural and political *status quo* of the receiving culture. Translation functions here as a gate-keeping device which reinforces a set of familiar and ideologically friendly ideas rather than as a faithful rendering from one language to another. Such ideological shifts may take place in any type of text although they are most commonly observed in religious, social and political fields. Consider the following example from the French magazine *Le Nouvel Observateur* (23-29 November 1995)

(7)   Jerusalem, les trois amours de Dieu
      (Jerusalem, the three loves of God)

It is evident that the writer is referring to the status of Jerusalem as the city in which the three religions, namely Judaism, Christianity and Islam, are gathered. The problem here relates to the way the religious character of this Holy

City is represented. A linear translation into Arabic of the French would read as follows:

> (7a) al-quds, `ashiiqaat Allah al-thalaatha
>   (Jerusalem, the three loves of Allah)

It is very unlikely that the Arab translator would choose this version for it might be perceived to challenge the ideological (religious) values of the TL reader. A more likely translation would therefore be:

> (7b) al-quds mahd al-diyaanaat al-thalaatha
>   (Jerusalem, the cradle of the three religions)

The salience of religious ideology in Arabic compared to English is very clear in the above example.

In the 1950's a committee was brought together, chaired by the well-known Egyptian writer and thinker Taha Hussein who was also the minister of education, to translate Shakespeare's plays into Arabic. It is worth mentioning that the influence of Islam was more dominant at that time. The following section of *King Henry VI* (1959:11-12):

> (8)   Bedford: His ransom there is none but I shall pay:
>   I'll hale the Dauphin headlong from his throne;
>   His crown shall be the ransom of my friend;
>   Four of their lords I'll change for one of ours.
>   Farewell my masters; to my task will I;
>   Bonfires in France forthwith I am to make
>   To keep *our great Saint* George's feast withal.

is rendered by M. Fathi (1959:25-26) as follows:

> (8a) bidfurd: lan yadfa` fidyatuh hunaak siwaay, sa'ajurr waliiya al-`ahd
>   min fawq `arshih wa sayakuun taajuh fidyat Sadiiqii wa kul sayyid
>   min saadaatinaa sa'astabdil bih arba`a minhum. al-wadaa` ayyuhaa
>   al-saada sa'adhhab 'ilaa faransaa li-'ada' waajibi wa sa 'uqiim hunaak
>   al-'al`aab al-naariyya iHtifaalan bi `iid al-qidiis jurj

> (Bedford: Nobody will pay his ransom there but me. I shall grab the heir to the throne out of his throne and his crown will be the ransom of my friend and every master of ours I shall exchange him for four of them. Farewell masters I am going to France to do my task. I will make there bonfires in the celebration of *the Saint* George.)

There are a number of ideological shifts. The author of the ST used the possessive pronoun "our" as a determiner of the noun phrase "great Saint George" and the translator replaced it by the Arabic definite article *al* (the). This shift from the personal pronoun to the general definite article brings about a parallel shift of attitude. It creates a process of distancing similar in its functioning to

Gumperz' (1982:86) notion of "we code" and "they code". That is, to the ST reader Saint George is "our" Saint George but to the translator and new TL reader "the" Saint George is their or somebody else's Saint George. But translation (8a) ignores the fact that Bedford is speaking here and that the "our" reflects his attitude.

An extreme instance of the creation of distance for the ST in translation can been seen in the following:

(9) Bedford: *Now, quiet soul, depart when heaven please,*
     For I have seen our enemies overthrown.
     What is the trust or strength of foolish man?
     They that of late were daring with their scoffs.
     Are glad and fain by flight to save themselves.

(9a) al-'aan 'ayyatuha al-nafs al-muTma'ina irji`i mataa shaa'a Allah lakii
     ann tarji`i fa-laqad shaahadt inhizaam 'a`daa'ii yaala Hamaaqat al-
     'insaan maa thiqatih bimaDaa'i `azmih wa bi-quwwatih? 'uwlaa'ika
     al-ladhina kaanuu munthu qaliil yaskharuun min GHayrihim fii quHa
     wa jaraa'a qad baatuu yaludhuun bil-harab.

                                             (translated by Fathi 1959:117)

(Now O thou the righteous soul come back thou to thy Lord as He wishes.
I have witnessed the defeat of my enemies. What is the trust of foolish
man in the acuteness of his will and strength? They that lately scoffed at
others insolently and boldly are now fleeing.)

The underlined line in example (9) is replaced in the Arabic text by an allusion to verses taken from the Qur'an (Chapter *al-fajr* 27-28):

To the righteous soul Will be said: O (thou) soul, In (complete) rest And
satisfaction! Come back thou To thy Lord, well pleased (thyself), And
well-pleasing Unto Him!

                                             (translated by Ali, 1403 Hijra)

This translation consists of a different ideological path from the ST. The ST has been completely integrated into the TL and the resulting TT can be said to elicit a similar, if not a stronger response in the TL reader. That is, the identification of the TL readership with the TT might be stronger than that of the SL audience with the ST, given the sacredness of the Qur'an to the Arab reader. In this case, the desire of the translator to trigger a higher response from the TL reader overrides the necessity to be faithful in rendering a content which is not familiar in the TL and target culture and is unlikely to produce the desired response.

Translation could be seen here as a mere transfer of a sequence of Pavlovian cues in which the emphasis is placed on response (Silverman 1983). This process of domestication through alienation from the source language culture can be reproached with serving the TL and target culture. It fails in this respect to satisfy the criterion of cross-cultural openness which a translation could reasonably be expected to fulfil in addition to performing a communicative act. Even the communicative purpose of translation between two such culturally variant languages as English and Arabic can be hindered unless the transfer of cultural information is sought in parallel with the other purposes of translation. It is not, however, an easy task to re-create an equivalent response in the TL while maintaining the cultural load of the ST. Some translators simply find it easier or more exciting to invade the TL with SL peculiarities regardless of whether they fit into the general frame of the TL and target culture. This is the process often referred to as foreignization.

The technique of foreignization in translation involves the attempt to introduce ideologies enacted in the ST into the TL. The aim is to achieve faithfulness to and non-bias towards the SL ideology. Ideally, this process should take place without impairing the communicative goal for the TL reader who may be unfamiliar with or even resentful of an intrusive ideology. Consider the translation of another extract from Shakespeare's play *King Henry VI* (1959:44):

(10) Messenger: Stay, *my Lord* Talbot
(10a) al-rasuul: fal-tabqa yaa sayyidi *al-luurd* talbut

                                                  (Fathi, 1959:136)

The translator has here introduced a transcribed foreign word *al-luurd* (lord) into the Arabic text thereby filling a lexical gap at the TL level. The translator could have opted for a cultural transformation such as:

(10b) fal-tabqa yaa *sayyidi al-nabiil* talbut
      (stay *my noble man* Talbot)

Instead the choice was made to be faithful to the ST thereby producing a foreignizing translation (10b). Although the translator aims here at preserving the identity of the ST without affecting other qualities of the text such as response of the TL reader, this goal is rarely achievable because translation involves two languages which intrinsically reproduce conflicting cultural and linguistic ideologies. In the most extreme type of foreignization, the translator tries to reproduce willy-nilly the ST in the TL by preserving its foreignness and even occasionally using SL terms or expressions despite the existence of indigenous TL corresponding ones. For instance, on BBC Arab radio, the English title "Mister" instead of the Arabic counterpart *sayyid* is often attached to names of high profile Western politicians, especially heads of state, despite the fact that the news discourse is in Arabic.

Obviously, such a marked choice has its own ends and purposes. It could be used with political or commercial motivations. For example, it might aim to express difference from the Arabic counterpart which is not used to address heads of state but rather people of lower status. It might also be used as a commercial technique using markedness to make the text more attractive to the reader/hearer and therefore captivate the attention of a larger audience.

3. Conclusion

From the above discussion, it seems very likely that different language users, and this includes translators, will assign different meanings to the texts they read. We should, therefore, expect different summaries and translations of a given text depending on what the translator has considered important and relevant to the TL audience. Translators should be able to account for the many hidden implications in texts that indirectly express ideologically biased positions, avoiding subjective involvement and achieving an exhaustive identification of intentionally or unintentionally manipulated areas of meaning. Hence, a critical model is essential in the construction of any acceptable theory of translation of texts that are prone to be potent with ideological embeddings.

Seen from a critical perspective, the format or the construction of a text is bound to be constrained by the societal, institutional, and economic micro-dimensions of its context as well as by consumption. In this context, the use of a critical approach does not in any way indicate a negative evaluation of the process of translation. It is, after all, an interpretative strategy that seeks to understand all the meanings embedded in the language of the text.

Appendix

Transliteration System

The following Arabic transliteration system has been consistently employed throughout this paper.

Arabic	Transliteration	Arabic	Transliteration
ا	a	ط	T
ب	b	ظ	Z
ت	t	ع	`
ث	th	غ	GH
ج	j	ف	f
ح	H	ق	q
خ	kh	ك	k
د	d	ل	l
ذ	dh	م	m
ر	r	ن	n
ز	z	ه	h
س	s	و	w
ش	sh	ي	y
ص	S	ء	´
ض	D		

Vowels

Arabic	Transliteration
ـَ	a
ـِ	I
و	u
ا	aa
ي	ii
و	uu

6 Bilingual Translation as a Re-creation of the Censored Text
Rhea Galanaki in English and French

CLAUDINE TOURNIAIRE

Bilingual translation, as it is described in these pages, refers to the translation of one source text into two target languages. The main inspiration for this paper was my own, initially experimental, translation of Rhea Galanaki's first collection of poems from modern Greek into English and French, as part of an MA dissertation. I have, since then, reviewed the texts for publication purposes, which meant that the two (English and French) versions had, at that later stage, to become autonomous. The main purpose of this paper, however, is an examination of the merits of translation into two parallel, complementary texts. In this particular case, the chief arguments in favour of the bilingual approach derive from the fact that the source text was subjected to censorship. It is therefore appropriate to concentrate on bilingual translation as a way of reflecting multiple layers of an original text complicated by inherent constraints and conflicts due to censorship, although the relevance of such an experiment to the translation of poetry in general may be worth considering. Let us also bear in mind, from the outset, that the bilingual approach is but one type of multiple translation, and that the latter can take on an infinity of forms (if one includes, at one end of the spectrum, intralingual translation through the confrontation, for instance, of different registers, or, at another extreme, translation into other media than that of the written word). As will be seen in due course, bilingual translation allows two languages to cooperate in such a way as to capture different aspects of the original, thanks to their own idiosyncratic tendencies.

Rhea Galanaki was born in 1947 and is now best known as a novelist. Her first two collections of poems, *Plin efharis*[1] (I adopted Roderick Beaton's English title *Albeit Pleasing*, whilst opting for *Non sans charme* in French) and *Ta orykta* (*The Minerals*), were written during and immediately after the years of military dictatorship in Greece, and the former first came out in print in 1975.

---

[1] In accordance with common practice among Greek literature specialists today (see Beaton 1994:xii-xiii), the transliterations included in this paper and in the bibliography, rather than following an established system, attempt to render the Greek phonology as closely as possible (with the exception of established English spellings of proper nouns, such as the name of the poet Cavafy), whilst taking Greek spelling into account, as, for instance, in the alternative spellings of the same vowel sound as *i* or *y*. The apparent inconsistency in the spelling of the author's first name as *Rhea* in this paper and *Rea* in the title of the dissertation is due to the author's personal request, some time after the dissertation was completed, that an *h* should be added so as to avoid possible mispronunciations; in all other references to her I have come across, however, the spelling *Rea* seems to prevail.

This was the only time when Galanaki wrote in verse. After 1975, she turned to prose poems, then to fiction. Although her first novel, *O vios tou Ismaïl Ferik Pasa* (*The Life of Ismaïl Ferik Pasha*), brought her fame and was almost immediately translated into French, the poems remained relatively obscure and had never yet been translated. What makes the two collections of verse particularly interesting is the conditions of censorship under which they were written. In November 1969, the Greek military government had introduced a new Press Law, replacing preventive censorship with a system of self-imposed censorship whereby authors, publishers and editors became fully responsible for what came out in print (see Beaton 1994:266-275 for an account of the major effects of censorship on literary production at the time).

The first point of this paper will be an examination of some of the questions translators may ask themselves when approaching censored poetry. These issues arise on both a global and a local level. Multiple translation will then be offered as a possible answer to some of these questions, with the help of a specific example. A third section will examine some of the issues raised by bilingual translation. Finally, there will remain the question of whether this whole approach can be of benefit to the practices of poetry translation in general. One of the chief concerns, throughout the argument, will be the translator's task, to some extent mirroring and mimicking the author's own predicament, in negotiating a balance between the constraints of censorship and the urge to re-create the source text. All translations quoted hereafter, unless otherwise indicated, are mine.

On a global level, censorship in the text can affect the choice of a translating strategy in at least three possible ways. First of all, transplantation of a censored text into a different social context raises the wider question of historicizing translation. This, in turn, is usually linked to the question of "foreignization", as opposed to "domestication", of the text. These two terms, coined by Schleiermacher as far back as 1813, refer to the two opposite strategies of enhancing the foreignness of the source text through its translation, or, conversely, making it seem as familiar as possible in the target culture (see Schulte and Biguenet 1992:42). Historicizing translation (as described by, amongst others, Lawrence Venuti) aims at a foreignizing effect through archaisms or other devices emphasizing the time elapsed between the writing of the source text and that of its translation (see Venuti 1995:234-75, on translations of Provençal poetry by Ezra Pound and Paul Blackburn). In the present case, the translator may initially ponder the question of how far the transplantation of a text into another period and culture should entail the erasure of the marks left on it by specific circumstances. In practical terms, the answer to this question determines how the translator will treat those elements in the text (supposing they can be identified) that can be attributed to censorship. In Galanaki's early collections, censorship directly affects, amongst other things, the overall structure of the texts. The poems are short (six lines at the most), and written in highly elliptic syntax, with frequent blanks between lines. Numerous semantic features seem to reflect the formal constraints imposed on the text (a number of images and

symbols play on the themes of enclosure or mutilation). Galanaki's own statements after the fall of the dictators confirmed that what she calls the "secretive"
form of the poems was due to the constraints of censorship:

> My earlier poems were very, shall we say, secret poems ... You have the
> feeling that if something remains [in the text], if you give something away,
> it must not be recognized by the censor.
>
> (Interview, 1987, quoted in Van Dyck 1990:180)

The view, put forward by many translators and academics, that a translation
is especially worthwhile if it contributes a fresh input into a target culture, would
require that a censored text which has interiorized external constraints through
a number of formal and semantic features, be translated according to a similar
agenda into the target language of a freer nation (this, of course, is especially
relevant to the younger generations of Western European readers, for whom
political censorship may not be a familiar situation). Above all, the statements
placed at strategic points in the text are sufficient proof that the creation of the
poems is inextricably linked to the constraints that are brought to bear on them,
as indicated in the first and final lines of the collection:

Our anxiety
sinuous sealed mouth

I give you an apple, you do not touch it, what you cut is a shadow.

I decided, on all of these grounds, that the translation should be a historicizing
one, and that the overall structure, and such other constraints on the text as
ellipsis and cases of truncated syntax, should be preserved, little or no conces-
sion being made to the conventions of the target languages. The aim was to
respect the cryptic appearance of the poems as much as possible, at the cost of
alienating target readers hoping for a more fluent rendering of the Greek.

Once a decision on form has been made, a translator must then come to
grips with the interpretation of the text. This, however, poses problems of its
own, for the censored text calls for a questioning of two central concepts: those
of authorial intention and empathy between author and translator. It is always
impossible, whatever the authors themselves may tell us about their intentions,
to verify the sincerity or accuracy of such statements. Yet one generally assumes that the text in its final shape, regardless of how easily it lends itself to
interpretation, is as the author wanted it to be, at least at a particular point in
time. In the case of a censored text, authorial intention takes two opposite directions, for it aims at the expression of a message, whilst attempting to suppress
it. This, in turn, affects whatever empathy may exist between author and translator. The questions one may ask oneself are "should I, as a free translator
writing for a free audience, free the text of its shackles, systematically looking
for a subtext, or should I respect the author's efforts to blur the message?" and
"does the de-censoring of a text constitute another form of violation?" To go

back to our example, Galanaki admits that she tried to communicate something to her reader whilst hiding it from the censor. In other words, the text is written in such a way as to divide its own audience. The author-reader relationship is thus of a conspiratorial nature. And, presumably, the translator sides with the intended reader, rather than with the censor. Most importantly, the poems are subjected to *self*-censorship, and only the author's own hand is involved in whatever is written. It seemed, as a consequence, that the conspiratorial nature of the initial relationship should, in such a case, be reproduced, as far as was possible, for the benefit of the target reader (the translator dealing with poetry subjected to other forms of censorship may well arrive at different conclusions). All of this, of course, raises the question of how a so-called "free" audience may respond, given the distance that separates it from the source text and its background. An attitude of deliberate elusiveness on the part of the translator, artificially simulating unreal (to her) dangers, may be considered exceedingly elitist, alienating part of the audience in the process of reaching others. Yet it is worth pointing out that although Galanaki's poems voice the predicament of a far larger community than that of persecuted intellectuals, her language, both during and after the years of dictatorship, remains sufficiently obscure to alienate many contemporary native readers.

A third area of reflection – on the extent of political concern in the poems – arises directly out of the above observations. The translator may tend, especially when dealing with censored poetry by a politically committed writer, to interpret the poems as political texts. This raises the question of whether translators should allow themselves to be biased (supposing that such a thing can be avoided). Should, however, a distinction be made between the kind of bias whereby a translator decides to translate a text as a political text (translation itself then constituting a political act), and the *assumption* that because the text is subjected to political constraints, it is predominantly political? The very elusiveness of the language can lead the over zealous translator to ignore the possibility of non-political, even frivolous concerns. This paper will attempt to show that multiple translation can help to stimulate the evolution of the relationship between the translator and the text.

What do these global issues imply on a local level? If the translator opts for a foreignizing translation, and wishes to leave the text in a cryptic state, this probably implies that foreign words, or any parts of the text with specific cultural connotations, are left intact. This certainly helps to suppress the message, but it conflicts with the expressive function of the text, and with the translator's interest in, say, potential political allusions. The Galanaki poems, like much modern Greek literature, make use of myth and ancient history as a set of codes. As Galanaki herself admits, mythological or historical figures are to be understood as masks:

> I know that these characters of mine were often used as masks, giving the reader a few basic points of reference about the person I wanted to describe whilst hiding them, so that he would understand and I would conceal.

After which I would go on to develop my mythical character.

(Interview published in *Diavazo* 69)

This subjects the translator to more specific constraints than those brought about by the rendering of, say, archetypal imagery, or the translation of foreign words with general cultural connotations. Such foreign references act like codes, meaning (to quote the Shorter Oxford dictionary 1996:335), "a system of words arbitrarily used for other words and phrases to secure brevity and secrecy". These codes imply certain conventions, such as a common knowledge of myths and an understanding of how they are to be perceived. Greek myths are certainly central enough to the Western cultural heritage to retain much of their power in translation. Yet their reliability in Galanaki's poems is impaired by two factors: first of all, myths became so heavily used in the language of the establishment that their traditional meaning had become corrupted (one famous example was the myth of the Trojan Horse, often used as a metaphor for the threat of communism; this, in turn, coloured any subsequent reference to this particular image, which was then perversely picked up by a number of dissident writers, such as the poet Jenny Mastoraki, who turned the Trojan Horse into a fairground toy in the 1972 collection *Tolls*). Secondly, some of the codes are inherently ambiguous. In the case of Galanaki's poems, examples of this are to be found in the figure of Medusa; or in historical figures such as that of Theodoric the Great (a political leader in the late Roman empire, not only relatively obscure, but also difficult to assess from a moral standpoint). The translator is thus faced with the following difficult tasks: preserving foreign elements along with their full metaphorical potential; avoiding a simplification of complex messages (supposing that the target audience are vaguely familiar with the myths, they may wrongly assume them to be homogeneous); last but not least, having to contend with the instability of codes in the light of any preliminary assumptions on the political function of the text. One may think, by contrast, of the codes used in BBC wartime broadcasts (which were entirely obscure to the uninitiated, but entirely clear to their intended audience).

Ultimately, the translator who does not want to domesticate the language of the text may still have to domesticate part of its meaning. In the previously mentioned case of Theodoric, for instance, it may be important that the general theme of tyranny should be communicated, somewhere in the text, to the target reader, without this happening at the cost of an over-clarification, or plain erasure, of the central metaphor. From this moment onwards, the translator's task is to re-create, albeit in veiled terms, the concealed parts that lie just within reach of the native source text reader.

Multiple translation comes in at precisely this point, for it may provide a way of capturing the conflicting intentions of the original. Concentrating, once again, on global effects, it would seem that the use of two or more target texts might provide the target reader with a partial decoding, under certain conditions. The latter would, of course, need to be adjusted and refined in their application according to the historical context of the translation; the whole issue of what constitutes so-called sensitive material is an ever-shifting ground.

The first condition is that all target texts remain cryptic, because when ambiguity is one of the hallmarks of a text, disambiguation amounts, especially in the case of poetry, to an impoverishment; and because the disambiguated text is semantically stable, and may fail, therefore, to refer the reader to alternative texts. It is not a case, for instance, of saying "A" with one target text, "B" with another, but "A" or "B" with one, "B" or "A" with the other. One of the most creative aspects of multiple translation is the dynamic interplay between different responses to a single source.

The second condition is that the texts should not compete with one another, because their goals would be different: where one target text might obscure the original meaning even further (by opting, for instance, for a literal translation of foreign terms), another provides a degree of clarification (by offering, for instance, a potential political reading). Thus in one of the poems, the Greek word *hitonas* (Greek tunic) can be translated by the accurate, but almost equally opaque English term "chiton", rather than the ordinary term "tunic". The English version, however, relies on the French to supply a more interpretative approach. Because this particular poem alludes to the themes of knowledge, enforced silence and mutilation (the statues wearing the dark tunic have had their arms amputated), the French translates the "dark tunic" as "plis obscurs", relying on the dual meaning of the word "plis" as folds in a garment, or as written messages.

The third condition is that the texts should not aim at a coherent whole. Different target texts may point in opposite directions. The two translations of the poem "The sound of a drop of oil" discussed hereafter evoke contrasting images and moods.

The final condition is that the method should reflect on the source text itself. Ideally, the multiple approach makes different target texts interact so as to recreate, in this case, the initial conflict between the expression and suppression of a censored message. It also highlights the heterogeneous aspect of the source text, keeping ambiguities alive for the benefit of the target reader; as a result, it paradoxically questions the status of the source text as a political text. I thus came to the conclusion that the political nature of the constraints imposed on the poems masked a more idiosyncratic interest, on the part of the author, in ambiguity and deferral of meanings. This peculiarity is corroborated, not by Galanaki's explicit statements, but by her lasting preoccupation, in her later works, with ambivalent characters, androgyny, cases of dual identity, abrupt narrative changes and open-ended plots (all of them typical of modernist writing, but so central to the texts in question that they stand out as hallmarks of Galanaki's work). Although she immediately sheds the cryptic verse form after the fall of the colonels, the more linear and, one might expect, explanatory medium of prose is still placed, even in her historical novels (*The Life of Ismaïl Ferik Pasha* and *I Shall Sign Louis*), at the service of meanings that are persistently deferred.

On a local level, the multiple approach works in two ways. It preserves, in all target texts, the outer constraints of the poems in terms of structure, elliptic constructions, foreign lexis and opaque metaphors. Within these boundaries, however, it allows the translations to deviate from one another in terms of syntax, lexis, register, and so on, so as to activate alternative readings and relationships with the source text.

The following example (poem 16 in the collection) shows how two versions, mutually foreign yet collaborating, can retrace and re-create the divergent directions taken by a seemingly coherent source text. In transliteration, then translated literally, the poem goes as follows:

O ihos mias stagonas tou ladiou
kai to thrymatisma tou iliou se hromatisto gyali
kathos hamogelouses ki ixeres
gia ta erotika kai gia ta nikifora somata

The sound of a drop of the oil
and the fragmentation of the sun in/on the coloured/stained glass
while you [singular] smiled and knew
about the erotic and about the victorious bodies.

For all its clumsiness, the literal translation reflects the anecdotal simplicity of the source text. One ambiguity is already evident, however, in the alternative translations of the adjective preceding "glass" (*hromatisto*). The poem will in fact begin to revolve on itself with the final word, for there is no indication as to whether the bodies (*somata*) are dead or alive (there is another Greek word that would clearly refer to a corpse, and yet another that could only apply to a living person). The positioning of the word draws attention to it, and the plural form is equally appropriate in the two contexts of love and war. Because of the positive impact of the preceding adjectives (although "victorious" is indicative of conflict), the translator could legitimately overlook the elusiveness of *somata*. But the above-mentioned adjective *hromatisto* (which could denote the stained glass in a church, as well as any coloured glass) reinforces doubt; as, in fact, the word for "fragmentation" (*thrymatisma*): the hasty meaning of "fragmentation", automatically chosen by the translator in close proximity to the word for "sun", comes last in bilingual dictionaries, after such meanings as "crumbling", "smashing", "shattering". The interpretative process has reached a crossroads.

Translation through a single target text (I concentrate here on English examples) would need to rely heavily on the elusive word "bodies" to awake some doubt in the target reader's mind. The adjective *hromatisto* would inevitably be disambiguated, into either "coloured" (or other equivalent term) or the more specific "stained". In other words, the single translation may be too static to do justice to the original. Yet it may be argued that the source text itself has no further meaning than meets the eye, even if the native reader is likely to spot the same grey areas as the translator does. The bilingual tool, however, has the potential to bring all tensions to the surface. I therefore worked towards the following translations:

> The sound of a drop of oil
> and the sun shattered on stained glass
> as you smiled and remembered
> the bodies lying in love and victory.

> Le bruit d'une goutte d'huile
> (The noise of a drop of oil)

> et le soleil éclaboussant le verre chatoyant
> (and the sun splashing the glass shimmering)

> comme tu souriais en pensant
> (as you smiled whilst thinking)

> aux corps amoureux, aux corps victorieux.
> (of the bodies in love of the bodies victorious.)

The strategy implemented in the two texts involves lexis, syntax and sound, in order to produce two divergent sets of images and feelings, the French favouring a vivacious, the English an altogether more sombre mood. Beside the already mentioned lexical issues around such words as *thrymatisma* and *hromatisto*, in English the addition of "lying" exploits the ambiguity of the supine position (of loving or dead bodies). The French has "éclaboussant" (splashing) and "chatoyant" (shimmering or glowing, referring to a coloured object), where the English has "shattered" and "stained". The effect created by the two active verbal forms in French, as opposed to the passive ones in English, is reinforced by the resulting repetition of sounds. This semantic use of syntactic features crosses boundaries between fields normally kept apart, but I was reassured in discovering, some time after finishing the translations, that Galanaki herself was aware of such possibilities (in her review of a poem by Mantos Aravantinou, set in the Paris of May 1968, she comments on the high number of intransitive and passive verbs, and the ensuing lack of "any transfer of a revolutionary act" (in *O Politis* 1983).

It was only much later that I came across Galanaki's article (in *I Lexi* 1983) on the poem "Apo gyali hromatisto" ("Of coloured glass"), by Constantinos Cavafy. This poem, which made a strong impression on her in her formative years, was written in 1925, in the wake of the disastrous Greek defeat by Turkey and exile of Greeks from Asia Minor. It describes a painting, displayed in a Constantinople church, of the coronation of emperor John VI in the fourteenth century, at a time when the empire was so poor, following numerous defeats, that the crown jewels had been pawned to Venice (hence the "coloured glass"). Cavafy's poem is a homage to dignity in adversity. I therefore reviewed the translations in the light of these new findings. Yet there seemed to be no need to alter them. The church setting evoked by the "stained glass" had become purely coincidental, for the title of Cavafy's poem, quite irrelevant to its sacred setting, refers to the jewels. Since the older text was itself poised between conflicting emotions (affection for the dignified wedded couple, mourning over their losses), Galanaki's text remained equally ambivalent. Even the coincidence between love and death, summed up in the word *somata*, was relevant to the historical context of the painting (war is the backdrop to the imperial wedding).

The English and French translations deviate only slightly from the source text (if one excepts the addition of "lying", which visibly alters the original), but considerably from each other. Indeed, only a reading of both translations side by side can reveal the full potential of the source text in generating tension. Moreover, although this inner tension has been shown to exist from the outset, the bilingual method has brought it to the fore in a way that the Greek cannot do so decisively. The translation has not created a new text, as much as it has re-created an existing one in an exploded form.

Ideologically, multilingual translation is the clearest way for a translated text to present itself as exactly that. More relevant to the specific case of the ambiguous text is the availability of two or more linguistic systems. Interlingual differences can be exploited in a number of ways. The translator can make use of morphological differences, such as the number of available tenses; the absence or presence, and number, of genders, and compensatory measures available to a language which is devoid of them (for instance, the fact that there are three genders in Greek, two in French, none in English, can be seen as a disadvantage, but can also be manipulated in various ways); lexical differences, in terms of greater or lesser specificity, or relative strengths in different fields; potential connotative meanings; contiguous denotative meanings; homophony and homonymy, which constitute powerful triggers for parallel interpretations; registers, which can determine, for instance, whether a given interpretation is to be taken as ironical. Ultimately, the apparent pitfalls of interlingual transfer can be exploited in all sorts of possible manners.

In this instance, because ambiguity was to be preserved, the devices I used were often expected to work subliminally, and relied on suggestion. But whether one likes it or not, there can never be any guarantee that the translator's tricks will fulfil the exact function they were intended for. Besides, there is no reason why communication of meaning should be any more predictable between translator and target reader than it is between author and source reader. Furthermore, what applies to the text also applies to the language, since one has to allow for the way in which individual translators relate to a given language. Which raises the following question: how consistent should the languages be in their respective tasks?

In the case of a single translator, the fact that all target texts partake in the same project implies an inevitable degree of consistency in terms of interpretation and feelings about the source text, and, of course, in terms of language.

One may find that certain translators are prone to using certain linguistic devices, and that such tendencies transcend language barriers. To go back to the question of how different languages interact, I found myself using French (my native language), most of the time, for the more interpretative versions, whereas the English usually offered a more external (and superficially faithful) reading of the poems. One reason for this might be that I tackled the English first before shifting to French (so that the latter tended to be more exploratory). It may also be that the interaction between two translations reflected the relationship between two languages in my personal experience. This is not to say that the opposite might not sometimes apply. Particularly when translating a censored text, there might be a case for feeling more at ease in the more distant of the two languages, and more inhibited in the mother tongue, precisely because its expressive potential is greater. Another interesting case to study would be that of the truly bilingual translator. Would such a person prove less consistent, or offer other reasons for consistency? The fields of bilingualism and literary translation, when considered together in the particular context of multiple translation, point to tracks that are well worth exploring. Ultimately, consistency for its own sake should not be seen as presenting any advantages. I personally allowed individual poems to dictate how each language was going to deal with them.

Since the bulk of literary translation only exists in monolingual, single-target-text form, is the approach described here only useful to a minority? And is it suitable only when dealing with censored poetry, or can it be relevant to other projects as well? The latter seems to be the case, in the sense that this particular method merely magnifies issues that are or should be central to all translation of poetry, and which I see as being fourfold: firstly, a view of translation as a relative rather than absolute process, subject to changes, inevitably biased, and addressing a specific audience (at the risk of alienating other readers); secondly, a reflection on the source text itself as something elusive, heterogeneous, and begging to be recreated in ever-changing forms; thirdly, a reliance on the audience as an active participant, encouraging them to explore possible meanings and leaving them to consider, or indeed to reject, potential alternatives; fourthly, an awareness of language as a set of effective, yet highly personal mechanisms, and of interlingual differences as aids, rather than obstacles to the translating process.

7 Realizing Theatrical Potential
The Dramatic Text in Performance and Translation

SOPHIA TOTZEVA

In the theory of drama translation the problem of the theatrical quality of dialogue was first discussed in relation to the translation of Classical Greek dramas.
As soon as Shakespeare's plays advanced to a key position in European discourse on drama and theatre, the dichotomy of drama as literature on the one
hand, and as script for the theatre on the other, was recognized and reflected
upon. Even when, in recent semiotic approaches, theoreticians refer to theatricality as a relation between dramatic text and performance, the term still
represents an implicit, undefined and indefinable quality of a dramatic text,
where conceptualization is in fact made more complex by literary and theatrical
communication.

This paper is an attempt to provide a model for the general operations
involved in the two transformation processes of translation and theatrical performance, to discuss their implications on theoretical and practical levels, and
to establish the hypotheses which guide these processes. The concept discussed
here can thus be considered a tentative approach to a partial theory of theatricality, a problem which has in fact been raised by theorists of both theatre and of
dramatic translation but has seldom been extended beyond a generalized discussion or the notion of deictic dimensions in dialogue. In more concrete terms,
I wish to test some concepts and procedures elaborated by contemporary semiotic and semantic theories by using contexts, implications and presuppositions
as experimental devices to construct a model which will serve to validate, refine
or question these notions, in order to discover the system that underlies the
structures of dramatic texts.

The main problem such an approach encounters is the very wide range of
aesthetic norms to which the texts belong; this makes it difficult to posit a set of
characteristics of dramatic texts and also to determine a level of systematic, nor-
mative or structural analysis. The approach adopted here is a systematic one.
Though it is not easy to define on a systematic level the extremely wide-ranging
aesthetic constraints on dramatic texts, the only way they can be defined is in
fact in terms of a systematic description of their aesthetics. That is, they must be
described as texts conceived for possible theatrical performance, as dominant
verbal sign-systems which rule and integrate all other theatrical sign-structures.

In my approach (see also Totzeva 1995), *theatrical potential* (TP) refers to a
semiotic relation between the verbal and nonverbal signs and structures of the
performance. In a dramatic text this semiotic relation is already to some extent
present as a concept through given theatrical codes and norms, although the
performance does not need to follow it. Theatrical codes and norms, however,
need to be understood and investigated as a particular historically-based system
for creating meanings. If we focus on the virtual relation between the verbal and

nonverbal signs inherent in a performance, which goes beyond certain theatrical norms and codes and is called up by the strategies of the text, TP can be seen as the capacity of a dramatic text to generate and involve different theatrical signs in a meaningful way when it is staged. The concept of TP aims to clarify how the various structural characteristics of a dramatic text stimulate and regulate the integration of theatrical signs to create intersemiotic meaning structures; for, after all, it is only the written dramatic text that provides the literary communication and allows the creation of all the different meanings which can be rendered through theatrical signs. In this sense, although the study of this particular problem aims at the construction of a theory of drama translation and the determination of the notion of theatricality in drama, the final result of the enterprise will in fact be a description of text structures as a paradigm which is instantiated in a particular text.

The problem for translation as an interlingual transformation of the dramatic text is therefore how to create structures in the target language which can provide and evoke an integration of nonverbal theatrical signs in a performance. My aim is to focus systematically, and strictly for purposes of translation, on the linguistic structures of the text with regard to potential theatrical communication. This issue appears essential for both translation and staging as transformation of the dramatic text.

To exemplify the problems involved I shall consider the following short passage from *Der Besuch der alten Dame* (*The Visit*) by Friedrich Dürrenmatt (1990:81). The passage is taken from the third act, in which the mayor tries to persuade Ill to shoot himself in order to prevent his fellow citizens from killing him. The Old Lady has offered a great deal of money for the murder of Ill in revenge for his having jilted her in their youth. To make Ill's decision easier, the mayor has even brought a rifle. However, it costs the mayor a sleepless night to make this suggestion and he can hardly utter it aloud. In German the passage reads as follows:

> DER BÜRGERMEISTER: *nimmt das Gewehr wieder zu sich* Schade. Sie verpassen die Chance, sich reinzuwaschen, ein halbwegs anständiger Mensch zu werden. Doch das kann man von Ihnen ja nicht verlangen.
> ILL: Feuer, Herr Bürgermeister. *Er zündet ihm die Zigarette an.*

And the English translation by Patrick Bowles:

> MAYOR: *taking back the rifle* Pity; you're missing a chance to redeem yourself and be a more or less decent human being. I might have known it was too much to ask you.
> ILL: Have a light, Mister Mayor. *Lights cigarette for Mayor.*

Feuer can refer here to two different nonverbal signs mentioned in the stage directions and presented on the stage: *cigarette* and *rifle*. Thus the word is able to evoke a double meaning: as a command to shoot and as an offer to light a cigarette. Depending on which reference is chosen to be presented in the performance the acting will differ.

The remark *Er zündet ihm die Zigarette an* referring to the general context calls for more acting than the situational context of "smoking a cigarette" alone evokes. It presupposes that during or immediately before the former utterance the mayor has taken out a cigarette. That he does not light it immediately indicates his mental state. In the entire situational context, the cigarette suggests a range of behaviour such as nervousness, hopelessness, embarrassment, concern. By offering him a light, Ill makes him aware of his discomfort.

In another context, the word *Feuer* can establish a different level of meaning referring to the rifle and so to the background situation: there is a hunt going on for the Old Lady's black panther. But she used to call Ill himself "Black Panther" in their youth and this creates a parallel between the hunt for the animal and the impending murder of Ill. This explains why Ill feels that he is in danger. On a symbolic level, the whole city is hunting for him. The word *Feuer* referring to *Gewehr* could be treated as a command to shoot. The mayor will react to this meaning of *Feuer* with either surprise or shock and he may, for example, raise his hands to express this.

The production by the Sofia Satiričen teatăr in 1990, directed by Plamen Markov, staged this double meaning: the mayor reacted to the offer with an anxious gesture of raising his arms. The production by the Vienna Burgtheater in 1992, directed by Hans Hollmann, conveyed only the first meaning, the lighting of a cigarette, but the reference to the background context, the hunting of Ill, marked by the firing of the rifle, was not rendered by the acting. A theatrical production can shift these meanings to other structures, expressing them in the background situation through other signs. The omission of this reference does not necessarily require a negative evaluation; across the range of meanings, the performance selects for the stage different theatrical signs and codes according to the actual or chosen theatrical norm.

Thus it is of great importance for the dramatic text and its TP to offer and to retain the potential meanings and the potential ambiguity in a translation. Obviously this can happen in our case only if the word *Feuer* has the same semantic value and semantic collocation in the target language. The translator would be very lucky if this were always the case. In Bulgarian, only the diminutive form of *Feuer* (*ogănche*) is used for smoking. As a command to shoot the normal form *ogăn* is used. So what does the translator do? One possible solution is that used in my own translation (followed by my own back translation):

> KMETĂT: *otnovo vzema puškata Žalko*. Izpuskate šansa da izmiete srama si, da stanete donjakade porjodăčen čovek. No tova ot vas ne može i da se očakva.
> ILL: Ogăn, gospodin kmete. *Zapalva mu cigarata.*

> (MAYOR: *taking the rifle back* Pity; you're missing the chance to wash away your shame, to become a halfway decent person. But then nobody can expect that of you.

ILL: A light, Mister Mayor. *Lights his cigarette.*)

The choice I have made using the form "Ogăn" (fire) as an order to shoot and not as an offer to light a cigarette, affects the TP of the text, and through that, the potential interpretation through theatrical signs. The situation of smoking a cigarette is, however, presented on the stage clearly enough on the nonverbal, visual level. I preferred the command to shoot in order to create the reference to the background context on the verbal level as well. By choosing the word used in the command I may have stressed this sense too much and have "manipulated" the performance towards this interpretation.

What I have outlined above is an orientation towards a context-marked model of theatricality in a dramatic text. Context is used here as a term in its widest sense. It covers all schemata, frames, scripts, systems and networks that we refer to when contrasting the units that actually occur in a piece of discourse, or can be inferred from it, with those units that do not occur. Context can be defined as a set of premises used in interpreting an utterance. This approach is particularly concerned with effects of contexts, presuppositions and implications in the dramatic text involved in the establishment of indirect, context-determined meanings, of which only a selection will be represented in the target language or performed on stage.

Considering several contexts – of situation and characters, as well as general (internal) and pragmatic (external) contexts – it is possible to isolate different clues, that is, concrete semantic items in the text which suggest and allow a very dynamic contextualization. Words such as *Feuer* I call *aesthetic dominants* in the text. The problem for the translator is not only to retain and render them but first of all to recognize and select them. The aesthetic dominants are not fixed in the text structures, it is a matter of interpretation and of a dynamic setting.

The various transformations of the text – interpretative, interlinguistic (translation), intersemiotic (theatre) – are based on these aesthetic dominants. Depending on where the aesthetic dominants are set in textual structures they may refer to a whole network of contexts and generate multiple semantic references and thus different meanings. The greater the ambiguity of the text the greater the number of levels on which meaning can be created and then be selected for the performance. This multiple interpretative contextualization also occurs in narrative texts or in poetry. But what is specific to the dramatic text is the permanent double reference of utterances to two communication systems, an internal and an external, which theatre provides in addition to other multiple contexts. Every utterance has therefore at least two simultaneous settings; it refers both to the internal and the external communication systems of the theatre, and these permanent simultaneous references to dynamic multiple networks of contexts make theatrical contextualization a very dynamic process. Signs can easily change their pragmatic relations. If a dramatic text allows the verbal signs embedded in the meaning structure of the performance to develop these dynamics, it has a high TP. In other words, TP registers the openness of the dramatic text to the inner dynamics of generating theatrical meaning.

The set of contexts establishes multiple meanings and leads to a greater density of information in the text, in particular when placed in the intersemiotic structures of the performance. Contextual effects, as a necessary condition for TP, allow the text to generate non-representational dimensions of mental processes. The greater the contextual effects, the greater the relevance of information.

The dramatic text also allows multiple forms of semanticization by allocating the message to two linguistic systems: dramatic dialogue and stage direction. The dialogue text and the non-dialogue text together constitute the meanings of the dramatic text for which theatrical signs can be found. I view the TP of the dramatic dialogue as a specific relation between the dialogue and the non-dialogue text, whereby the information structures are shifted mainly on to the dialogue. In this particular relation of high TP, the non-dialogue text is reduced or removed, but in a significant way. In other words, its place in the dialogue is retained by gaps, which may be marked or unmarked. The dialogue refers forcefully to the different contexts, especially to the situational context, and it governs the pragmatics in such a way that it can take on the functions of the stage direction.

Dramatic texts also exhibit a further type of dual reference: to literary and to colloquial communication. The dialogue is marked as spoken language, which is thus bound in a conversational situation, but it still remains aesthetic language and therefore ambiguous and self-reflexive. On the one hand, as spoken language, dramatic dialogue is marked by a range of specific structures of spontaneity. It is contextually anchored in a situational context shared by communication partners. The close reference to the situation requires communicative behaviour. As a representation of real talk, it provides nonverbal signs, paralinguistic and gestural, which accompany spoken language. On the other hand, TP is characterized, as we have seen, by aesthetic ambiguity. A dramatic text can develop a wider variety of ambiguous meanings because of the capacity of theatrical communication to embed one utterance in many different and dynamic contexts. In this respect, TP can be said to have its origin in the aesthetics of the dramatic text more than in the particular stylistic characteristics of spoken language.

This distinction between TP based on communicative pragmatics and TP based on aesthetics corresponds to the treatment of dramatic dialogue as both spoken and aesthetic language. In principle, the process remains similar irrespective of context. Discourse can be placed in a situation and an intertextual network with the aid of clues from any textual level. However, relevance markers, that is, distinctive features all through the macrocosm of both spoken and literary structures, govern communicative behaviour patterns. The claim made here is that the TP is based on textual strategies of varying complexity.

Besides the ambiguity and self-reflexivity of aesthetic texts, other characteristics of theirs, noted for example by the Russian Formalists, include formal patterns which distinguish them from non-literary texts. These patterns and distinctive features of the dramatic text may be systematized into two opposite tendencies of *similative* (recurrent) and *reductive* (elliptical) structures.

The reductive structures include ellipsis or semantic gaps (either marked or unmarked) and provide an economy of expression with multiple signification. However, the different forms of communication which the dramatic text provides, from both the aesthetic point of view and in its reference to colloquial language, reveal deficits and shortcomings, which are manifested by both semantic gaps and syntactic gaps. This explains why dramatic texts, when read, are seen as something incomplete or only partially realized. In the process of interpretation, the recipient fills in the deficits with meanings, supported by contexts and presuppositions or implicatures. The integration of the external and internal communicative systems provides a special cognitive reception process of assumptions, presuppositions and implications by establishing contextually supported implicit meanings. The strategies of the dramatic text which are based on similative and reductive structures also enable different degrees of informativeness both among the characters and between stage and audience. This explains the extreme indirectness of the semiotic process in theatrical communication.

Similative features of different kinds are, for example, isotopic, repetitive or defective patterns. As aesthetic dominants they have recurring items such as clues in isotopic patterns or a deviation (interference) in repetitive or defective patterns. The same principles of generation which are pertinent on the microtextual level in reductive structures and in their opposites, similative structures, such as isotopic, repetitive and defective patterns, can also be observed on the macrotextual level.

A text structure having a high TP might for example involve the unexpected completion of gaps from two different contexts. These might be two different contexts of the characters or the context of a character and the external context of the audience. These two meanings may come into collision with one another and sometimes produce a comic effect. An example from *Reigen* (*La Ronde*) by Arthur Schnitzler will exemplify this; the relevant sections have been italisized:

> DER GATTE: Es wär ja auch kein Malheur, wenn du einmal – mit deinem Geliebten –
> DAS SÜSSE MÄDEL: Natürlich wärs kein Malheur. *Aber ich hab kein Geliebten.*
> DER GATTE: Na geh.
> DAS SÜSSE MÄDEL: Meiner Seel, *ich hab keinen.*
> DER GATTE: Aber du wirst mir doch nicht einreden wollen, daß ich ...
> DAS SÜSSE MÄDEL: Was denn? ... *Ich hab halt keinen* – schon seit mehr als einem halben Jahr.

And the English translation by Eric Bentley:

> HUSBAND: Well, it wouldn't be a tragedy if you'd been – with your boyfriend ...
> LITTLE MISS: Sure it wouldn't be a tragedy. *But I haven't got a boyfriend.*
> HUSBAND: Go on!

LITTLE MISS: Cross my heart, *I haven't.*
HUSBAND: You don't mean to tell me I ...
LITTLE MISS: What ... *there hasn't been anyone* – for more than six months.

Of particular interest here is the similative pattern of the Little Miss's utterances with marked gaps: *Aber ich hab kein Geliebten. Meiner Seel, ich hab keinen. Ich hab halt keinen* (I haven't got a boyfriend. Cross my heart, I haven't got one. I haven't got one). The repetition or variation of the same pattern is here of meaningful significance because the Little Miss stresses not having a lover at all. In destroying this pattern the translation loses or at least weakens this meaning of the similative structure. Such an omission is often caused not because a re-creation in the target language would be difficult but because its relevance for the TP is not recognized. It would be possible to keep a similar pattern in English, but it is completely destroyed in this translation: "But I haven't got a boyfriend." "I haven't." "There hasn't been anyone –"

The third variation of the elliptic structure "there hasn't been anyone –" arises in response to the grammatical structure of the following unexpected completion of the elliptic utterance: "for more than six months". It is unexpected because the Little Miss completes the phrase not as expected by the Husband or the audience according to their contexts, that is, with: "at all", but according to her own staging as an innocent with: "for more than six months".

Of the two patterns which here provide TP – the similative (repetition) and reductive (elliptic) structure – the preference is given to the reductive structure and to the filling of gaps in an unexpected way, not only because of the comic effect they evoke. The omitted utterance: "You don't mean to tell me I (am your first lover)," whose completion is unambiguous, and the pronounced utterance by the Little Miss, to the effect that she has not had a lover just for the last six months, collide and evoke a new meaning: the Little Miss is not the real innocent but the opposite. The constraints of the target language lead the translator to give preference to just one of the two meaning structures in the source text: the reductive or the repetitive. The repetitive structure is omitted and thus the insistence on her role as an innocent is weakened and the effect of the collision of two opposite meanings reduced.

Also of great importance and difficulty for the translator are other reductive structures, especially non-marked gaps like presuppositions, which occur widely in dramatic texts and create a specific theatrical information structure with precise differences for every character and for the audience. A dramatic text does not necessarily specify where, when and who but it can tell us about the what and why, or it can omit descriptions of place and time, merely presupposing this information. It often begins with a scene involving action and dialogue, and it is left to the receptor to infer the setting in which such action and dialogue could be occurring.

Utterances are always linked to environments. When we judge the acceptability of an utterance we try to find a situation for the appropriate nonverbal communication in which that utterance could be used. If we can find such a context we consider the utterance acceptable. In this way, the internal communicative pragmatics of dramatic dialogue established by the speech situation evokes stage signals without describing but just presupposing them. And the necessary re-creation of these presupposed meanings in literature or in theatre is regarded here as the TP of the dramatic text.

An example from *Anatol* (*Farewell Supper*) by Arthur Schnitzler (1978:48) serves to illustrate what could be called presupposed and implicated information, as well as showing where exactly it is located in the text and how the translation focuses these items and turns them to aesthetic dominants. The scene occurs early on in the play and the recipient does not have much information about the situation or relations between the characters:

> MAX: *wie Anatol in die Mitte des Zimmers zurückkommt* Und – wenn *sie* gar nicht kommt!?
> ANATOL: Warum denn "gar nicht!" – Jetzt – jetzt ist's zehn Uhr! – *Sie kann ja überhaupt noch gar nicht da sein!*
> MAX: *Das Ballett ist schon lange aus!*
> ANATOL: Ich bitte dich – bis sie sich abschminkt – und umkleidet! – Ich will übrigens *hinüber* – sie erwarten!

And (the English translation by Frank Marcus, with my comments):

> MAX: *as Anatol comes back into the room* And – suppose *she* doesn't turn up? (A woman is expected.)
> ANATOL: Why shouldn't she? It's – exactly ten o'clock now! *She couldn't possibly have got here yet!* (She is occupied until ten o'clock.)
> MAX: *The ballet* finished *a long time ago*! (She has something to do with the ballet. She must be detained by something.)
> ANATOL: I ask you – by the time she's taken off her make-up and changed! I'll walk *over* to wait for her! (She dances in the ballet. The opera is opposite the Hotel Sacher in Vienna. She might dance in the Opera.)

The highlighted items deserve particular attention and serve as a starting point for the transformation of the text structures in translation. In this example explication of the presupposed meanings is avoided. In other target languages not so close to German, such as Bulgarian, the recreating of implications easily becomes a problem. For example, it is difficult to render the implication in: "Ich will übrigens *hinüber* – sie erwarten!" (I'll walk *over* to wait for her!). In Bulgarian it could be: "Šhte otida otsrešta da ja posreštna" or "šte otskoča da ja posreštna". As solutions both are rather problematic and lead to compromises on different levels, such as explication or difficult pronunciation. To explicate these aesthetic dominants, which evocate implicated information, would disturb the cognitive process of the recipient, but it would also reduce the required acting needed for establishing the speech situation or in other words, the TP of the text.

The tendency to retain deficits, gaps, omissions and reductions goes against the unavoidable processes of completion which underlie every transformation. A transformation leads to a completion through the interpretation of presupposed and established but not directly expressed information. In translation, this is done through verbal signs and in a theatrical text through nonverbal signs. This process is provoked by the change of medium and this raises a number of problems for the transformation. These two opposing processes can be systematized as expansions (in translation) and enhanced theatrical intensifications (in performance) on the one hand and as reductions and on the other hand as gaps.

As gaps and incompletenesses of different kinds are part and parcel of aesthetic communication, the deficits have to be kept to some extent in translation or in theatrical performance in order to guarantee the aesthetic cognitive processes of indirectness. In theatre, the different sign systems may modify each other. As theatre is a system of heterogeneous and hierarchically structured sign complexes, any transformation presupposes the selective emphasizing or weakening of the multiple meanings offered and created in the dramatic text in a simultaneous and successive presentation.

In particular, a concept of translation in which the translator tries to render and create within the structures of the target language all meanings realized in the dramatic text leads to a reduction of TP. The result is often an expansion of the text, as meanings of grammatical structures are expressed by semantic structures. In an ideal case the translator will select only some of the meanings in the source text and trust the expressive power of the source language, using omissions and implications, in order to keep the reductiveness of structure necessary for the indirectness of aesthetic and especially of theatrical communication with its inherent multiplicity of meanings.

A further reason for the reduction or loss of TP in translation is frequently a narrow concept of textuality, where text is understood not as a complex of communicative signals, but only as a complex of verbal signs. However, text as a structured sign-complex could involve nonverbal elements as well. The dramatic text only includes verbal signs, but is marked by strong communicative pragmatics and refers to different dynamic contexts. Its way of creating meanings therefore involves nonverbal signals to a greater degree than is the case with other literary texts. The meanings of these nonverbal signs arise out of the very nature of the specific information structures of the text discussed above.

In cognitive processes it might be necessary to verbalize nonverbal signals by drawing on contexts, implications and presuppositions. But in processes of transformation the opposite might be the case: one can reduce verbal signs or cancel them, leaving them implicit in the context. In this way, the notion of complex meanings takes on other dimensions: the recipient is not faced with a loss of meaning if omitted signs are taken over by contexts, or rather by implications and presuppositions. For the producer, and especially for the translator, this selective stress on meaning provides greater freedom to deal with the meaning structures of the source text, as long as he or she is conscious of not eliminating already generated meaning but rather of exploiting more fully the expressive forces of the target sign-system, that is of the target language and the theatrical sign-system.

8   Changing Horses: Nabokov and Translation

JENEFER COATES

All translators are writers, but not all writers are translators. By the time Vladimir Nabokov had published his translation of Aleksandr Pushkin's *Eugene Onegin* in 1964, he had achieved world-wide fame, and notoriety, as the author of *Lolita*, which had appeared in Paris in 1955. The scandal caused by *Lolita's* sensational subject-matter clouded the acclaim that Nabokov won for his scintillating style and he thus sprang to prominence in the Anglophone world with an ambivalent literary persona: a brilliant writer of dubious judgement. Nevertheless, the prospect of his translating Pushkin's Russian masterpiece held out great promise. Nabokov's skill as translator, however, would be measured by his reputation as writer and his translation proved to be almost as controversial as *Lolita*, igniting one of the most impassioned literary disputes of the century, and one which continues to smoulder on, decades later.

The controversy centred on the way in which Nabokov chose to convey Pushkin's witty, elegant rhymed verse: instead of the smooth domesticated poesy of previous translators, Nabokov offered up a word-for-word literalist version, which was outweighed by voluminous notes and commentaries that ran to six times the length of the text they annotated. To many critics, Nabokov seemed to have lost his belief in the possibility of translation, becoming what Steiner later called a "monadist" (Steiner 1992:77), and he was greeted by a chorus of disapproval led by his erstwhile friend, the American writer, Edmund Wilson. Had his four-volume translation been the fruits of labour by some unknown professor of Russian, it would have been read in a different light and probably praised as a work of brilliant but eccentric scholarship. But so far as the literary world was concerned, it was by a writer who had catapulted out of obscurity a decade earlier with a suspiciously brilliant novel that had been banned as pornography. The reader of a translation must place trust, faith, in the translator. Having used literary pyrotechnics to cloak dark obsession in *Lolita*, Nabokov was now suspected of the reverse: of concealing a luminous original beneath dull literalism in *Eugene Onegin*. By presenting a canonical work in an idiosyncratic manner, Nabokov's literary motives were called into question; by rendering fine verse in "bald and awkward" literal form, he had failed to do justice to Pushkin's sublime art; by making subjective interventions in his commentaries, he raised doubts about his scholarship; and finally, by refusing to re-create the expected sparkle and wit of which he had shown himself capable in earlier translations of Pushkin's verse and most especially at length in *Lolita*, Nabokov stood accused of witholding his gifts, of placing his own interests as a writer before his obligations as a translator. The ranks of hostile critics are still growing: Robinson (Robinson 1991:243) for example has called him an "aversionist" and Hofstadter (Hofstadter 1997:258) has heaped fury upon fury to conclude that "people are strange". Taken as a whole, these criticisms indicate not only what is expected of a good translation, but what is expected of a good translator. Yet if literal translation is reconsidered in the terms made famous by Lawrence Venuti (Venuti 1995:148), as "resistant" or even "dissident", fresh light is cast on Nabokov's motives as well as his readers' reactions.

Whereas Pushkin had compared translation to the post horses of civilization, Nabokov, acknowledging his version's failings as a work of art, modestly called his vast project "a pony". Many reasons for his switching of horses midstream have been conjectured, but to understand fully how Nabokov came to make his last translation of another man's work so deliberately "unreadable", it needs to be set in the context of his own life as a translator and author. He was continually engaged in translation throughout his life and wrote numerous articles, commentaries and polemics on the subject. Nor was translating an activity exogenous to creative writing: it came to be an increasingly dominant element within it. But with each successive change in outward circumstance – exile first from Russia to Europe, where he mostly wrote in Russian, and a second exile to America where he switched to writing in English – his views on translation also underwent change.

Nabokov's translations fall into three categories, each governed by a distinct approach, and each broadly coinciding with a phase in his own creativity: as a writer of Russian translating others mainly into Russian, he was an enthusiastic domesticator; as a writer of English translating others into English, mainly for student use, he became an adamant literalist; and finally, as a writer of English translating his own early Russian work into English and late English work back into Russian, he paraphrased and rewrote on the grounds of absolute authority, and he took the creative liberties that by then he denied to others. As Jane Grayson (1977) has shown, these changes occurred so patchily, it is hard to trace a pattern. She suggests Nabokov's change of tack was brought about by the need to reinvent himself as a scholar following adverse publicity as the author of *Lolita*. Yet he had adapted translating strategies in response to a number of changing restraints and circumstances before that time. His apparent contradictions, which have attracted accusations of hypocrisy, disappear when examined in a wider context.

1. Early Translations

Born in 1899, Vladimir Nabokov had grown up as what he termed "a normal tri-lingual child": English in the nursery, French in the library and Russian everywhere else. His privileged life in a wealthy liberal family came to an abrupt end with emigration in 1919 and his father's assassination by right wing extremists in Berlin two years later. School in St Petersburg was followed by university at Cambridge, England, on a scholarship. Nabokov became the leading writer of an inevitably close-knit émigré community which continued, despite losing the vast majority of its readers through political repression, to nurture the flame of Russian culture and language in exile. The Soviet ban on Nabokov was only lifted officially in 1986, nearly ten years after his death.

Nabokov had begun translating early, working to and from English, Russian and French. He made his first translation at the age of eleven, of Mayne Reid's *The Headless Horseman* into French alexandrines. His choice of texts points to the usual affinity between translator and text, but here it had clear significance for Nabokov's development as a writer. Translating offered a form of literary apprenticeship as well as the opportunity for creative appropriation (he rejected the term "influence"), and traces of everything he translated can be found in his own work through direct, encoded or parodic references.

So long as Nabokov was primarily a writer of Russian, he produced the smooth and elegant translations that he would later come to repudiate. He did not scruple to Russianise, for that was consistent with his aims as a writer consciously enriching his linguistic heritage through inventive and original composition. Appropriative translation was in any case a vital element in the establishment of a Russian national culture: Pushkin, Turgenev and Dostoevsky, for example, had all translated.

Most notable of the prose texts that the young Nabokov translated from the French was *Colas Breugnon* by Romain Rolland, which he published in Russian as *Nikolka Persik* in 1922. This was undertaken following a bet with his father that a translation of such complex writing could not preserve its rhythm and rhyme and Nabokov later described it as a "Vesuvius of words, an eruption of the old-French lexicon … an interrupted game of rhythmic figures, assonances and internal rhymes, chains of alliterations, rows of synonyms" (Boyd 1992:176). Though written in the twentieth century, it mixed ancient and modern French in a rollicking, playful Rabelaisian style which presented numerous challenges to the translator. In particular, it required trawling through dictionaries for appropriate archaisms, an exercise setting a precedent for the pedanticism that would be regarded as one of Nabokov's literary sins both as translator and writer. His habit of drawing on a broad lexical range in translation was thus begun early, although that range seems restrained when compared with the even broader lexicon deployed in his own work.

Another important early translation was Lewis Carroll's *Alice in Wonderland*, which Nabokov was commissioned to work into Russian in 1922. It was published as *Ania v strane chudes* in 1923. The intellectual puzzling and wordplay, dream states, chess and nonsense that characterize Carroll's texts would find echoes in many of Nabokov's fictive worlds.

In this early phase, Nabokov employed a variety of domesticating strategies: he Russianized by turning the eponymous Colas Breugnon into Nikolka Persik and the English Alice into a Russian Ania, while Alice's recital of Shakespeare becomes Ania reciting Pushkin, and William the Conqueror is replaced by the medieval Grand Prince of Kiev, Vladimir Monomakh; pounds are converted to roubles, and so on. But Nabokov's enthusiasm could occasionally lead to excess: he out-punned the originals and devised longer strings of alliteration than strictly necessary. Translating at this time thus offered him the opportunity to display his own youthful powers of invention and linguistic virtuosity, while he

aimed at fidelity of tone and the creative recapture of the spirit of the text –
aims that he would condemn in due course, as circumstances changed.

During the 1920s, still living within the Berlin émigré community, Nabokov –
who wrote under the pen-name V. Sirin – translated French and English poetry,
mostly into Russian. Among the poets he worked on were Rupert Brooke,
Verlaine, Keats, Yeats, Shakespeare, Rimbaud, Supervielle, and de Musset,
traces of all of whom were woven into his own writing. These translations were
still what he later termed "graceful imitations", carrying the implication of appropriation and domestication, of enlarging and enriching a body of literature
through the importation of foreign writings. Nabokov was consciously contrib-
uting to aspects of the Russian literary tradition that had been neglected by the
prevalence of textual content over style. The foreign texts he imported through
translation therefore reflected both his identity as a Russian writer, and the impulse to draw the European heritage into Russian culture, tendencies which
were condemned after the Revolution as bourgeois, with the complex forms of
art he espoused being dismissed in Soviet Russia as elitist or "formalist".

In 1938, with the rise of Nazism, Nabokov and his Jewish wife fled Germany for France. Anticipating a further move to an Anglophone country, he
had already begun to switch languages. Embarking on *The Real Life of Sebastian Knight* in English in 1938, he wrote a novella in Russian the following
year. The latter would be posthumously translated as *The Enchanter* (1986) but
it was the first attempt at a theme of illicit infatuation which would be greatly
elaborated in English in *Lolita* during the following decade. The Nabokovs finally left Europe for America in 1940.

2. Transition to America

Until this halfway point in his life, Nabokov seems to have regarded translation as a mixture of diversion, literary callisthenics and a chance to display
transcultural interests. Translations of his own work made by others appear not
to have caused him upset. But with the switch to using English as a primary
creative medium and his increasing mastery of it, his views began to undergo
change. Abandoning Russian had caused a double sense of loss: the vast potential readership in Soviet Russia had long been inaccessible through censorship,
but now the last vestiges of his highly literate if shrunken community of émigré
readers was left behind in Europe for good. Russian would thenceforth be kept
alive as an idealised literary form, practised only in private and cut off from a
living community of speakers. Moreover, Nabokov's English-speaking readers
would have no idea of his past reputation as a leading Russian writer. As he
would write in "On a Book Entitled Lolita" (1956), his postscript to the American edition of *Lolita*: "None of my American friends have read my Russian
books and thus every appraisal on the strength of my English ones is bound to
be out of focus … My private tragedy, which cannot, and indeed should not, be
anybody's concern, is that I had to abandon my natural idiom, my untrammeled,
rich, and infinitely docile Russian tongue for a second-rate brand of English …"

But an unpublished note remarks: "The déménagement from my palatial Russian to the narrow quarters of my English was like moving from one darkened house to another on a starless night during a strike of candlemakers and torchbearers." The loss of his "natural idiom" had deep consequences, for despite the appearance of equal proficiency, his English was then the weaker of the two languages. If the switch to writing in the weaker language was difficult, translating out of his native culture into an adopted one would be equally fraught with difficulties. It was as though he had passed through the looking glass himself.

Two related aspects of American intellectual life in the 1940s surprised him. One was the general ignorance of Russian culture, the other was the low standard of British and American translations that his students were required to use (he complained, in uncharacteristically expletive language, about "Constance Garnett's dry shit" for Gogol's *Inspector General* (Boyd 1992:45)). Indeed, so many translations failed to capture the individual qualities of Russian writers that an Anglophone reader was unable to comprehend the lines of literary development, or the reasons for almost every Russian writer expressing a debt to Pushkin. Remedying this loss would become one aim of translating: for despite the forced abandonment of Russian, Nabokov remained loyal to its heritage. Literary esteem played a part too, for by unfolding the rich specificity of his native culture, Nabokov sought to gain it the respect and admiration he felt it deserved. Translation thus became a professional and psychological necessity both for his survival as a foreign writer whose heritage was unknown and for his livelihood as a teacher.

As a writer Nabokov faced many fresh obstacles: if his early work was unknown to his new readership, so too were the traditions from which he drew inspiration. Many modernist and symbolist writers remained untranslated: Bely's influential Joycean novel *Petersburg* (1916), for example, only received its first English translation in 1958, and then in so bowdlerized a form that affinities with Nabokov's work were almost indiscernible. And no version of Pushkin had ever managed to convey his special Mozartian poetic qualities. Nabókov needed to educate his new readership.

He found work in American universities: to begin with, teaching basic Russian language and literature in translation, and later European classics, particularly modernist texts. Teaching would provide Nabokov's main source of income for almost two decades, while literary activities would be fitted into summer vacations during which he travelled in search of butterfly specimens for his work in lepidoptery, formerly pursued as a serious amateur, but now taken to a professional level.

The fictions he composed in English during this period were enriched not only by reference to the works he taught in translation but by a wider understanding of the way texts were constructed. For in the classroom Nabokov came face to face with readers for the first time, observing what they grasped and what eluded them, particularly in translated texts. Familiarity with originals enabled him to comprehend the entire range of conceptual frameworks that shaped the initial creation of a text, its infinite interpretations and readings, its many translations and finally its reception. And he noted the further textual changes frequently introduced by editors, annotators and printers along the way. These competing interventions were reflected in the intricate structures he began to devise for his own fictional narratives.

3. Early Translations into English

Nabokov began in America by translating Pushkin's verses into English with such success that his new friend, the eminent American critic and writer, Edmund Wilson, declared them in 1941 "the best Pushkin translation and the best translations of poetry of any kind I ever saw" (Karlinsky 1979:42). They were included in the volume of poetry by Pushkin, Lermontov and Tiutchev that Nabokov published under the title *Three Russian Poets* in 1945 (a revised, enlarged edition was published in 1947). Beyond this, Nabokov now only made translations into English for teaching purposes and began to explore ways of transliterating and translating that remained as close to the original text as possible. He would later reject even these literal versions as too readable: part of his mission was to take students to the text and its creator, to fill a gap that had been widened by over-smooth translations. Behind this approach lay his belief in the specificity of experience and its transmutation into art. His withdrawal from advocating conventionally domesticated translation was prompted by realization that the specificity of the original would thus be represented by an alien imitation, and that the smooth and elegant Anglo-American versions encouraged by publishers and critics preferred the false voice of an "impersonator" to the original artist's, whose authenticity had got lost. Translation thus became a form of resistance to cultural appropriation. It was also to become a form of resistance to the theories that proposed the death of the author and denied the concepts of authenticity and originality. Though a grateful refugee, Nabokov found himself in what he felt was a philistine America where the intentions of remote European artists were both respected and ignored, so that dull translations could be accepted in place of brilliant originals. Here lay the seeds of contention that were eventually to blossom into the theory presented in his Commentary to *Onegin*, almost a quarter of a century after his arrival in America.

Nabokov's important friendship with Edmund Wilson began in 1941. The support and kindness Wilson offered the newly arrived Nabokov is attested by their long correspondence (Karlinsky 1979) where advice over jobs and contracts is interspersed with often heated discussions of diverse literary matters. Their differences tested their affections from the start. Wilson was something of a dilettante trying to learn Russian (which Nabokov would call publicly a "hopeless infatuation" with the language). They offered each other instruction: Wilson chided Nabokov on misuse of English, while Nabokov countered with lessons on Russian. Nabokov longed to produce a scholarly translation of *Eugene Onegin* but felt he needed a native collaborator; Wilson declined. That the latter refused to acknowledge Nabokov's Russian prowess was due to ignorance as well as literary and political rivalry, for Wilson could never fully abandon the latent progressive views so deplored by the unwavering liberal Nabokov, as their thunderous exchanges around 1948 indicate (Karlinsky 1979:194). Suspecting Nabokov of bourgeois frivolity, Wilson never approved of his quirky and playful style. In 1955 he reproved Nabokov for "sloppy" writing in *Lolita* (Karlinsky 1979:289). The publication of *Lolita* proved a turning-point: Wilson disliked the work and appeared to resent the celebrity it brought Nabokov. He sourly noted Nabokov's new cheeriness. But Wilson had already registered distaste three years earlier by threatening to "read [Nabokov's] complete works and write an essay on them that will somewhat annoy him". He never did so, but their divergent literary views would come to be focused on the matter of Russian versification. Having been aired from time to time in private correspondence they would be publicly expressed in expanded and apostrophized terms when Wilson launched his bitter attack on Nabokov's translation of *Eugene Onegin* in 1964, which brought their long friendship to an end.

4. Teaching

One of the main tasks Nabokov set himself as a teacher of literature was the improvement of "reading skills". Eschewing the sociological and historical in favour of close structural analysis, he focused on textual detail, enjoining students to "cherish the details", to approach the text "with open senses". Famously oversubscribed, the courses were designed to create better readers who would not recoil from difficult syntax or abstruse vocabulary, would appreciate wordplay, archaism and neologism, novel images and apt metaphors. He taught students to be prepared, dictionary at elbow, to read and read again a complex passage in order to savour its hidden meanings, its polysemy and its layers of reference, as well as its more conventional surface stylistics. After such instruction in aesthetics students were equipped to negotiate the kinds of problem that translation and the reading of translation presents. Nabokov was, of course, also educating them to become the ideal readers of his own kind of writing.

His pedagogy was not, however, an isolated activity: it was rooted in his approach to the appreciation and creation of all art. Despite consistently opposing utilitarianism, he was possessed of a strongly didactic streak which runs through almost everything he wrote and uttered. It is often deliberately obscured by superficial comedy. Pushkin's dictum that "La morale est dans la nature des choses" points to the sophistication and depth of understanding that was expected: Nabokov showed, he did not tell. Constructing complex narratives that only make sense at the deepest level, for example, he urges the careless or confused reader, through ludic and adversarial asides (such as addressing "the re-reader of this passage" in *Ada*), to follow the convolutions of text, mis-trust appearances, be wary of deception or observe the minutiae of details – all borrowings from the detective genre so frequently parodied, and all ideal prescriptions for the reading of a difficult translation.

With such a mission, therefore, it was not surprising that he found so many

Anglophone translations wanting. The product of an often patchy grasp of Russian language and culture, they were characteristically over-fluent and do-mesticating, obliterating the very stylistic particularities that in Nabokov's eyes gave a work its value. He would usually embark on teaching a new text by drawing attention to mistakes in the translations being used: his lectures, pub-lished in book form (Nabokov 1981) carry reproductions of the copious changes and comments annotating his teaching copies.

Nor should it be a surprise, in this context, that he himself produced one of the most difficult, indeed "dissident", of English translations in his *Onegin*: it was not an aberration but was, rather, a response to a lack of understanding that he regretted. It was also continuous with his own style, which similarly eschewed smoothness in favour of defamiliarization, inviting the reader to participate by decoding an intricately wrought text. Many of his stylistic effects compare with strategies that translators regularly deploy: paraphrasing particulars, reinventing proper nouns, prising open cliches, rendering the familiar strange, and the strange familiar, employing archaic and non-standard terms that strain towards their source, or leaving traces of source languages visible. Not only was Nabokov a resistant translator, he was probably the most resistant English prose stylist of this century.

For many years Nabokov explored different possibilities for collaboration in translating into English, but most joint ventures ended badly until Nabokov's son Dmitri was trained as "docile assistant" to produce literal versions for re-working. Perhaps, as Beaujour suggests, (in Alexandrov 1995:720) intralingual rewriting was closer to the composing process than interlingual translating. Nabokov was undoubtedly driven by a need to keep final control.

One venture that failed involved Roman Jakobson, the Russian linguist, who wished to publish Nabokov's translation of the *Slovo o polku Igoreve*, an el-egant but literal version he had produced in 1952 for teaching at Harvard. They disagreed, however, over the authenticity of this highly poetic text whose au-thorship is shrouded in doubt, and they were further divided by politics. Nabokov therefore eventually published his own version alone under the title *The Song of Igor's Campaign: an Epic of the Twelfth Century* (1960). In its foreword, he refers to his earlier work of 1952 as "purely utilitarian – to provide students with an English text" and "much too readable" which, consistent with the trans-formation of his views, he had revised to render it still more literal and unreadable. Some of the *Slovo*'s stylistic features (the quest, the battle, per-sonification and pathetic fallacy) may be found in *Lolita*.

5. Self-translation

Nabokov made many changes in translating his own novels, employing an im-mense range of techniques to shift the text towards the target readership (Grayson 1977:167). While he never revised Russian fictions, he made different versions of English texts, sometimes taking a work into translation and back translation: *Otchaianie* was written in 1932 and published in 1936. It was translated into

English as *Despair* in 1935 but underwent further rewriting for re-publication as *Despair* in 1966. Another text began life as *Conclusive Evidence* in 1951, was translated into Russian under the title *Drugie berega* in 1954, and then underwent rewriting into English to be published as *Speak Memory: An Autobiography Revisited* in 1966. Although he used collaborators when translating into English, Nabokov worked alone when translating into Russian.

The fame that Nabokov was to acquire through *Lolita* in the late 1950s would spur a public demand for his earlier work. Nabokov thus found himself simultaneously translating his own youthful novels into English while composing new ones, with the result that his oeuvre reached readers in a curious order: mature compositions were interspersed with newly translated juvenalia. Indeed, one of the last titles to appear in English was *Mary* in 1970, the translation of his first Russian novel, *Mashen'ka*, written in 1926. Texts were selected randomly for translation according to market demand and their promotion as "a new novel by the author of Lolita" distorted perception of his development and confused his readers. This unusual chronology would affect the reception of his translation of Pushkin.

Nabokov is commonly accused of self-contradiction in his theory and practice of translation by preaching fidelity while practising freedom. But many factors affect the process of translation. In her comparison of original texts with their translated counterparts, Jane Grayson (1977:59) points to the numerous instances in which Nabokov makes adjustments by rewriting or rephrasing to create different effects. Self-translation, he protested, involved the mature writer revisiting the "greener fruits" of his youth. Familiarity with the text's original inspiration permitted the author alone to make adjustments and create fresh effects for a different readership. He tended to bring early works into line with late ones. Such creative licence was categorically denied to everyone but the author: translators, collaborators, or "paraphrasts" as he came to call them, were required to remain as faithful to the original as possible. Though perceived as an insult to translators everywhere, this stricture signals the degree to which Nabokov acknowledged the appropriating imperative within the creative act of translating. It was only when facing threats of misappropriation by an Anglophone culture himself, that his resistance had appeared to grow and he had begun insisting on authorial control.

Nabokov himself admitted to feeling constrained when translating other people's work. He regarded it as secondary to the primary activity of creative writing, and a chore that drained him of energy required for his own art, leading him to complain that it "requires another section of the brain than the text of my book, and switching from the one to the other by means of spasmodic jumps causes a kind of mental asthma" (Nabokov & Bruccoli 1989:42). It was thus somewhat irksome to be asked in 1955 (before *Lolita*'s publication) to translate Lermontov's *Hero of our Time* as part of a publishing deal to keep his own name before the public. He also entered discussions to translate Tolstoy's *Anna Karenin* (as he insisted on calling it) but that was never completed, though some of the energy he might have expended on it, one could argue, was transferred to *Ada* (1969), which embodies a sustained parody of Tolstoy's masterpiece.

Nabokov's anxiety about the transition to writing in English affected the style and structure of his compositions. In response to criticism of the stilted and clumsy language in *The Real Life of Sebastian Knight* (1941), his first novel in English, he suggested that its "assumed author ... writes English with diffi-culty" (Karlinsky 1979:51). So began a series of memorable foreigners and outsiders such as Humbert, Pnin and Kinbote whose non-standard linguistic virtuosity spills over into foreignisms or odd syntactical constructions. Uttered by non-native speakers, their odd discourse falls plausibly within character rather than leaps out as mistake. By hiding behind this gallery of non-English charac-ters, Nabokov himself could indulge in exuberant wordplay and tricks – what Suzanne Jill Levine calls "the dormant baroque" (Levine 1991:vii) – which tended to run counter to Anglo-Saxon literary norms. The rhetorical tone of *Lolita* (1955:9) signals this tendency: "Lolita, light of my life, fire of my loins. My sin, my soul." Nabokov allows his characters to express their voices directly by constructing nested or framed narrative structures: Humbert keeps a journal, for example. Meanwhile, an authorial personage, who may be distinct from the narrator, tempers hauteur with irony and pathos to distance himself from his other characters and their misperceptions and mistakes. Nabokov's confession in 1941 that "What tortures me when I try to write 'imaginative' prose in Eng-lish is that I may be unconsciously copying the style of some second-rate English writer" (Karlinsky 1979:51) suggests a motive for borrowing techniques that Pushkin had already used in *Eugene Onegin* a century earlier. He, too, had used parody and humour to reveal essential inadequacies in his creatures.

Translation was itself to become a topos of increasing importance in his writing: woven into the drama of the narratives, it is openly discussed by pro-tagonists in *Bend Sinister* (1947), *Pnin* (1957), *Pale Fire* (1962) and *Ada* (1969), with direct allusions to Shakespeare (for example, *Hamlet*, *The Tempest*, *Timon of Athens*). Translation becomes a central metaphor that is obvious in *Pale Fire* but less obvious in *Lolita*, where the European Humbert "misreads" the Ameri-can Lolita.

Nabokov's concept of language appeared gradually to move beyond con-ventional linguistic systems to enter the realm of semiotics. His important short story *Signs and Symbols* (1947; reprinted in Nabokov 1984) expanded the idea of translation to encompass the reading of meanings into things beyond words. This expansion had wider implications for his fiction which D. Barton Johnson has explored at length in his *Worlds in Regression* (1985) tracing the way in which Nabokov makes one conceptual scheme or world open onto another in infinite regression. Sometimes this effect is achieved across different languages; sometimes it works through memory, or mirrored images, or written texts; some-times through madness, delusion or obsession. Characters interpret their own or someone else's world through their own constrained mental apparatus, yet they may be merely projects of another character's imagination. Kinbote in *Pale*

Fire (1962) interprets a poem and its creator through paranoid delusions; the poem itself opens with the image of a reflection in a window pane. Characters are locked inside monolingual systems whose conceptual boundaries are unbreachable; polyglot characters fare somewhat better, but are prone to mistakes. Constructs such as these are clearly related to problems of translation in the wider sense.

For Nabokov, monologic writing was such a constraint that he tended to subvert standard utterances at every turn with multiple discourses: jokes, asides, puns, parodies. Even in discursive prose, Nabokov reached for the arcane, the archaic, the scientific or the abstruse if he felt that was the most apt or precise way in which a specific notion had to be captured: he constantly sought the particular and shrank from the general. By blurring the edges of language and creating polyglot texts, weaving in increasing quantities of untranslated words and phrases, even whole passages of French or Russian (as in *Ada* (1969)), he rendered the limits of each language more palpable. The text grows more strange and, in Venuti's sense, more "resistant" or inaccessible to the English reader. This process of alienation caused discomfort to many readers, who disliked being turned into translators, expected to play games or decode clues, and many recoiled from being tested and found wanting. Nabokov's clever displays of complex ideas were too elitist in an era of mass and pop art. But they provide evidence of the continuity of ideas between his own writing and his views on translation.

6. Nabokov's Pushkin

The competing myths and associations that accrue to canonical works of art raise manifold challenges for translators. Pushkin occupied a unique place in Russian literature. He was a poetic icon who had created the modern literary language by fusing Russian with French into a lively, flexible, natural discourse from which the nineteenth-century Russian canon would grow. Pushkin was a poetic genius of supreme technical skill: he combined rhythm and rhyme, clarity and conciseness, natural elegance and wit to create an effortlessly light and radiant text: a challenge to any translator.

But further problems arose with the figure that Pushkin presented to the world beyond. Having been strongly influenced, along with the rest of Europe, by Byron, he feared being dismissed as merely a "Byron in a Russian cloak". Translators, however, particularly those working into English, attempted to recreate him as precisely that, ignoring his own specifically Russian genius. Seeking to conserve Pushkin's unique rhyme scheme and rhythm, earlier versions of *Eugene Onegin* by Babette Deutsch (1936), Oliver Elton (1937) and others, and a later version by Walter Arndt (1963) which Nabokov devastated in review ("Pounding the Clavicord", Nabokov 1973:231), all resorted to padding and contrived phrasing which are foreign to the limpid eloquence of Pushkin. They had failed to capture the dialogism, the multiple voices and registers, the deliberate shifts, the mistranslations and the misperceptions. And above all they failed to bring out that most innovative but influential of devices, the authorial voice that was crucially distinct from the eponymous hero's. These sins were further committed in the "waltz and schmalz" rendering of the poem in Tchaikovsky's opera, the bowdlerized version through which the educated public had probably gained greatest familiarity with Pushkin's name, though not his true poetic art.

Eugene Onegin, a "novel in verse", consisted of eight chapters composed of 14-line stanzas with a specially devised rhyme scheme. When Nabokov wrote in his Commentary to his own translation of the work (Nabokov 1964:viii) that the translator "must have as much talent, or at least the same kind of talent as the author that he chooses" he knew that he was one of very few qualified to undertake the task. It was clearly not beyond his powers in terms of skill, since he had made fine translations of Pushkin previously. But a number of constraints inhibited him.

For a poem such as Pushkin's *Eugene Onegin*, rooted in a specific culture at a specific time, composed by a poetic genius using language at a specific point in its evolution, no equivalent form in another language could hope to be found. It could be re-created in a number of ways – through pastiche or parody, for example, or according to some conjecture of what Pushkin might have written as an Englishman then, or what a Pushkin might have written now, but Nabokov rejected them all. "Beyond genius and knowledge [the translator] must possess the gift of mimicry and be able to act, as it were, the real author's part, by impersonating his tricks, demeanor and speech, his ways and his mind, with the utmost degree of verisimilitude", he wrote in his essay "The Art of Translation" (Nabokov 1981:319-20).

This statement contains key words in Nabokov's aesthetic values. For in his view, fakes, frauds, mimicry and impersonation were signs of deceit, inauthenticity and, ultimately, evil, and so Nabokov balked at creating an artifical, westernized Pushkin. Like most Russians, he regarded Pushkin as an Olympian figure, a kind of pole star that not only guided him through the darkness and loneliness of exile but offered a standard of artistic purity by which all else was measured. Nabokov's fictional characters lived or died according to their knowledge of Pushkin's verse: to misquote was the sign of a flawed soul. In a lecture given in Paris in 1937 (attended by James Joyce) under the title "Pouchkine: ou le vrai et le vraisemblable" (translated by Dmitri Nabokov for the *New York Review of Books*, 31 March 1988, under the title "Pushkin, or the Real and the Plausible") Nabokov had declared:

> Those of us who really know him revere him with unparalleled fervor and purity, and experience a radiant feeling when the richness of his life overflows into the present to flood our spirit ... To read his works ... and to reread them endlessly is one of the glories of earthly life.

7. Translating *Eugene Onegin*

In the opening pages (p. 9) of his Introduction to his translation of *Eugene Onegin*, Nabokov placed, significantly, a poem he had addressed to Pushkin in the style of an *Onegin* stanza. In it, Nabokov expressed his sense of self-disgust by likening translation to serving up the poet's head "on a platter ... and profanation of the dead". Nabokov, however, not only refused to make Pushkin palatable for an Anglophone readership out of respect for the poet, but he also appeared to hold in contempt those readers who expected him to do so. The Americans depicted in *Lolita* and *Pnin*, it should be recalled, were narrow and complacent, with little imagination or compassion for outsiders. Nabokov's American Dream was something of a nightmare, with endless *poshlost*, travesty and trivia. Though he despaired of being "properly" read, Nabokov refused to make his texts easier for public consumption. His Pushkin would be likewise difficult, accessible only to those with determination.

According to his own statements and his biography, Nabokov originally conceived his *Onegin* translation around 1949 as an interlinear version for students of Russian, but it never appeared as intended (Boyd 1992:318-355). Three lines of text were supposed to run parallel: the Cyrillic, its roman transliteration and an English literal rendering. The syllables of each word would be aligned as closely as possible with the Russian. The footnotes (some of which ran to several sides) were to be somehow printed on the same page. Since no format could be found to accommodate this impossible arrangement, the translation initially appeared in 1964 as four separate volumes in hardback, which was later slimmed down to two in paperback. The complete translation consisted of almost 1500 pages: the eight chapters of verse occupied around 250 pages, while the notes to them ran to 800 pages, with some 250 pages of Translator's introduction and additional notes on the poet and the poem. There was an index of over 100 pages. Though only a few sides long, Nabokov's Foreword contains a rhetorical question that proved to be explosive: "Can Pushkin's poem, or any other poem with a definite rhyme scheme, be really translated?" His answer (1964:vii) contains the formulation of three categories of translation:

> *Paraphrastic:* offering a free version of the original with omissions and additions prompted by the exigencies of form, the conventions attributed to the consumer, and the translator's ignorance. Some phrases may possess the charm of stylish diction and idiomatic conciseness, but no scholar should succumb to stylishness and no reader be fooled by it.

> *Lexical:* (or constructional): rendering the basic meaning of words (and their order). This a machine could do under the direction of an intelligent bilinguist.

> *Literal:* rendering, as closely as the associative and syntactical capacities of another language allow, the exact contextual meaning of the original. Only this is true translation.

To many translators these categories are an insult, and many have commented on the extent to which Nabokov failed to apply them consistently to his own practices. But as Nabokov well knew from his days as a "paraphrast" and as the re-writer of his own texts, the re-creation of a work of art in a new language did bring about a conflict between loyalty to the source culture and the demands of the target culture. Resolving that conflict required an intervention by the translator that Venuti has called "invisible" (Venuti 1995:19).

Another contentious point is the meaning of "literal", which is easily tested by comparing any two literal versions of the same text – there are frequent differences. Nabokov was particularly keen to omit what he called *otsebiatina*, solecisms and unnecessary padding, which suggests the Russian word *sebia*, meaning "self". Here again, Nabokov points to the translator's subjectivity.

When Nabokov brought *Onegin* into English, his aim, according to his biographer, was a translation that "deliberately eschew[ed] every stylistic grace in order to render with ruthless fidelity the exact verbal meaning of Pushkin's lines, at the cost of all their magic" (Boyd 1992:318). "I had to sacrifice to completeness of meaning," Nabokov wrote in his Foreword (Nabokov 1964:x), "every formal element including iambic rhythm whenever its retention hindered fidelity ... To my ideal of literalism," he continued, "I sacrificed everything – elegance, euphony, clarity, good taste, modern usage and even grammar – that the dainty mimic prizes higher than truth." Rhyme he considered "an absurd dictatorship which it was impossible to reconcile with exactitude." His aim was to avoid domestication, encourage *ostranenie* or strangeness, and take the English text as close in meaning and syntactical order to the original Russian as he could manage. Though not designed to stand alone but in conjunction with the Russian to which it was a complement rather than a supplement, Nabokov's translation aimed to pull English readers over towards the foreign, to jolt them out of the comforts of cliché and equivalence and into the dangerous thickets of alien terrain, as if taking a journey abroad.

Nabokov had perceived Pushkin in his own image: an intellectually sophisticated, scholarly cosmopolitan. By discarding the worn image of a provincial, romantic socialite, he had constructed Pushkin as a modern writer, irreverent and ironic in the style of Sterne, with a modern narrative voice that separated author from text – a voice which had been effaced in other English translations. This was partly due to the translators' deafness to nuance, partly to their oversight of authorial intentions and partly to a failure of literary imagination. Nabokov's playful, muscular Pushkin bears many similarities to the authorial persona Nabokov projected in his own writing. By emphasising the dialogistic, intertextual qualities of *Eugene Onegin* not only did Nabokov create a textuality shared by his own work, but he created a literary forebear that he wished his readers, especially readers of *Lolita*, to associate with him.

Nabokov's magisterial but frequently digressive notes shed novel light on Pushkin the poet and created an unparalleled context for the poem. A common complaint has concerned Nabokov's intrusions into them, as though he were parodying his role as scholar and mocking those for whom serious comment should always be solemn and impersonal. He drew fascinating but immodest parallels between Pushkin's creative processes and his own. Statistics on imports of French champagne were offered along with detailed bibliographic and linguistic details. Discarded variants of Pushkin's lines were compared with their final versions. The sources Nabokov attributed to Pushkin suggested a mind formed by French and German translations, unable to read English, which offended those who saw Pushkin as a homegrown Russian, or who detected rivalry between the polyglot Nabokov and his subject who was made to appear dependent on translations, on reading texts at second-hand. Perhaps, however, Nabokov was here attempting to amplify his idea of translation as agent and catalyst, with the artist or poet as synthesizer of cultural imports. This would have fitted in with his notion of paraphrasis in cultural transfer, whereby the translator should remain servile and constrained by the source, but the artist alone was free to create a work that "sings and soars" by paraphrasing in a new context, using the "new props" of his experience. As his trust in conventional translation waned, belief in another kind of cultural proliferation gained strength: the idea of spirality and synthesis, which Nabokov began to embody in his novels by means of intertextual references and verbal mirroring and patterning. It is possible, though, that the mischievous Nabokov's Commentary was designed to subvert the conventions and authority of scholarship, in the same way that his fictions broke the conventions of literary genre and his Pushkin translation tilted at the conventions of "good" translation. "Dissident" is not an inappropriate label.

The row that erupted over its critical reception entertained the literary world for many months. Those with a knowledge of Russian tended to commend Nabokov. Writing in *The Observer* (29 November 1964) John Bayley concluded: "A better commentary on a poem has never been written, and probably not a better translation of one." Although it was difficult and bumpy, conceded Anthony Burgess: "If we want to read Pushkin, we must learn some Russian and thank God for Nabokov ... We have the feeling throughout of a new literary experience ... a new poetic *frisson,* as though Russian were fertilizing English" (*Encounter* May 1965). Later, Alexander Dolinin (in Alexandrov 1995:122) wrote "...the translation not only faithfully reproduces the meaning of each line but, in addition, retains a vestige of Pushkin's *sound* play and thus creates a poetic *image* of the original which can be appreciated in its own right". Dolinin also questioned Nabokov's self-imposed restraint of eschewing formal elements and provided examples of "perfect iambic clones" that were achieved along with poetic phrases that recall the beauty of the original.

But upon its first appearance, many others expressed dismay and declared it variously elephantine, clumsy and pedantic, for in place of the expected wit and glitter they found dusty archaism and forced syntax. The strongest attack was fired from Edmund Wilson, who shocked Nabokov by rehearsing their private arguments in public, loudly deploring the "bald and awkward language which has nothing in common with Pushkin" (*New York Review of Books*, 15 July 1965). Wilson singled out for derision such unusual words as "mollitude" and "sapajou" and the invented "scrab". Archaic and abstruse, they betrayed

Pushkin's elegance of diction, he felt. But Nabokov had long resorted to the arcane and antique, and was attempting here, as he had explained in his Foreword (Nabokov 1964:x), to reproduce the gallicisms and neologisms that presented especial difficulties in Pushkin. In spite of himself, Wilson displayed the claws of imperialism by demanding a smooth text, for what clearly enraged him was Nabokov's stubborn refusal to hand over a domesticated Pushkin for Anglophone delectation. Despite being hailed as an American writer, Nabokov had never entirely surrendered his identity to the new world: his work on *Onegin*, the last text he would translate besides his own, is testimony to the deep ambivalence he felt towards his adoptive language and culture and the loyalty he retained towards his native roots.

Nabokov was finally moved to write "A Reply to My Critics" in which he retorted "Only suspicion and bloodhounds await the gaunt, graceless literalist groping for the obscure word that would satisfy impassioned fidelity" (Nabokov 1973:241). Although intending *Onegin* for study, he felt it still "fell short of the ideal crib. It is still not close enough and not ugly enough ... I wish to put on record my utter disgust with the general attitude ... towards literalism." But while admitting to its inadequacies and regretting that it was "stiff and rhymeless", he stood by his scholarship: "If told I am a bad poet, I smile; but if told I am a poor scholar, I reach for my heaviest dictionary," he retorted.

As Boyd showed (1992:492-499), the cross-fire between Nabokov and Wilson provided great intellectual entertainment, but it was as sad as it was diverting, for the quarrel ended their long friendship.

8. Links between *Lolita* and *Onegin*

Nabokov's translation of Aleksandr Pushkin's *Eugene Onegin* was a crucial project in the oeuvre of a bilingual writer, recognized in 1966 by his forecast that "I shall be remembered by *Lolita* and my work on *Eugene Onegin*" (Nabokov 1973:106). Not only did his *Onegin* create a monument to the founder of the modern Russian canon, it changed Pushkin scholarship forever. No translator or student of Pushkin can ignore it, for by revealing the transcultural, European roots of Russian literature it changed, and lengthened, the perspective. It also strengthened the bridge between the Russian and English canons, to both of which Nabokov belonged, for it indicated how Nabokov's art had descended from Pushkin's. The work that crossed that bridge was *Lolita*, whose intertextual nature makes it important to both cultures simultaneously.

The deep connections between *Lolita* and the complete translation of *Onegin* (poetic text together with notes and commentaries) illuminate cross-links between Nabokov's creativity and translation. It is usually assumed that because *Lolita* had appeared first, the Pushkin translation was begun later. But his correspondence (Karlinsky 1979:42) and biographical data (Boyd 1992 and Alexandrov 1995:xxx) indicate that there was a crucial overlap of work on both projects for several years. Preoccupation with the *Onegin* project started in the 1940s, with work on the text begun around 1949, reaching completion in 1957.

Nabokov revised proofs of the poem to render it more resistant for final publication in 1963. By comparison, *Lolita* was also begun around 1949, completed by 1953 and published in 1955. Nabokov's destruction of drafts prevents examination for links between the two that might have been more explicit in earlier versions of *Lolita*.

Lolita had begun life in 1939 as the Russian novella *Volshebnik* whose manuscript Nabokov thought was lost. It may be conjectured that, in re-creating his Russian text in English, Nabokov grafted themes from Pushkin onto it in order to re-create, in highly paraphrastic and distorted form, the *Onegin* that he was translating "officially" in strictly literal terms. This might account for his views on "spirality" and artistic synthesis. Priscilla Meyer has posited *Lolita* as a "transmogrified" translation of *Onegin* (Meyer 1987:13-38), but if it is not that or a very free or inspired translation, then it is certainly a parody of free translation, a calque of misperception, misunderstanding and miserable romance. As a pair of interrelated texts, they stand at opposite extremes of the spectrum of possible translations: the literal *Onegin* is as close to its original Russian as possible, while *Lolita*, with its intricate perversities, seems as remote as may be imagined. Yet the two texts bear striking similarities: the "fancy prose" of the one, the "novel-in-verse" of the other; the shared gallicisms and neologisms; the layered structures and intertextual references; the parody, humour and multiple registers; the loathsome hero and anti-hero, the pathetic but morally triumphant heroine; Romanticism and unrequited infatuation, the epistolary episodes and shooting scene; the topological exploration and social panorama. Humbert quotes and misquotes from French texts referred to in *Onegin*, his mistakes evincing the same authorial scorn for bad readers and poor translators as Pushkin showed.

If the two texts are indeed related as suggested, then their order of publication is highly misleading. For, contrary to common perception, Nabokov wrote *Lolita* after translating *Onegin*, and was thus not the accomplished writer of note and notoriety who was judged to have sabotaged a rival poet's work through deliberate misrepresentation, but rather a hesitant translator who chose to channel his anxieties and powers of invention into his own work rather than risk distorting or misappropriating the sacred verses of a beloved poet. Perhaps we shall never establish the truth. But what clearly angered some critics was losing Pushkin and gaining Nabokov.

In the end maybe there was indeed a battle for artistic survival: the energies Nabokov might have invested in resurrecting Pushkin's art were instead poured into the creation of *Lolita*, which does indubitably pulse with all the inventive sparkle that the bonily literal *Eugene Onegin* lacks. In Pushkin, Eugene Onegin, the weak poet, shoots Lensky the pathetic one. In *Lolita*, Humbert the bad poet shoots Quilty the evil one. Might Nabokov have felt he had left Pushkin for dead by failing to bring his poem to life? It is the kind of question Nabokov ridicules and forbids us to ask. However, Sergej Davydov's view that "Nabokov's translation, accompanied by three volumes of meticulous commentary, will remain as the most enduring monument raised to Pushkin on American soil" (Davydov in Alexandrov 1995:495) surely marks the kind of success that any translator, and maybe any poet, would be glad to enjoy.

9 Pushing the Limits of Faithfulness
A Case for Gay Translation

ALBERTO MIRA

1. Gay Studies/Gay Translation: the Politics of Faithfulness

Feminism, post-colonialism and gay studies are three different directions in contemporary literary studies that strive to assert the symbolic centrality of the traditionally marginal. In each case, a discursive identity that was hitherto studied exclusively in terms of otherness is given prominence and reappraised as central. Classical ideologies of literary history, with their claims for universality and absolute value, provided a stable framework for translators by stressing the importance of linguistic or rhetorical devices (such as word order, metre and metaphor). There were, of course, debates on how to translate and what the best approach to translation was, but there was also a general agreement on the composition of the literary canon and a belief that there was a "right" interpretation. Post-modernist critical interventions affect the translator in focusing, among other things, on the politics of language and literature. The translation of homosexuality will also benefit from this shift in emphasis. Such political concerns affect translators in many ways: in choosing texts and framing their work, in emphasizing certain features within those texts and in legitimating translators' social identity as relevant to their task. The latter is a key issue that has too often been unconsciously ignored (or actively disregarded) in the field of translation studies. The existence of a different cultural context in which homosexuality is "produced" can be a constraint on the translator. The case of Spanish homosexuality can be used as an illustration of this: gay-positive translators may lack the language (or the political conditions) to reproduce gay-positive meanings in the original. From a different point of view, it is not simply a question of lack of conditions, but also of a different terminology and cultural differences, that make impossible the rewriting of homosexuality in the translated text in such a way that it remains faithful both to the denotative meanings and to its political value.

Recent inquiries into the concept of "faithfulness" reveal it as fundamentally flawed: riddled with ideological discourse and unstable when taken as a starting point for the translator (Venuti 1992). After multiculturalism and deconstructionism, faithfulness can no longer be regarded as an absolute concept, for textuality itself is regarded as a chain of differences with no absolute links. Faithfulness becomes a limitation for the translator. But it is even more limiting when translators are aware of the political value of language and wish to activate it in their versions.

In the following pages I attempt, first, to theorize the intersection between "gay identity" as a specific cultural construct and language as a chain of unstable signifiers. This makes it possible to set forth the conditions in which such identity is written and therefore can be translated. But I would like to suggest that the very specificity, political and definitional, of gay identity will present the translator with a number of problems that can be solved only through, first-ly, awareness of recent investigations into the conditions of homosexuality (basically its very instability as a cultural construct) and, secondly, a willing-ness to deal with the political effects of language in an explicitly political way. My reflections on the specific ways homosexuality works in language are put forward as a contribution to recent debates on the concept of "faithfulness". Traditional views of faithfulness can be constraining for gay-positive transla-tors, keeping them from preserving some of the more politically active meanings of gay literature. The gap between different cultural constructions of homo-sexual identities is illustrated specifically in the case of the 1975 translation into Spanish of Mart Crowley's gay text, *The Boys in the Band* (1968), Spanish culture lacking at that time a clear equivalent of gay identity. I will focus on the gap in delimitation of homosexual identities existing between Anglo-American and Spanish cultures, but my conclusions may readily be extended to other cases in which a similar gap exists. I would like to show how in this particular case the translators were trapped between two constraints: on the one hand, the lack of a "gay language" in Spain with a similar status to the one in the original, on the other, the claims of faithfulness that prevented them from being too creative in overcoming some of the problems the translation of this play poses.

The more radical versions of the so-called cultural turn in translation studies will argue that there is a need for explicit interventions in the text. This is espe-cially clear in the case of feminism and translation where several investigations have opened up the field. On the one hand, Barbara Goddard (Goddard 1990; 1991) and others have rethought the implications of the links between feminine identity and the act of translation; on the other, Carol Maier (Maier 1994) has reflected on the translation of women's texts by women as a cultural practice. Textual intervention, a taboo in traditional theories of translation, is here praised rather than condemned. In a key article, Louise von Flotow (1991) points out several strategies for textual intervention that not only emphasize female trans-lator visibility in the selection of texts, the prefacing and footnotes, but also challenge received notions of faithfulness ("hijacking"). However in von Flo-tow's discussion one can see the more problematic side of feminist proposals: feminism is often in danger of becoming a canonical ideology in itself, and it is therefore dangerous simply to extrapolate its conclusions and suggestions for the translator's practice to gender studies at large and gay studies in particular. Sherry Simon seems to be adopting a similar perspective in her study, mislead-ingly entitled *Gender in Translation* (Simon 1996). Even if the title proposes "gender" as the book's subject, an essential feminine identity is its only con-cern, and its analysis seldom provides a framework for the discussion of translation from the point of view of "gender studies". Both feminism and gay studies can be framed within this discipline, and the specificity of each group cannot be overlooked. It would nevertheless be a mistake to disregard the latter by giving undue academic prominence to the former and my main concern in this paper will be to bring forward specific ways in which gay studies might provide the translator with new creative strategies for the translation of gay texts.

The main problem with Simon's approach lies in a narrow starting point that leads to a limited definition of feminism. "Femininity" is presented as an absolute, essential identity that will necessarily find a textual reflection in style and therefore can be decoded by translators. When we turn our attention to less clear-cut gender categories, the practicality of her procedure is less obvious. Homosexuality is relatively new as a subject of study in the field of literary theory. One of the distinguishing features of such identity is that it cannot be perceived without resorting to discursive (and therefore contingent) definitions: if femaleness is a signifier that can be anchored in unambiguous characteristics and a measure of agreement exists as to its definition, definitions of homosexuality depend completely on the methodological framework used. This results in an open-endedness that may be used by translators to their advantage in order to convey in their work a gendered position. Yet any attempt to provide a theoretical basis for gay translation needs to articulate the relationship between homosexual identities and writing. As Lee Edelman (1995) proposes at the starting point of his key work *Homographesis*, the very notion of "homosexuality" was created in the nineteenth century as something completely different from previous delimitations of same-sex desire. "The Homosexual" thus became a textual entity, that is, a category of individual which can be read and diagnosed. Edelman's delimitation of the homosexual as text is the first step towards shaping the issue of homosexuality in writing and one of key importance for the translator who has to be able to read the signifiers in an informed way and, more importantly, to be able to transfer them to a different cultural context. Edelman's collection of essays follows through this idea of homosexuality as textuality and formulates some of the conditions in which that reading takes place together with some of its effects. Historically, homosexuality was first constructed as an "otherness", and therefore as something to be looked at, explained and interpreted. Homographesis is proposed as a neologism that refers to the way homosexuality is both inscribed textually and read. There are some issues that merit highlighting here. First, Edelman refuses to start with a given definition of homosexual identity: following Michel Foucault's *History of Sexuality*, homosexuality is nothing until it enters into discourse, and then its rules are the rules of its textuality; homosexuality is not viewed as an essence that somehow precedes writing, its meaning is produced as a result of ideological discourse. Second, homosexuality is treated in his work as an umbrella signifier, under which we can distinguish a number of distinct homosexual identities. Post-Stonewall "gay" identity is only one of them. Homophobic constructions of the homosexual or even psychoanalytical delimitations are two further examples. From Edelman's account, a new layer of complexity is added to the two tasks normally faced by the translators, decoding and encoding: they will also need a further delimitation and activation of specifically homosexual, and therefore fundamentally unstable, meanings within the text to interact with other textual demands (rhetorical, syntactic, lexical, stylistic, cultural, etc.).

Gay studies has largely contributed to a better understanding of homosexual codes. Of course, as an academic discipline, gay studies is still controversial, and its credibility is often questioned both in and, especially, outside academia. It rarely receives the same treatment as feminism and post-colonial concerns (Tierney 1997); for translators in particular, largely dependent on the market (driven by non-academic motivations) and haunted by traditional notions of faithfulness, explicit intervention is made more difficult to justify, as the pressures for adoption of mainstream strategies are strong.

As a result of this, if the following reflections are to be useful to practising translators, my starting point cannot be found exclusively in scholarly arguments, even if gay studies is to provide the main theoretical basis for the translator's task. Bringing homosexuality in translation out of the closet has to be regarded, first and foremost, as a political gesture. A clear example of how the scholarly and the political are articulated can be found in the translation of Oscar Wilde's *The Importance of Being Earnest*. Gay studies has consistently decoded the supposedly hidden homosexual meanings in the play (for instance, see Craft 1990). From the cigarette case to the concept of "Bunburying" or the verbal style of the male protagonists, to give three distinct examples, a number of signifiers in the play, linguistic and otherwise, point toward a homosexual subtext that may or may not have been intended and may or may not have been perceived by Wilde's audiences. None of these signifiers translate easily into Spanish and, more generally, into any other language with different homosexual codes. Making explicit the pun on "Bunbury" would be going too far when it is common practice now in Spanish not to translate names; a cigarette case is not universally read as a signifier of homosexuality and its significance might even go unnoticed today by British contemporary audiences; likewise with Algernon's camp patter: it is not unequivocally read as homosexuality in Britain and it is even less likely to be recognized as such even for people well versed in homosexual codes in other cultures. It could be suggested that if even contemporary British audiences are going to miss the homosexual elements in the play, why not leave the whole question alone. Again the answer could only be political: if we believe they *can* be there, it is easy to bring them out in production. At any rate, there is the question of their *potential* to work as an element in a homosexual subtext that will definitely be lost in translation. High camp itself has a problematic status as "gay language" when we are dealing with it as translators. In traditional Spanish versions of Wilde's play, all the possible implications are either genuinely missed or actively ignored: after all, there are no "proofs" and, as conservative academic wisdom hints, gay scholars have vested interests in publicizing homosexuality. Somehow, heterosexuality has managed to present itself as "objective" whereas homosexuality is represented as subjective. But even a recent Spanish translation (Villena 1995) done by a gay man, the Spanish poet and novelist Luis Antonio de Villena, avoided any attempt to bring out the homosexual potential in "Bunbury" and let the rest of the signifiers take care of themselves: nothing specific was done to point up homosexual connotations.

The point here is that, given the uncertain status of homosexual representation at the time of writing, and given the threat of censorship or even jail, the textual coding in the play cannot be explicit and unequivocal. Villena may not have found enough evidence to justify what would have been regarded as a blatant intervention in the text. But the problem is that in most cases no amount of research will produce conclusive proof for the existence of a homosexual sub-text, whether intended or perceived. On the other hand, the translator may choose to bring these meanings out. The intention may be merely artistic and creative: that is to say, the translator tries to find a different way to make signifiers inter-act, emphasizing certain meanings so as to produce a fresh vision of the text. More often, however, the emphasis is politically motivated, for the presence of homosexuality in a canonical text, even if subtle and underplayed, contributes to the visibility of homosexuality in culture at large. In the case of Villena's translation, he has intervened in the play's title. The actual title of his transla-tion *is La importancia de llamarse Ernesto (siendo formal y moderadamente ambiguo)*, which can be back-translated as *The Importance of Being Earnest (When One Is a Formal Person and Moderately Ambiguous)*. The play on "am-biguity" is interesting here: even when Villena shies away from intervening in the text itself, he imaginatively introduces a cue in the title, a key framing struc-ture to the play, in order to set the atmosphere for gender uncertainty.

As the above example illustrates, gay studies has a political agenda to appro-priate both writings and figures that identify as gay as well as those attempting to conceal their homosexuality: the latter model is as central to the definition of group identity as the former (see Aliaga and Cortés 1997). Homographesis is in itself a political concept as it shows awareness of the manipulations to which homosexuality is subject. By reading homosexuality into a given text, its politi-cal character is emphasized and can be activated by the translator. But encoding homographesis in a different language presents a number of problems.

In the past thirty years Britain and the United States have seen the rise of a discourse around homosexuality that is radically different from any other cultural codes associated with homosexuality in other historical periods and cultures: this new gay identity shares some features with traditional models, but is performatively distinct from them in trying to seek an integration into mainstream culture. Gay historians, such as John Boswell, Alan Bray and David Halperin, point out that there is nothing essentially new in the existence of cultural codes based on homosexual orientation: homosexuality was already a cultural trait widespread in such cultures as eleventh-century France and seventeenth-century England and Classical Greece, to name but three that have been researched by these authors (Boswell 1981; Bray 1982; Halperin 1990); whatever the actual contents of homosexual identity, whether acts, rituals, legal status or language, it has always been something that made a group of people think that they were different from straight society, a difference that went beyond sexual practices and that was always influenced by delimitations of class, lifestyle, age, economic status, and so on. It is in this sense that most of the elements that made up homosexuality can be put in discursive terms. Such signifiers constitute the general marks of homographesis. But, as well as proposing a general homosexual umbrella identity, historians insist on the specificity of each model in its own time and cultural background. Codes, slang, rites and symbols are always specific and out of this specificity come the difficulties in translation, for homographesis will only point towards gayness in a given context. This means that any version of discursive homosexuality is encrypted in specific, context-dependent codes. Such codes will be lost in translation unless translators activate them.

Anglo-American culture has been among the most successful in creating linguistic codes to denote homosexuality, as a play like *The Boys in the Band* clearly illustrates. But how can the specificity of Anglo-American gay identity be defined in terms of writing? Far from being a series of underground codes shared by a minority that make communication at the margins of institutional discourse easier, Anglo-American gay culture from the sixties is constantly trying to reach into the mainstream, to achieve a central position in popular discourse. For gay culture, making its presence explicit is as important as its very articulation in terms of language and cultural references. Its codes have become less cryptic, closer to a jargon to which non-specialists now have access.

If gay identity is thus described as a mainly Anglo-American phenomenon and if, furthermore, we regard such a phenomenon as something politically positive – defenders of gay identity would say that it is a tool to fight unspoken prejudice and build a fairer, less oppressive society – then it may, and from a more politically committed perspective, it must be exported to other cultures with less effective homosexual identities. Even if this attitude does have an element of imperialism, one cannot help but sympathize with it. The gay movement in Spain, France, Italy, lacks the coherence and strength of its Anglo-American counterparts, its ability to appropriate history and literature, to create narrative myths, forms and common dreams. Its ability to achieve any results in the fight against discrimination and changing attitudes is, therefore, very limited.

Gay homographesis demands translation and yet is stubbornly resistant to it. In order to suggest a way forward for translators, it will be useful, first of all, to identify the areas in which gay homographesis is most clearly manifested.

2. Gay Homographesis

Gay intertextuality is without doubt one of the privileged areas in the construction of a written homosexual discourse. Post-modern theory has emphasized the role of intertextuality in the process of writing: texts are seen as intertextual compounds, made of references to other texts, genre structures or traditions. Gay intertextuality presupposes, first, the appropriation of certain literary texts that may subsequently be quoted in other gay texts. The effect is the impression of complicity with the reader: in acknowledging shared references the distance between reader and text narrows and the text is perceived as "gay friendly". Gay identity therefore becomes anchored in a cultural tradition. The conditions in which homosexual identities develop in different cultures have made the agreement on a universal gay canon virtually impossible until very recently – it is precisely the development of gay identity that will make this feasible – and therefore many of the references used in gay intertextuality will necessarily be obscure in the target language. If we allow them to remain so (by merely preserving their semiotic meaning), an important mode of gay signification (their performative functions) in the text will be missed, even if its integrity as an aesthetic object can be preserved.

The second area in which gay homographesis can be appreciated in English is in the use of camp. The debate on camp is a complex one, and several arguments have been put forward about its relevance in the construction of gay identity. Authors in Moe Meyer's collection *The Politics and Poetics of Camp* (1994) argue that camp is *the* gay style. Meyer and his contributors appropriate camp for gay politics and find numerous historical instances of the articulation between the two. Elsewhere, critics have dwelt on the way camp becomes a marker of homosexuality without explicitly mentioning it. The specificity of camp as a gay language has been pointed out by Susan Sontag in her seminal "Notes on Camp" and later, in more depth, by Eve Kosofsky Sedgwick (1990), Thomas E. Yingling (1990), Jonathan Dollimore (1991) and David Bergman (1993) among others. According to all of these authors, camp cannot be confined to the twentieth-century: texts by reportedly homosexual authors, from Matthew "Monk" Lewis to Oscar Wilde, lend themselves easily to camp readings. Interestingly for the translator, camp also seems to be transcultural, for how else could we describe the excessive ornamentation and mannered style of writers such as Lorca, Lezama Lima and Virgilio Piñeira, Severo Sarduy, even Góngora or Goytisolo, to restrict ourselves to the Hispanic world. The suggestion that camp is transcultural is, however, problematic. In a recent collection edited by Mark Simpson, *Anti-Gay* (1997), the authors argue that the widespread recognition of the Anglo-American gay model is due almost entirely to its success on the market. An initial distinction has to be made between camp as form and camp as a conscious signifier of homosexuality. If Hispanic homosexual authors may be using language in a camp mode, it must also be taken into account that, because the connection between camp and homosexuality is not explicit in Hispanic culture, its performative power as gay language is greatly diminished.

In all academic accounts camp is related to a particular post-modern notion of language as a chain of signifiers; in contrast with Saussurean linguistics in which the link between the word and its meaning is fixed, in camp surface meaning is emphasized rather than conventional meaning. The translation of camp stands therefore against traditional notions of faithfulness which emphasize meaning and economy. Again, translators can choose to ignore gay camp in texts like Ronald Firbank's *Valmouth* or E. F.Benson's *Lucia and Mapp* series, and decide to translate concepts precisely, trying to make sense, instead of producing linguistic nonsense based on linguistic excess: in this case, the gay-performative aspects of the text, linked to the very rhetoric of camp, are neglected.

A third aspect that deserves attention is the framing of the translated work. How is the published text offered to its readers? Does it identify with a gay perspective or does it treat homosexuality as otherness? One of the achievements of gay homographesis has been the control of a network of gay publishing or, at least, of gay-aware books. There are several ways to "homosexualize" a text: a gay-friendly image on the cover, or even an image which posits an explicitly gay gaze, extracts of reviews from gay publications on the back cover blurb, camp style in general presentation. In translation, these elements have tended to be missing, even in cases when such strategies have not prevented the original text from achieving mainstream success. Spanish publishers are notoriously cautious on this particular issue and still seem to be reluctant to narrow the range of target customers. Homosexuality is still regarded as uncommercial, and editions of translations from landmark gay fiction works such as Alan Hollinghurst's *The Swimming Pool Library*, Dennis Cooper's *Frisk* or Edmund White's *A Boy's Own Story*, to give three clear instances, have completely ignored the gay reader. They are presented as mainstream novels that just happen to feature homosexuality. This move to erase gay homographesis de-politicizes some of the values in these texts.

Given these areas of action, the gay-aware translator will, as suggested, experience difficulties bridging the gap between languages. The traditional paradigm of faithfulness to the semiotic values of the language will hinder rather than enhance the impact of translation, as it does not allow for a serious consideration of the politics of language. Different languages express the political dimension of homosexuality differently, and the Anglo-American model cannot be simply projected seamlessly over other languages. Spanish is a case in point, and the example described below will be used, firstly, to study the problems of translation of gay homographesis in 1975, at a time when the very idea of a gay identity in Spain was but a faint echo of events happening abroad, and secondly, to reflect on the possibilities of a gay appropriation of the play twenty years later, when social conditions had made the rise of gay identities possible.

The original production of *The Boys in the Band* opened in New York in 1968 and it has been regarded both as the last instance of pre-gay homosexual identities and as the earliest manifestation of the Stonewall spirit, ante-dating the actual founding moment of the modern gay movement. Indeed, the very idea of translating this particular play could be questioned: its initial critical reception was problematic, even if it was an instant success among gay audiences; gay-identified critics dismiss it all too quickly (Clum 1991; de Jongh 1993), choosing to regard it as an example of homophobic representation of homosexuals as tortured outcasts. Audiences, on the other hand, still seem to enjoy its camp humour, clearly identifying with the characters and events. The choice of a largely gay cast certainly had much to do with this success. The text shows nine characters, eight of them self-identified as gay, representing a broad range of homosexual types at the end of the sixties. Of course, self-identification is not easy for all of them: Donald is undergoing therapy and both Michael and Harold express themselves in a ruthlessly insulting way which cannot conceal their guilt. The place of this play in the gay canon is something few critics feel comfortable with. Choosing to translate *The Boys in the Band* has clear political implications, as it is a well-known text which puts forward a debatable representation of gay identity. But, it could be argued, if the play works for gay audiences, it must be possible to find a gay-positive reading in spite of protests from the critical establishment. The issue of the explicit presence of gay characters and the politics of the representation of their gayness will necessarily be something prospective translators have to consider.

In the text, gay homographesis is double-edged. On the one hand, the text can pander to homophobic views of gay identity: homosexuals as grotesque, shrill individuals, unable to find a place in "normal" society. For translators into linguistic communities with weak gay cultures, this is a very real risk, as the language used about homosexuality in such cultures tends to be homophobic. Yet there is a way to read the play that would emphasize gay people's cultural specificity and the lively, provocative character of gay culture. The play's potential to evoke uncomfortable responses from homophobic audiences must be a starting point for the gay-aware translator. Identifying the elements such audiences find shocking is easy: gay style and culture is not just presented, they are flaunted; moreover, this flaunting creates the feeling of an articulate community which homophobes, content with the pathological model, find difficult to accept. This exhibitionism is manifested in the richness of its gay intertextual references. For the translator, this is one of the keys to a gay-friendly reading of the text.

3. *Los chicos de la banda* and Gay Translation

The Spanish version of *The Boys in the Band*, *Los chicos de la banda*, by Ignacio Artime and Jaime Azpilicueta, opened in Madrid in 1975, in the last months of Francoism, an especially repressive period, when all dissidence, sexual or otherwise, was regarded by the government as a threat. Obviously, the framing of the published translation was not, could not be, gay-friendly. The published playscript is presented in such a way as to avoid any gay identification, and, judging from the stills from the actual performance, something similar happened with the acting and artistic direction. The picture on the cover shows Alan, the straight character, looking at three couples, all men, dancing, therefore emphasizing their strangeness. Homosexuality is presented as an otherness both in the introduction and the dust jacket blurb: a number of references to "this painful issue" or "this social problem" clearly construct a heterosexual enunciative position that looks at gayness from the outside, rather than inviting any identification with it. There is even an explicitly homophobic joke by cartoonist Manuel Summers that dispels any doubts as to the editor's attitude to the play's subject matter. The edition is mostly a manifestation of homophobic homographesis: gay-positive potential is ignored in order to pander to reactionary audiences.

In this way, the Spanish playscript was consciously trying to offset the positive effects mere representation could have on audiences; this was a tacit acknowledgement that unbridled flamboyance could be catching. It was very difficult to find anti-homophobic language in Spain in 1975: the homosexual liberation movement, which in Britain and the United States was actively creating a new language enunciated from a gay perspective, was invisible, almost non-existent, and homosexuality was severely punished. The only way one could refer to homosexuality in a positive way was through the language of science or by resorting to pity, and although both modes do appear in reviews of the play, neither is used in the play itself. A discourse to deal with homosexuality in the first person had not been created, and therefore the ways in which the play could be gay-positive resisted translation.

Gay intertextuality is at the root of this particular play's gay rhetoric. *The Boys in the Band* constructs gay identities rooted in quotations from classic films (*Sunset Boulevard*), camp performances (Maria Montez, Barbara Stanwyck), popular songs (Cole Porter's "Down in the Depths of the Nineteenth Floor"), the gay tradition (William Inge) and myths (Judy Garland), to give only a few examples. None of these intertextual references are specifically homosexual, in the sense of focusing on male-to-male desire. But all of these have been appropriated by American gays, and in the play they all work as signifiers of gay homographesis. Moreover, they can be identified as such by non-gay-identified audiences. In the Anglo-Saxon cultural context the association between gayness and, for instance, *Sunset Boulevard* is not presented as accidental: its constant recurrence has made it natural. The performative function of such references is to celebrate this identity, and failure to translate them necessarily eliminates this element from the translated version. Some of these references have been missed by the translators. One example is the classic ending of *Sunset Boulevard* quoted by Emory, who is coming out of the bathroom after throwing up, in Act II: "I am not ready for my close-up, Mr De Mille. Nor will I be for the next two weeks" (p.52). The Spanish translators miss the implicit gay value of the reference: "Hoy no podré rodar ese primer plano, señor Polanski" ["I won't be ready for that shot, Mr Polanski"] (p.72). There is, admittedly, an attempt to make sense of the reference: the translators seem to take it that average audiences would not know who Cecil B. De Mille is, or indeed where the quotation comes from and choose the name of a more popular director. *Chinatown* (1974) may have been the reference they had in mind, given the time of the translation, evoking a certain old-fashioned glamour that Emory would at that moment feel unable to emulate; more problematically, audiences could associate Polanski with horror films (*Repulsion, Rosemary's Baby, The Fearless Vampire Killers*), and the joke loses all vestiges of gay content. Neither *Chinatown* nor Polanski's horror films are gay classics and the gay relevance is therefore lost in translation. In several other examples we can see how gay references are systematically missed: a reference to Butterfly McQueen, the young black maid in *Gone with the Wind* is ignored altogether; the ironic phrase "he's straight as the Yellow Brick Road" (a reference to the winding path to the Emerald City in *The Wizard of Oz*, one of the key popular texts for American homosexuals of the seventies) becomes in the translation, "tan normal como David Bowie" ("as normal as David Bowie"). In all these cases the translators, following the dictates of a particular view of faithfulness, felt they needed to replace a reference in English by a *similar* reference, understandable in Spanish. But they have not done this creatively, ignoring the importance of gay-friendly language present in the source play. Occasionally, however, a coincidence makes a reference work as gay homographesis in Spanish. Cole Porter's "Down in the Depths of the Nineteenth Floor" is so emphatic in its expression of self-pity through contrast between worldly success and emotional failure that it has been used in several camp acts as the epitome of the torch song; its author's homosexuality places it even more firmly in the gay canon. Again, the translators opt for a change in order to make the reference less obscure (in Spain in the 1970's, neither the song nor Cole Porter would have meant anything at all) and they choose "Mi hombre", the Spanish version of "Mon homme", which was also translated into English as "My Man", again an example of over-the-top emotional masochism which retains similar associations with Spanish camp performance.

In the instances mentioned above, the semiotic meanings of the text will lend themselves to translation through imaginative use of literary strategies. Yet translators cannot hope that the political-performative character of gay writing will take care of itself when gay identity is transferred to a different cultural context. In other words, it is not as important to reproduce intertextual references in translation as to maintain its identity-reinforcing performative value. The former would be central in the traditional paradigm of "faithfulness". After all, when the author chose to mention *Sunset Boulevard*, Cole Porter, Butterfly McQueen or Barbara Stanwyck he meant exactly that, and his choices, as the supporters of traditional views on translation would claim, must be respected. As pointed out by feminist translators, footnotes clarifying the gay relevance are a solution in these and other instances. Our main objection is that we are dealing with a theatrical text here, and the gay connection would be missing in performance. But, more generally, explanatory notes do not function in the same way as other text-integrated solutions as they emphasize the scholarly character of the text and therefore deprive it of some degree of immediacy. The translators have, however, opted for Polanski, "My Man", silence and Bette Davis respectively. In this they show awareness of the gap between cultures and attempt to preserve semiotic meaning by being flexible with faithfulness. But gay relevance is still lost in some cases, when, given the cultural conditions of the target culture, it should really have been emphasized in order to achieve a similar effect. Gay-aware translators have to go beyond this narrow conception that remains faithful to the original words but is detrimental to the politics of the text.

The manifestation of gay homographesis through camp use of language is apparent throughout the play. Not that an awareness of gay slang is completely absent in this version. On occasion, Artime and Azpilicueta seem to overcome their tendency to downplay or marginalize the specificity of gayness and use their knowledge of such jargon in Spanish. (The question of knowledge of gay slang as something that becomes suspicious has been studied by Eve Kosofsky Sedgwick (1991) and may be relevant for those interested in studying translations of gay homographesis. Translators may choose to ignore their knowledge of gay slang in order to avoid being themselves identified as gay.) The Spanish text does feature some specific Spanish homosexual slang. Even if this does not constitute such a recognizable discourse as its Anglo-American counterpart, there are some words that come closer to the latter in performative function. One of them is "entender", literally "to understand", a term normally used by gay individuals referring to homosexual identity. "Pedro entiende" does not just mean "Pedro is gay", but it also hints at the speaker's gayness. This is used to good effect at a certain point in the translation when it could have been easily missed. In the original, the main characters are discussing a third:

> "Listen, asshole, what am I going to do? He's *straight*. And *Square City*! (*"Top Drawer" accent through clenched teeth*). I mean, he's rally vury proper. Auffully good family"   (p.15).

Both the word "straight" (a term mostly used in the sixties strategically by gays to suggest heterosexuality's otherness) and the camp style here identify the speaker as gay: the former in a semiotic way, the latter in camp performative mode. Whereas the translators have attempted to solve one of the problems posed by this passage, they have ignored the other:

> "Calla, idiota ¿qué voy a hacer? ... Es normal. No entiende. Y además, es un tremendo puritano. Estirado, de esos podridos de ricos y de buenísma familia"   (p.32).

A back translation might read: "Shut up, you fool, what can I do? He is normal, he doesn't know about these things. Filthy rich and from a very good family". Admittedly, the loss here is mostly nuance: references to tone, the character's feigning an accent, but nuance is usually what makes camp language so relevant. Camp is also lost elsewhere, gay wordplay particularly being missed. When Bernard, a black gay man comes in, he is welcomed with the words "It's the queen of spades" (p.25). It could be suggested that camp offsets racism in this particular instance. The nearest equivalence the Spanish translators could find is "Llegó la oveja negra" (p.42) ("Here comes the black sheep"). Later, another camp reference to Bernard, in this case a whole paragraph, is omitted: "Hi, Bernadette. Anybody ever tell you you'd look divine in a hammock, surrounded by louvres and ceiling fans and lots of lush tropical ferns?" (p.25). This is seemingly replaced by a reference to "humor negro" (p.45, "black humour"). The ambiguity characteristic of camp language is therefore replaced by an overtly racist pun with connotations not present in the original. There is, indeed, a very thin line beween camp style and the grotesque aspects homophobic readers like to see in it, and the translators do not seem to be aware of the difference. Where the English goes for gay-identified camp, the Spanish prefers grotesque jokes that lend themselves to homophobic readings. The result of these changes and omissions is not only to deprive the play of part of its richness as a gay text, but also to encourage a vision of the gay characters as viciously racist, something the original is careful to avoid.

There are many other instances in which camp is played down. When the "Cowboy" character complains of a "weak grip", Emory comes in with a sharp reply: "A weak grip. In my day it used to be called a limp wrist" (p.43). The Spanish translation is faithful to the meaning, but again loses the appropriateness of the joke: "Tú lo que tienes es la muñeca tonta" (p.63). "Muñeca tonta" does not really mean anything very concrete, and in any case it is not something one would associate with homosexuality. The character in the original is re-appropriating one of the features attributed homophobically to gay men. The problem with the expression "muñeca tonta" is that it is never used in that sense, and therefore the political power of camp is again lost. Similarly, the character of Harold, who appears at the end of the first act, is perfectly characterized linguistically in the original as camp. This is done not only through the choice of words and sentence structure, but also, in the script of the play, through the use of italics: "*But he's beautiful*. He has *unnatural* natural beauty. Not that that means anything" (p.56). Again, the translation is clumsy and it deprives the character of a specific linguistic style: "Pero es guapo. Tiene una belleza natural ... absolutamente innatural. Y eso significa mucho" (p.76). This could be back translated into English as: "He is handsome. He has a natural beauty ... absolutely unnatural. And that means a lot". Apart from an obvious misinterpretation in the last phrase, the choice of words in Spanish underplays the excess of the original: "guapo" is a colourless choice for "beautiful", the wordplay on "natural/unnatural" in the original is spoilt with a hesitation in the Spanish. And "innatural" is cacophonic and not too elegant. "Sobrenatural" (supernatural) would have been a more daring alternative, for even if it does not follow the original so closely it does retain its connotations, and it is easier for the actor to use emphatically.

The one stylistic feature of camp language which the translators have worked to preserve is effeminacy. True, camp is often perceived as effeminate in Anglo-American culture, and most dictionary definitions refer to this. Gay studies has interpreted this link in transgressive terms: gays are able to go beyond received notions of gender roles, whereas homophobic critics and readers have seen it as a mark of decadence or perversion: gay men cannot stick to the demands of their biological gender. But even if the link is there, effeminacy and camp cannot be equated. While *Los chicos de la banda* generally misses some of the wordplay and sense of humour of camp, it preserves the effeminacy of characters, making homophobic readings easier. In this version, characters often refer to each other as "she". This insistence is easier in Spanish than in English, as adjectives are gendered in the former. It could be argued that the translators are trying to compensate here for the loss in the general colourfulness of the language elsewhere. But my point is that, in any case, gay homographesis has been replaced by a style easily subject to homophobic readings, pandering to audiences with an anti-homosexual bias. The issue of whether effeminacy should be appropriated or not by the gay movement is only partially relevant here: at the time it was not in Spain. Even if it had been, it is a question of balance, of whether we construct gay identity with reference to a cultural structure that is politically activated or exclusively in terms of gender role reversal.

With all its good intentions and obvious flaws (mainly from the point of view of gay homographesis), the existing version could not work now (or would do only as a homophobic text), and just as the original needs new stagings and new ideas to bring out the full potential of the characters, so a new translation could stress the positive aspects present in the 1975 version. A new translation for any future production of the play, therefore, will require an effort to include possibilities opened up by twenty-five years of gay visibility both in Spain and elsewhere. For instance, the camp element could be stressed through sharper replies in Spanish, whenever possible: it should not be necessary to reproduce them only in the cases when they appear in English. The injection of humour and the introduction of contemporary gay jargon would help to bring the play closer to gay audiences. Some jokes missed in the 1975 version could be replaced by others when total faithfulness is not possible. But this acknowledgement of the need for creative translation should not ignore the original's potential to address gay audiences and create a sense of community. Time has made Spanish audiences more aware of gay culture and, even if an important vernacular set of intertextual references has not yet been created, there are a number that can be used. Faithfulness to the period can also become a constraint for translators. Prospective translators might also consider updating the play and setting it, for instance, in the early (i.e. pre-AIDS) eighties: indeed, this was the moment when gay culture in Spain was at a similar stage of development to American gay culture at the time when the play is set. The eighties see the rise of a new international gay canon in popular culture. Intertextual references could be included that made sense both in the play's original setting and in Spain (examples of such references could be: Village People, Donna Summer, Calvin Klein or even Madonna). The early eighties, after all, are still recognizable as "the past", so we are not risking a radical change in the time perspective between audience and characters.

4. Concluding Remarks

Translation needs to grow as perceptions of any given text mature: faithfulness can never be a fixed formula that offers translators a stable framework for their task; whenever it is regarded as an absolute need, the translation's success as literature in its own right is diminished. In attempting to translate homosexuality this is further complicated when, as I have attempted to show, faithfulness to the political values of the text takes precedence over pure philological faithfulness to the original. Accepting the centrality of the performative element in gay literature makes the old notion of canonical translations of a given text increasingly untenable. Gay translators have become aware, to a larger extent than some of their colleagues, that, like specific readings of literary works, translation too belongs in a specific temporal or spatial context. One might even emphasise further the constant need for new translations (or re-readings) by suggesting that *The Boys in the Band* would require different approaches, depending on the place where it is going to be performed, in order to capture the sensibilities of different audiences in, say, Barcelona or Burgos.

A knowledge of gay homographesis and its codes, possibly through gay theory, and maybe also through cultural experience, would help to fill the gaps that become apparent when translating homosexuality between cultures: it is the gaps that provide a framework for creativity. As usual in translation, it is a matter of doing one's homework, instead of resorting to the facile excuse that gay affirmative meanings are bound to be of secondary interest or are able to take care of themselves. They can't. Nothing ever does; meanings always need to be activated. But homosexuality presents itself as a specially blurred discursive element, strained by competing attempts at definition and rooted in particular cultures. The key concept here for translators is "awareness": there is a need to look closely at the way gay culture works in both the source and the target culture and translators must find imaginative, creative ways to bridge the gap. Ignoring the specific value of gay identity (and its place in contemporary Anglo-American culture) should not be an option. Translators faced with the constraints of gay texts cannot but integrate the points raised by gay theory and, at least, engage with them. No doubt there are other concerns in any text, and no one could wish translators to be political all the time. But without knowledge of the conditions under which gay homographesis is formulated, there is no way one can choose when to be political.

10 Moratín's Translation of *Hamlet* (1798) A Study of the Paratexts

JUAN J. ZARO

Leandro Fernández de Moratín's translation of *Hamlet* into Spanish, which was completed in the period between 1792 and 1794, and was published in Madrid in 1798 under the pseudonym of "Inarco Celenio", is considered to be the first faithful Spanish translation of a Shakespeare play. The only previous translation is the adaptation of Ducis' *Hamlet* (1770) by Ramón de la Cruz in 1772, which he entitled *Hamleto*. Moratín's translation of *Hamlet*, which was revised by Wilhelm von Humboldt himself (see Farinelli 1924: 112f), was not his only one: he also translated two plays by Molière (*L'école des maris*, 1808; *Le médecin malgré lui*, 1814) and Voltaire's *Candide* (1814; first published in 1838).

The importance of this translation in the European context has not been adequately acknowledged. For example, the most recent book on early Shakespearean translations, *European Shakespeares* (1992), edited by Delabastita and D'hulst, makes no reference to Spanish translations. Yet Moratín's *Hamlet* appeared at the same time as the German translation by Schlegel (1797) and predates other similar translations into Italian (Leoni 1819) and into Russian (Vronchenko 1828). It is also one of the most successful, with 33 editions published up to 1978 (Conejero and Talens 1992:56). Oddly enough, Moratín's translation has never been used to perform *Hamlet*. The play's first performance in Spain was in Madrid in 1825. The translation, based on the French version by Ducis, was made by Jose María Carnerero, who did not even take a look at Moratín's (Par 1936:71).

This paper studies the texts accompanying the translation (other sources for the study of this translation are: Adela Alfonso Fast 1975; Pilar Regalado Kerson 1989a; 1989b or paratexts (a concept first coined by Gérard Genette in 1962). They comprise the preface, the stage directions and, above all, the endnotes. In this particular case, the main focus is on the paratexts, not because the decisions taken by the translator are justified or explained (this being their usual function), but rather because – as I shall try to prove – this is an unusual case, in that they reflect the tension between the decisions made by Moratín as a translator and his theoretical beliefs about the concept of drama. The purpose of the notes was "didactic": they were meant to "illustrate" and "explain", but in fact they were used to make comments about a given text, and thus express opinions. Moratín had already used the device in an earlier work (Moratín 1812; quoted by Guido Mancini 1969:243). In other words, it is an example of non-acculturated translation which adheres to the codes of the source culture; its originality, however, lies in the fact that the translator has the opportunity to express his disagreement with the features of the source text. The preface to the first edition (1798) is in fact a declaration of mixed feelings:

This tragedy is one of the best by Shakespeare, and the one most frequently performed in the theatres of England. The admirable beauties,
easy to perceive, and the defects, that stain and spoil its perfections, make
an extraordinary and monstrous whole, composed of parts so different
from one another in quality and merit, that are hard to find in any other
dramatic composition of this or any other author or theatre; and, therefore, none is as appropriate to make us aware of Shakespeare's poetic
merit and the taste still prevailing in that nation (1944:473)[1].

Moratín states clearly his desire "to introduce the Spanish public to one of
the best pieces of English theatre" (1944:473), trying "neither to add defects
nor to hide those that I have found in the play" (1944:474), and in fact he achieves
a remarkably faithful prose translation whose only alterations lie in the sequenc-
ing (he introduces a new scene as soon as a character comes in or out), and the
naturalized characters' names (Claudio, Gertrudis, Polonio, Horacio, Marcelo,
Cornelio, Ricardo [Rosencrantz], Guillermo [Guildenstern]), and locations
(Elsingor, Wittemberga). To do this, Moratín translates straight from the English original, but admits to having looked at two French translations: La Place
(1745), which is in fact an abridged translation, and, more especially, Le Tourneur (1776) although he does not find in them "the help that he expected to
find" (1944:474). Cristóbal Cladera, a staunch enemy of Moratín's, wrote a
severe critique of the translation (Cladera 1800), in which he successfully demonstrated with a few examples how Moratín, perhaps unable to understand the
meaning of the English original, translated from Le Tourneur's French *Hamlet*.
In the case of Le Tourneur, Moratín said: "he did not make a perfect and faithful
translation" (1944:474). He goes on to explain why: Le Tourneur was a mem-
ber of one of the two "rival" French literary schools of the time, the "Corneille"
school, as opposed to the "Racine-Voltaire" school, which strongly disapproved
of Shakespeare's theatre. Le Tourneur, in his effort to present Shakespeare as a
genius, omitted or disguised all the "imperfections" in his plays (1944:474). In
consequence, Moratín "looks at those two translations with some mistrust", and
only "agrees with them in what he considers to be correct" (1944:475). It is
therefore in the endnotes that we can find the most substantial arguments for
and against Shakespeare, as well as Moratín's struggle to prevent his impressions from influencing his translation. However, these notes were modified in
the course of time. In his facsimile edition of Moratín's *Hamlet* (1991), Juan
Carlos Rodríguez compares the first edition (1798) and the second (1825),
analyzing the changes made by the writer himself. Twenty of the original notes
were either left out or shortened, and another of the paratexts in the first edition,
A Life of Shakespeare, in which Moratín described his plays, making some
derogatory comments on them, was also omitted. Rodríguez (1991:61) argues
that these changes were probably made as a result of Moratín's perception that
the literary scene of 1825 was completely different, and that Shakespeare was

---

[1] All translations are my own, unless otherwise indicated

far more widely recognized then than in 1798, when the translation was first published.

The notes have been classified according to their contents, and fall into ten categories. Notes are given here as numbered by Moratín according to Act and note number (V-1 is, for example, Act V, note 1) and quotations are my translations of Moratín's comments.

1. Notes about Words and Expressions Which Are "inappropriate to tragic sublimity"

Moratín criticizes samples of language which he considers either too popular or too vulgar to be included in a serious tragedy. This is the case with these two examples:

(Note I-2) Not a mouse stirring (I.i.10)
> This is "an expression very natural in a soldier but inappropriate to tragic sublimity" [this comment had already been made by Voltaire in his critique of *Hamlet*], and he attributes its presence to Shakespeare's "ignorance and passion".

(Note III-12) Let the galled jade wince ... (III.ii.249)
> In spite of Moratín's comment, "What sublime words for a tragedy! Le Tourneur did very well omitting them", the sentence is fully translated (*Al rocín que está lleno de mataduras*). In other cases, he denounces the irrelevance of whole episodes with respect to the play's main action, like Polonius' advice to Laertes:

(Note I-21) Give thy thoughts no tongue ... (I.iii.59)
> For Moratín, "this is very good advice, but it has nothing to do with the fable".

But this main criticism is about the comic touches in the tragedy. It should be remembered that Voltaire was amazed at Shakespeare's "comic interludes" because they did not fit in with his concept of tragedy. Although Moratín never attempts to omit or change them, he sometimes strives to find justifications:

(Note II-8) My liege, and madam ... (II.ii.86)
> Here, "Polonius is trying to make people laugh ... Those who attribute the mixture of tragic and comic to specific national characters are wrong, although it is the French who know better when to laugh or cry on the appropriate occasion because they have cultivated dramatic poetry with more accuracy". Yet, in another note (II-9), he admires Polonius' great comic features and stresses Shakespeare's talent, "had he lived in another era and with other principles".

He also criticizes the mixture of prose and poetry in tragedy, another of Shakespeare's great mistakes:

(Note II-10) But look, where sadly ... (II.ii.168)
  "Verse suddenly becomes prose ... why have these changes been made?"

2. Notes about the Appropriateness of Time, Space and Action

Obviously, the unities of place, time and action are not followed in *Hamlet*.
Moratín criticizes both the slowness and the excessive length of the play, caused
by irrelevant episodes which are a waste of time:

(Note III-4) Speak the speech, I pray you ... (III.ii.1)
  "What a slow pace! What is told in five acts could be told in three".

(Note I-14) My lord, I think I saw him yesternight ... (I.ii.189)
  "The play should have started here. What precedes this is unnecessary".

With regard to place, Shakespeare's great fault is to be vague about the loca-
tion of the tragedy:

(Note I-13) But what is your affair in Elsinore? (I.ii.174)
  "Up to now, nobody knew where the action was taking place".

But he also points out how some attempts to avoid the "disgusting" locations of the play were unsuccessful due to the low level of theatrical culture of
the English public:

(Note V-1) Is she to be buried in Christian burial? (V.i.1)
  "This is all ridiculous. Garrick tried to suppress this disgusting scene, to no
  avail, except among the right-minded people".

But it is the graveyard scene that Moratín finds the most faulty, especially as
far as the characters' behaviour is concerned:

(Note V-7) Take thy fingers from my throat ... (V.i.262)
  "Here, a prince and a great Danish lord can be seen fighting inside a grave,
  kicking a corpse, grabbing each other's neck and hair, and punching each
  other". The rest of the note, omitted from the 1825 edition, went on as
  follows: "If Shakespeare [according to some] imitated Nature, we may
  infer that in his time, princes went walking in graveyards, talked to grave-
  diggers, and had fights with lords. Shakespeare often imitated Nature with
  great felicity; sometimes he copied it exactly as it is, and at other times he
  abandoned himself to the excess of his feverish and free imagination,
  making ideal and monstrous paintings that resemble nobody". The duel
  scene is also a great mistake, because "this general slaughter does not enhance the tragic effect, but diminishes it by splitting interest instead of
  concentrating it" (V-5). This last scene is just the culmination of a series of
  badly constructed episodes in which characters are irrelevant or misplaced.

(Note I-3) Look where it comes again! (I.i.40)
  "If the tragedy starts with a ghost, how is it going to end? Why does he not

appear in front of Hamlet at the very beginning, instead of wasting time frightening soldiers?"

(Note I-8) We have here writ to Norway, uncle of young Fortinbras. (I.ii.17)
"Fortinbras has nothing to do with the tragedy's action".

3. Notes about the Absence of Rigour and Verisimilitude
In his very first note, Moratín describes how the action of *Hamlet* takes place in very early times (3390-3370 BC), as retold by Saxo Grammaticus in his *Historia Danica* (*c*.1200; published 1514). Since he takes this literally, most historical and contextual references in the play are misplaced:

(Note I-5) Fortinbras of Norway. (I.i.82)
"A king that never existed".

(Note I-6) In the most high and palmy state of Rome ... (I.i.113)
"How is it possible that Marcello and Bernardo know who Caesar was, if he had not yet been born?"

But these inconsequentialities are not only the result of spatial or temporal misplacements. Sometimes, the characters themselves say or do things which are either inappropriate for their condition or simply unbelievable:

(Note I-7) It was about to speak when the cock crew (I.i.147)
"The cock should be included in the list of characters" [paragraph omitted in the 1825 edition]. "How is it that Horatio, a learned man, believes in supernatural powers? Do not forget that the play was intended for a low-class London public".

(Note I-27) I set it down ... (I.v.107)
"It is incredible that Hamlet, at night, in a deserted place, should write things in a book".

4. Notes on England and the English
Moratín started his translation while he was in England. He arrived there on 27th August 1798, fleeing from the horror of the French revolution. He learnt English very quickly, read many books and saw many plays. His impressions of England can be found in his *Apuntaciones sueltas de Inglaterra* (in Moratín 1867-1868). (Other sources for the study of Moratín's impressions on England are Susi Hillburn Effross 1965; Robert Johnson 1970; Pedro Ortiz Armengol 1985.) He was immediately attracted to Shakespeare, but rejected the norms of English theatre, which had developed independently of the models adopted on the continent. In this respect, he notes in his diary:

> The extravagances of the Spanish, the Italian and even the Malabar theatre are nothing compared to those of the English one; if the French were not mad, I would never have come here to see the immortal plays of Shakespeare. (p.138)

On 1st February 1793, there is a note about the translation:

> What a devilish language these people have! Although I translate easily, there is no way to speak or understand what they say. I go every day to the British Museum to see books ... (1973:150)".

He left England on 9th August 1793. He travelled to France and Italy, where on 6th August 1794, he wrote to his friend Mélon: "I have just finished translating *Hamlet*, the English play. What a tragedy" (1973:175). The notes include some cultural references to English popular culture, as well as some digressions on the English people's behaviour and temperament:

(Note IV-7) Saint Valentine's day (IV.v.48)
The celebration is explained and compared with an old Spanish tradition that Cervantes included in his play *Pedro de Urdemalas* (1615).

(Note V-1) Is she to be buried in Christian burial ...? (V.i.1)
"English people love horrors and stupid jokes, philosophical speeches, highflown language, battles and burials, witches, ghosts, fights, triumphs, music, torture and corpses. This is a small consolation for those nations which have not bred a Bacon or a Newton."

5. Notes Demonstrating Admiration for Shakespeare

Moratín cannot conceal his admiration for Shakespeare, expressed very clearly in quite a number of the notes:

(Note I-19) Youth to itself rebels, though none else near (I.iii.44)
"This, and many other sentences which can be found throughout the play, contain such a substantial and important doctrine that it is not necessary to draw the reader's attention to them".

(Note I-25) What if it tempt you toward the flood, my Lord ... (I.iv.68)
"All the poet's mistakes so far can be forgotten: Here, his talent pervades all ..."

6. Notes on Previous Translations

The notes only include references to Le Tourneur's translation, although, as indicated above, Moratín also read La Place's version:

(Note I-31) Ha, ha, boy! say's thou so? (I.v.149)
A critique of Le Tourneur's translation. It seems that the French translator omitted the colloquial and familiar expressions here and rewrote them in a much more formal style. For example, "old mole" [I.v.162] becomes "invisible ghost" in French.

(Note III-26) Would from a paddock ... (IV.v.191)
"Le Tourneur forgot to translate this paragraph".

7. Explanatory Notes

The main purpose of these notes is to help readers follow the course of the story. Nevertheless, Moratín is constantly evaluating the action, although this does not mean that the translation is affected. Far from it: these notes are included to explain what readers might find difficult to understand given the faithfulness of the translated text with respect to the original:

(Note I-33) How strange or odd so'ever I bear myself ... (I.v.170)
"Here, Hamlet announces his purpose to feign madness".

(Note II-4) My lord, as I was sewing in my closet ... (II.i.77)
"The prince is now pretending to be mad, but this artifice will be of no consequence, since Hamlet proceeds with great care at all times".

(Note II-11) For if the sun breed maggots in a dead dog ... (II.ii.181)
"From now on, some of Hamlet's expressions will lack sense, but we must realize that he is pretending to be mad".

8. Notes on Improper Language

Moratín's idea here is that improper language must be identified and translated, in some cases, or omitted in others. Although he makes sure to point out what scenes are omitted in the performance – Act II, scene i and the passage "Then you live about her waist" (II.ii.235) – both are included in the translation. The only omitted passage is the sentence "That's a fair thought to lie between maid's legs" (III.ii.121), translated as *Qué dulce cosa es ...* [What a fair thing it is ...], because "it might offend the reader's modesty" (Note III-7). Moratín points out how, in spite of these things, Shakespeare "is the most decent and chaste writer of his time" (Note II-13), perhaps comparing him with his contemporaries.

9. Quotations from Shakespearean Experts

Paratexts and metatexts on Shakespeare from several authors (Warburton, Eschenburg, Steevens, Le Tourneur, Johnson ...) are often quoted in the notes:

(Note III-15) 'Tis now the very witching time of night (III.iii.396)
"According to the old superstitions, the night was profane and the day clear and pure [Warburton]".

(Note IV-2) The body is with the king, but the king is not with the body (IV.iv.27)
Explanation of different interpretations, made by Eschenberg, Stevens and Le Tourneur, about the meaning of this sentence.

The number and variety of these sources is remarkable, and proves how thoroughly Moratín researched for his translation. In this respect, Deacon (1996:304) points out the "historicist" character of his approach, and his attempts to find new meanings to the play's more obscure passages.

10. Notes on Specific Translation Problems

Moratín's decision to translate faithfully leads him to point out the specific problems of the target text and the strategies adopted to solve them:

(Note IV-11) Down-a-down, and you call him ... (IV.v.170)
"My translation is arbitrary, because there is no sense in these words. This is comparable to the *jota, cachirulo*, and other Spanish popular tunes".

(Note V-5) I think it be thine, indeed; for thou liest in't. (V.i.125)
Explanation of the double meaning implicit in the word *liest*, that makes this passage so obscure.

Conclusion

The notes accompanying *Hamlet* reflect vividly the tension between Moratín's creativity as a translator – based on his intellectual belief in the neo-classical approach to theatre, which he consciously applied to his own plays – and the self-imposed constraints derived from his profound admiration for Shakespeare. But there is also another source of constraint: in his *Preliminary discourse* to his comedies (1792), he advocates a complete reform of the Spanish theatre based on the models provided by other European countries, particularly France. On 20th December 1792 he wrote to the Spanish Prime Minister Godoy offering to carry out the project himself (1973:141). The purpose was to create a new theatre that would contribute to a moral regeneration of the Spanish nation based on foreign models. To imitate Europe was the path to "modernization", and this process meant the adoption of neo-classical rules and a discipline on the part of the author which, to a large extent, had previously been absent from Spanish theatre.

Nevertheless, perhaps these convictions, considered by critics to be one of Moratín's most important contributions to Spanish literature, were not as strong as they may seem. I suggest that Moratín, possibly influenced by his unexpected, but direct, contact with England and the English people, decided to translate *Hamlet* himself in spite of his prejudices because he identified with and respected another model, which was different, but as European as the French one, and which could also be imitated in Spain in order to further the nation's integration into Europe. The omission of some of the notes and the other paratext (*A Life of Shakespeare*) in the 1825 edition is, in this sense, highly revealing. (It is remarkable that, as late as 1825, the neoclassic ideal, though weak, is still much in vogue in Spain. Perhaps the almost complete absence of, for example, genres like the Gothic can be explained by an aversion to the fantastic as described by writers like Moratín, who were rooted in the neo-classical tradition. When this influence disappeared, it was already too late for the Gothic to flourish.) His translation, therefore, can be considered as a landmark in the history of Spanish literature, firstly because it is virtually the starting point for direct contact between the two literatures. According to Montesinos (1960:154-268), the only English authors translated before 1798 are Jonathan Swift's *Gulliver* (1793),

Samuel Richardson's *Pamela* and *Clarissa* (1794-5) and Henry Fielding's *Amelia Booth* (1795-96) and *Tom Jones* (1796). Most of these are indirect translations from the French. Secondly, it was important because in one sense, and probably contrary to Moratín's intentions, it marks the end of the hegemonic French influence, providing a new model that would slowly permeate the hitherto insular and inward-looking literature of Spain.

11 "A danger and a veiled attack"
Translating into Nazi Germany

KATE STURGE

> Every translation lent or sold means income for the English author
> and the English publisher, means taxes for the Empire, means weap-
> ons and ammunition against Germany!
>
> (*Die Werkbücherei* 1940:1f)[1]

There is evidently more to the reception of translations than a consideration of
the faithfulness and beauty of the translator's work – and not only such material
issues as those mentioned in the extract above, taken from a Nazi librarians'
journal. In such journals, translation is regarded as a potential danger to the
integrity of the target language community, a danger often framed in terms of
contamination and invasion. In this paper, I will examine some reviews and
articles on translations into German during the National Socialist (NS) period,
focusing on the attitudes to translation contained in these texts as illustrative of
different stances towards the importation of "foreign" elements into the target
culture.

Investigating the discourse on translation in the period, I shall leave aside
the study of the translations themselves. My interest is in what Gideon Toury
calls "preliminary norms" (Toury 1995:58) – decisions on what and why to
translate, and how translations fit into the surrounding cultural landscape – rather
than the "operational", or micro-level, norms that govern *how* texts are translated. Translators themselves, both as members of the receiving culture and as
agents of the importation process, are under strong pressure to conform to both
levels of norms: after all, even in a politically open literary system their translations usually have to fit the target culture closely enough to be ideologically
acceptable and commercially viable. The practice of translation by translators,
publishers and readers may, of course, be far removed from the evaluations of
its role by literary journalists; however, journalists' comments are interesting
because they touch on certain powerful criteria apparently being applied to translation as a channel for the influx of elements of other literatures. The context of
a totalitarian political system with highly regulated literary production means
such criteria may well be more explicit and unified than in an open system,
where informal, commercial considerations predominate. Indeed, at first sight
German literature between 1933 and 1945 might be seen in André Lefevere's
terms as an "undifferentiated" system, where status, economic security and ideological requirements are dispensed from one source (Lefevere 1996:17), resulting
in extremely strong constraints on translators and publishers and a relatively
coherent practice of translation. Without here being able to look in detail at the
practical conditions faced by translators and publishers in the period, I hope to

---

[1] All translations are my own.

show that, in contrast to Lefevere's model, there was in fact no single agent (or even a limited number of agents) controlling the production of translations but that translators and publishers had to police their own production to a very great extent, working within incoherent and contradictory norms. Even so, Lefevere's general emphasis on the economic and ideological determinants of translation policy is highly relevant in this context.

As a means of tracing possible correlations between translation policy and its surrounding ideology, I shall draw on Clem Robyns' proposal that attitudes to translation are part of the continuing work of a discourse as it "(re)produces its own borderlines and thus defines its own specificity with respect to other discourses" (Robyns 1994:57). Robyns proposes four ways of "meeting the alien":

> An attitude in which otherness is denied and transformed may be called *imperialist*, while one in which otherness is acknowledged but still transformed may be called *defensive*. A *transdiscursive* discourse neither radically opposes itself to other discourses nor refuses their intrusion, while a *defective* discourse stimulates the intrusion of alien elements that are explicitly acknowledged as such.   (p. 60)

These attitudes are not mutually exclusive but, on the contrary, can overlap and coexist within a cultural situation. The framework of these four stances does not always fit my material, where especially the division between imperialist and defensive stances does not hold clearly. Nevertheless, the emphasis on the translation as a focal point of discursive interference does help explain the deployment of a wider xenophobic discourse in Nazi comment on translation – and the passion with which my sources approach the question of whether and what to translate.

My contention will be that in a society whose official discourses (and these were in general the only ones with access to public distribution) were obsessed with issues of purity and autarky, the treatment of translation too will seek to support the fiction of cultural autonomy and adopt a hostile stance toward the alien. In fact, it might well present an extreme version of this stance. NS theories of literature were diffuse and contradictory – what Klaus Vondung calls a "heterogeneous conglomeration" of ideas (Vondung 1973:13) rather than a coherent ideology. However, core elements do emerge: different writers tend to converge in claiming literature as the "expression" of a national, or *Volk*, soul. *Volk* and its adjective *völkisch* refer to the racialized "folk" community imagined by German fascism. Because culture can only speak through the blood,

> no import of cultural "goods", no meddling by a foreign, or even an "absolute", spirit can create, can build life. Only the living *Volk* community has true creativity (*Bücherkunde* 1944:81; a literary journal published by Alfred Rosenberg's office. See below).

Strictly speaking, translations cannot be integrated into such a model of literature. Since the "soul" expressed is alien but the words used to express it are domestic, the translation must be a hybrid form, and as such anathema to an ideology of purity. Given that translations were published, bought and borrowed from public and, especially, commercial libraries in large numbers during the period, how did NS literary policy deal with this conundrum? In the following, I will first sketch aspects of the literary policy of the regime and its policy on translation, then examine articles and reviews of translations in an NS literary journal which may illustrate the complexity of the translator's perceived role in the process of literary importation.

1. The Control of Literary Production

The NS state attempted to regulate cultural production along two paths: on the one hand by promoting a managed, pro-NS production and on the other by destroying everything not consonant with NS ideology. The promotion of literature was set around a concept of literature as education, and specifically education to struggle. The approved book would express the German soul, working with elements like race, health, purity, leadership, manliness/womanliness, rural life in conflict with a demonized city – preferably within the frame of the soldier, peasant or regionalist novel, poetry or "action" theatre. These types of approved literature were promoted by means of prizes, marketing assistance and other financial support, but equally importantly by awarding politically powerful posts to approved writers. Little is written by NS ideologues on the topic of approved literature without appealing to the danger of extinction such literature supposedly faced. Alfred Rosenberg, for example, argued that truly German literature must be rescued: it was being threatened by, among other things, "rassenfremde" ("racially alien") literature, which had conspired

> to rob the German character of its last strength to resist its enemies. [...] In the place of what is fitting to the *Volk*, the rootlessly international is openly coming to the fore (Rosenberg, May 1928, cited in Bollmus 1970:27).

In other words, the literature to be promoted would remain firmly within the parameters of the *Volk* spirit, and the threat of internationalism was to be countered by the destruction of "mixed" literature.

This destruction (referred to as *Säuberung*, or "cleansing") made use of bans and confiscation of existing books, pre-publication censorship and the expulsion or murder of particular writers and publishers. Goebbels' Propaganda Ministry was the main, though by no means the only, body responsible; its decisions were implemented mainly by the Gestapo, which additionally often took its own initiatives (see Aigner 1971). However, literary production was not state-owned, and direct intervention by the state made up a small part relative to the entirety of control. A wider net was cast by a *gleichgeschaltete* ("brought into line", in other words Nazified) book trade, educational and library system, policed from within and watched over by Party institutions. For example, librarians' professional organizations swore allegiance to the NS state and took on the responsibility for carrying out its programme in the field, supervised by the local branches of the Party libraries' committee and the libraries' board of the Ministry of Education (Barbian 1995:119ff). From 1936 the *Liste des schädlichen und unerwünschten Schrifttums (Index of harmful and unwanted literature)* was available to the Gestapo and SS but was to be kept "strictly confidential" and unavailable to the book trade (see Aigner 1971). In the absence of an accessible, binding index of banned titles, those selecting books for libraries and bookshops also had to consider evaluations of books by other bodies currently in favour with the regime. Control was thus largely invisible to the reading public because it worked via the (non-) availability of books for sale and in libraries. Given that the implementation of control was unregulated and thus unpredictable, pre-emptive (self-) censorship had to be exercised. The book trade, for example, could not afford either politically or commercially to commit itself to a book which might be refused sale to schools and libraries or even confiscated. Thus the lack of clear-cut regulation, rather than leaving freedoms, probably encouraged a climate of fear which was for the most part able to contain the book market within acceptable boundaries.

This multilayered – not to say chaotic – system of control with overlapping responsibilities and rival institutions was typical of the NS state (as Bollmus 1970 argues). While lack of co-ordination opened some loopholes, overdetermination closed most, at the same time serving to disable potential competition to Hitler's personal power. Whether or not this system is interpreted as a deliberate ploy, it is important to notice that it meant the management of literary production was anything but monolithic. Instead, competing interest groups and personalities tried to exploit the confusion of competencies, and no unified policy or implementation existed. Individual publishers had to find for themselves a way to survive within an official ideology that was itself highly contradictory.

Translations were managed by the same confusion of powers as literature in general, but seem to have been more strictly regulated than other areas of publishing. According to Strothmann (1963:197), translations, in common with "political works", were subject to blanket pre-publication censorship right from 1933, although he suggests this may have been more of a formality until the outbreak of war; such censorship was extended to all types of publication only with the introduction of paper rationing in 1941-42 (p. 203). Lists of later banned works, particularly the 1943 index of popular fiction "unsuitable for young people and libraries", do show that despite apparently strict regulation, plenty of translations were being published right up to 1939. Once the war began, however, the position of translated literature changed: all imports from enemy countries were banned, with a special guide issued to librarians and booksellers separating language from nationality for this purpose (which English-language authors were British, which Irish or American, and which British but "exceptionally" permitted). It should be noted that the official focus on the source language of translations as a national, as opposed to a linguistic, category demonstrates a politicization of translation, an understanding of cultural importation as potential threat, which is echoed in the journal articles I will describe below.

2. Attitudes to Translation in a Literary Journal

Because the process of permitting translations was to be kept as discreet as possible, most decisions went through confidential memoranda between the Propaganda Ministry and specific publishers. Rather than attempting to trace the path of such decisions, I would like to look at the discourse on translation in one of the officially sanctioned or tolerated publications on literary policy. Its comments are neither coherent nor legally binding, but they do give clues as to what criteria were being applied in various parts of the system to judge the permissibility of translations. The reviews themselves will have been influenced by the reviewers' desire to follow a "correct" line so as to further their own careers as loyal academics visibly supporting the NS state (a role which could lead to considerable practical benefits in the shape of committee chairs, et cetera: see, for example, the case of Hans Hagemeyer discussed by Barbian 1995:165). Book reviews formed one among the many, and contradictory, sources of information available to librarians and the book trade in their task of deciding on the political and commercial viability of texts; political viability in that anyone involved in the book trade had to guard carefully their membership of the appropriate section of the *Reichsschrifttumskammer* (approximately, a "guild" of writers and associated professions), without which no professional activity was permitted and which could be withdrawn at any point by the Propaganda Ministry as a punishment for misbehaviour (see Barbian 1995:505ff), and commercial viability in that printing a book which was subsequently banned and/or confiscated naturally involved huge financial losses. Translators and their publishers, like all the other levels of book production and distribution, were in need of guidance to pick their way through the complexities of the regime's somewhat unpredictable responses to translation.

The journal I will investigate is the *Bücherkunde* (hereafter BK), published monthly between 1934 and 1944 as the organ of the literature branch of the Nazi Party's office for political education headed by Alfred Rosenberg. This Party institution laid claim (unsuccessfully, according to Bollmus 1970) to responsibilities similar to those of its State counterpart, the literature department of Goebbels' Propaganda Ministry. The Ministry had power over permissions and promotion, but Rosenberg's office reported on more books than any other body – around 50% of the average 20,000 works published every year (Strothmann 1963:217). The office published in the BK a monthly list of "recommended" and "not recommended" works from among those permitted, implicitly defying the official (secret) indexes drawn up by the Propaganda Ministry. The BK's position in the network of overlapping competencies should be borne in mind when investigating its statements on literary policy. It can particularly be seen in the pro- "Nordic" stance of the BK's earlier volumes (contrary to Goebbels' distrust of the "Nordic" idea) and its frequent, though always covert, criticism of government policy on publishing. The BK's much-vaunted monthly lists had no legal status, but it seems likely that its opinions would have influenced the book-buying policy of libraries and booksellers, and thus the strategies of publishers.

The eleven volumes of the BK, 1934 to 1944, cover various aspects of contemporary literature including debates on literary and political issues, panegyrics to approved authors, advertisements, reviews and, especially in later volumes, propaganda articles with only the flimsiest connection to a literary topic. Among the articles are some on translated literature in general and some on translations from particular language groups; the book review sections also include translations, with most reviews of translations concentrated in the years 1936-1938.

Translations from English are the most frequently reviewed (reflecting their dominance in the translated book market), followed by translations from French, then from Flemish. Various Scandinavian source languages come next; if we were to take them as one language group, as the BK undoubtedly did (for example, some books are labelled simply as translations from "Nordic"), they would match reviews on translations from English in number. Unsurprisingly, the predominance of English and French dies out in later issues, to be replaced by the languages of the "friendly" (meaning, in many cases, occupied) nations, with the solitary review of Japanese literature to be found in one of the very last issues (BK1944/5-6:78). BK reviews appear in categories under headings such as "Books on War" or "The British Empire", and translations usually appear in a separate section, entitled, for example, "From beyond our borders" (BK1938/12) or "Literature of our neighbours" (BK1938/8). Thus the translated status of the works is highlighted – they are not absorbed into the generality of books in German.

The BK does not take one clear line on translations – the attitudes visible in the articles and reviews are various and often enough contradictory. Drawing on Robyns' categories, I will seek to organize them along three trajectories: one stressing threat and maximizing difference, one stressing usefulness and highly ambivalent on difference, one based on lack in the target language culture. These positions are neither clearly separable nor internally coherent, but may serve as a means of looking at the multiplicity of possible translation norms articulated in the BK and their close relationship with the surrounding NS ideology of the alien.

3. Translation as Threat

If we begin with the discourse of threat, epitomizing what Robyns calls a "defensive" stance (1994:66), the first key term is that of the flood of translations onto the German market. The BK, along with Propaganda Ministry journals like *Die Bücherei* (1939/5) and *Die Werkbücherei* (1939/12), complains of a steep increase in translations into German during early 1939 (BK39/6:309). The problem is felt to be the fact that more is being translated into than out of German, in other words that the commercial and ideological trade balance of translations is negative. In particular, among translations out of German, anti-fascist authors rather than the state-backed literature are the most popular abroad. Thus, translation is failing to promote the new regime abroad; at home "the flooding of Germany with Scandinavian writing over the past years" (BK1940/6:161) is held to be pushing the "young, ambitious German writer" out of business (ibid).

The reader is reminded that by cutting down on Scandinavian imports, "we will not be the poorer but will even save a considerable amount of foreign currency". The piece ends with an appeal that echoes other wartime calls to buy homegrown goods: "First comes German literature, and only then foreign literature!" (ibid:162).

The emotive terminology of flooding/swamping, central to NS (and other) racism, suggests that it is not just the volume of translations into German which worries the BK, but also their potentially insidious nature. The metaphor of the flood depends on an opposition between the tide of foreign books and "us", the German readers, its victims. In the article on Scandinavian literature quoted above, the author further complains that the publishers of such translations apply "literary criteria that are alien to us" when choosing books for translation (BK1940/6:161). If publishers are irresponsible, then the literary critics must "lead the campaign against this flood" (ibid:162) by applying truly German criteria. This would be necessary to protect the German writer, but by implication also to protect the German reader: in another review, the reader is characterized as the innocent German about to be tricked into buying the book (BK1939/12:691). It is common for the BK to allude to the reader's need for protection and guidance; indeed, a helpless readership is vital to the construction of a benevolent guiding hand in the shape of the various state and Party offices. At the same time, the paranoid language of the reader as a victim of translation parallels the central NS theme of the German *Volk* as a victim of an alien conspiracy, in this case one mediated by the book trade.

The following extract from a long review of a collection of religiously-tinged Flemish stories edited and translated by Carl Heinz Erkelenz, *Unsere liebe Frau aus Flandern* (Leipzig 1938, reviewed in BK1938/12:689ff), may illustrate some of these points:

> [It is not our business to criticize bad Flemish authors.] But we do unambiguously demand of all German translators and publishers something which should really go without saying: if we wish to increase our German writing by the addition of works from kindred literatures, then those works must, firstly, bear the clear stamp of kinship. That means, among other things, that sectarian [i.e. Catholic] hole-in-the-corner literature, as a danger and a veiled attack on our German *Volk* community, must remain outside the Reich boundaries. And secondly, we will not tolerate the German book market being regarded as a junk-room for the rubbish produced by authors rejected [...] in their countries of origin (BK1938/12:690).

The emphasis on the first person plural in this extract asserts the community of German bookreaders as distinct from the foreign products (as usual conflating the "we" of the journal with that of the nation's readership). As mentioned above, these readers are presented as passive consumers, dependent on the good faith of the real agents, namely translators and, above all, publishers – in other words, those links in the translating process which can, unlike the readers' tastes, be

policed by the State. At the same time translators and their publishers are allo-
cated a highly suspect position outside the *Volk*, as mediators of a foreign
culture's "veiled attack". A similar claim is made equally strongly in a review
of a translation from French, Julien Green's *Mitternacht* (*Minuit*). The reviewer
complains that the translation's Viennese Jewish publisher has "horribly hu-
miliated the language that we love as part of ourselves" (BK1937/2:90) – again
the translator and the publisher of translations are cast as the enemy of domestic culture. The reference to the importer as Jewish further introduces an
association of the "Jewish alien" of anti-Semitic discourse with the threatening
importer of alien material, the translator/publisher of translations.

To return to the Flemish case, the reference to the German book market as a
repository for other literatures' cast-offs again stresses the relationship of hos-
tility felt to exist between source and target literatures, the assumption of a
closed system into which imports may be allowed to enter but only after careful
screening for quality. BK reviews often make reference to the "quality" of the
translation, but seldom is this elaborated further than with "sloppy", "masterly"
or similar labels. Far more often, quality is defined as the consonance of the plot
and characters with NS ideology, and in the passage quoted above, the emphasis on the relatedness of the source language suggests that when translations are
praised it will be for their success in reducing the foreignness of the foreign.
Thus, of Flemish culture, those aspects felt to be alien (religion) should be excluded and those felt to be kindred (race) admitted; a translating norm is
constituted that demands a highly selective approach to the content and tenor of
the source text by the translator. Other BK references to translations from Flemish likewise tend to evaluate the texts in terms of their adherence to an ideology
matching the NS literary surroundings, for example by picking or highlighting
subjects like the peasant soul which are not really different – a point I will
return to below.

So translations are reviewed in separate sections, almost always clearly labelled as imports and given special attention regarding the foreignness of the
content – the thrust of the BK's defensive stance is that translations need to be
carefully herded, kept sealed off from target language literature, their cultural
differentness and danger stressed again and again. The similarity with other
areas of NS political, and specifically racist, discourse is not difficult to see.

4. Translation and Differences

But alongside the strand of fear of the import there runs another motif: translations as potentially useful expressions of the relationship between source and
target language nations. Considerable emphasis is placed on the distance of
most source language cultures from "us Germans", but this is not necessarily
seen in a negative light, especially in the pre-1939 volumes. The value of translations in educating the readers about otherwise mysterious *Völker* is a point
frequently mentioned in their favour by BK reviewers. For example, the reviewer of a collection of Yugoslav novellas (BK1938/12:689) praises the insight

into the "true" (i.e. pre-modern) culture of this "new literary territory" – soon, we might add, to be more than just *literary* territory. A foreign policy agenda evidently feeds into such judgements. Similarly, the reviews of Finnish and Japanese texts in a 1944 issue (BK1944/5-6:79f) could be viewed as part of an education on the ways of new subjects and allies – again, the "understanding of the character of the Finnish *Volk*" (80) offered by one translation is the basis of the praise.

Of course, the understanding supposedly provided by translations is not neutral. In the case of French, and to a lesser extent English, literature, translations are usually considered informative inasmuch as they indicate the inferiority of the source language culture. AG Macdonell's *Selbstbildnis eines Gentleman* (*Autobiography of a Cad*) is felt to be useful in confirming the BK's worst suspicions about the English national character (BK1942/5-6:179); Julien Green's *Mitternacht* (*Minuit*) (BK1937/2:90) proves the decadence of the French. When translations furnish understanding of the foreign culture, this comes with the proviso that the image received by German readers must be accurate in NS terms; thus, the English must be accurately portrayed as degenerate snobs, the French as morbid and nihilistic, the Americans as stricken by social collapse, the Norwegians as really rather German. This is the accuracy criterion that the BK's reviews demand of translators, rather than one based on faithfulness to the source text. Indeed, the source text is assumed to *be* the source culture, the translated text an educational excursion, and the task of publisher and translator to select carefully so as to reflect the known realities of the other culture.

For the BK the usefulness of translations may, though, equally be to confirm the relatedness, the *lack* of difference, between source and target cultures. The amount of space given to those source languages considered to be related (i.e. Scandinavian languages and Flemish) is disproportionate to their numbers among published translations, where English dominated up to 1939. Among the literature of the kindred cultures, those authors are praised who can be presented as *völkisch* – and pro-German – in their approach. In other words, the virtue of kindred authors lies precisely in their closeness to German culture, in the case of Flemish authors their roots in "the shared *völkisch*-Low German reality" (BK1942/1:5). In this way, the source texts of some translations are not really foreign but merely "branches of our literature" (BK1937/2:95, on "Nordic" literature) – in this case, being hardly translations in the first place is what makes them acceptable.

The idea that the translation from Flemish or Danish is hardly a translation at all is reminiscent of what Robyns calls the "imperialist" stance (1994:60), which seeks to swallow the foreign text and deny its otherness. As in the cases he cites, this stance is probably not unrelated to a wish to swallow the foreign nation and territory too. However, here no typically imperialist claim is made for the universality of the superior nation's values, as only a select few nations are regarded as having access to the Germanic; others are held to have their own specific (and incurably inferior) moral universe. Nor is membership of a superior race immutable: even while it refers to "*Völker* related by blood and race" (BK1937/6:322), the BK is always careful to point out that much literature of these nations may only be masquerading as Germanic. The Norwegian Swedish writer Sally Salminen, for example, is still highly Nordic (and thus "Germanic") in BK1938/8:438, but by issue 1940/6, after an anti-fascist speech, she has joined the ranks of the racially alien. Typically for NS ideology, the notion of "race" here is paradoxical. On the one hand, the members of a *Volk* are held to be born into it; on the other they have to *become* members by consciously conforming to values elsewhere posited as innate.

Aside from clearly pan-Germanist claims, other aspects of BK reviews also appear to minimize the "good" foreign text's difference from home-produced literature. For example, plot is almost always judged in terms of its closeness to acceptable German storylines covering "important" themes: plenty of peasants; men who are men and women who are women (or who are destroyed by their attempts at emancipation); race and destiny as prime movers. "Irrelevant" themes would be society or manners (a common complaint against British literature, e.g. BK1937/2:94, on Evelyn Waugh). Like the judgements of plot, comments on the style of the translations share much of the ground of reviews of domestic texts, so that "artificiality" is criticized, "simplicity", "immediacy" and "truthfulness" praised. If the translator remains within these parameters, imported texts may be designated as "a welcome enrichment of our literature" (BK1937/ 2:93, on John Masefield's novels). The term "enrichment" recalls the imperialist quest for new acquisitions from abroad, and one reviewer even recommends that although "an excess of foreign cultural products is harmful to our own spiritual/intellectual life [...] a nation can profit greatly from the possession of the cultural treasures of others" (BK1940/6:159). In the context of the BK reviews, it appears that the "treasure" to be acquired from imported texts is the confirmation of the categories of NS ideology.

Thus translations are taken to be useful as a didactic tool, as long as they conform to NS knowledge of the foreign culture. In the terms of this knowledge, the otherness of the source language may be reduced to a matter of local colour if, as in the case of Flemish literature, this concurs with foreign policy aims. Yet even then at the core of each review is the anxious question: how foreign or not foreign is the text? This ambivalence is well illustrated by the case of reviews of translations from English. Here, while one book may prove the English are fundamentally Germanic, another will show they are fundamentally alien and corrupt, antithetical to the German nation. These judgements of translations, both made in terms of the English nation but drawing opposite conclusions, can be found coexisting already before the outbreak of war. Charles Morgan's *Der Quell* (*The Fountain*) demonstrates "how closely related the German and the British nature are, both having their origin in the same blood" (BK1935/12:393); Evelyn Waugh's *Eine Handvoll Staub* (*A Handful of Dust*) all too accurately portrays a "a decadent, rotten bourgeois society, full of lies, inner untruthfulness and lawlessness" (BK1937/2:94). In both cases, the translations are seen as expressions of an Englishness either more or less alien to the German, and the translators' success is measured according to the usefulness of these expressions for the NS context.

5. Translation and the Inadequacy of the Target Literature

Finally, there is an absence in the BK's comments that suggests another position, albeit only implicitly. This is what Robyns calls the "defective" stance (1994:60), where gaps in the home system are felt which need to be filled by imports. In the BK, a defective stance is present in an inverted, or denied, form, notably in the case of popular literature. There is almost no mention of this stronghold of translation – not even in the shape of the vehement attacks on it to be found in the librarians' journals. In the latter, popular genres (particularly the detective and the adventure novel, which were dominated by translations from English[2]) are condemned as corrupting, often explicitly in terms of their foreignness to the supposed German literary soul. An editorial in the journal for works librarians, *Die Werkbücherei,* condemns detective novels translated from English or using British settings and pseudonyms: "From now on we will refuse to tolerate any writing at all which indirectly or directly copies or propagates Englishness, the English way of life or English institutions" (*Die Werkbücherei* 1940:1). If popular literature had to be permitted, then a thoroughly Germanized form, with the Alexanderplatz police replacing Scotland Yard, should be provided. In this and other articles, the aggressive tone carries an unwilling acknowledgement of the success of an imported genre and the failure of the German system to fill the gap except with imitations.

But while the vices of popular literature are attacked frequently by librarians' and youth work journals, the BK steers clear of the topic. What we do find, though rarely, are rather anxious *denials* of inadequacies in German literature. For example, a review praising T.E. Lawrence's so-called colonial novels adds "but we Germans have no need – for example because of some lack on our part – to borrow from foreign nations, in the case of colonial novels just as little as in that of really good, realistic adventure novels" (BK1937/10:571). Precisely because translation is suspected to be caused by a "lack on our part", to be the sign of a weak culture – the BK argument appears to run – Germany cannot need translations because it is not a weak culture. The fear of weakness hinted at here is backed up by repeated assertions of Germany's need to pick only the very best of foreign literature and reject anything not reaching the high standards of indigenous literature. The claim is that imports are only extras, not

---

[2] The list of popular fiction banned for sale to young people contains 946 titles (excluding brochure-format series); of these 335 are translations from English and a further 320 are written under Anglo-American pseudonyms and/or have Anglo-American proper names in the title. Of the series, which include 2552 titles, the majority have Wild West American detective or other American themes. The *Deutshe Nationalbibliographie* data suggests that this reflects the proportions among popular literature as a whole in the period.

essentials, in the home system. Yet given the continued success of translation and imitation in popular genres, at least up to 1939, such claims ring hollow. Instead, the BK's denial appears unwillingly to admit a weakness in the regulated book market – and a failure to eliminate what another article calls the Germans' "unfortunate attraction to the foreign" (BK1940:162).

Thus, while the comments on translations as threatening or useful participate in the confusion within NS constructions of the foreign, the evidence of translations as filling a lack suggests another problem: despite all the (probably not unsuccessful) attempts to "educate public taste" (Goebbels, *Börsenblatt* 1933/112:335) and disparage imports, the existence and popularity of literature which glorified the foreign confronted the BK with a difficulty which could apparently be resolved only by an uncharacteristically discreet silence.

Conclusion

This has been a small investigation of just one of the many journals, the official voice of just one of the many and mutually suspicious clusters of power within the NS state. But its case seems to confirm that the construction of translation norms can be traced in terms of attitudes towards the alien in general. That the BK's reviews and articles cannot be simply subsumed under one stance does not, I believe, invalidate the approach; on the contrary, the instability and incoherence of the BK's comment on translation echoes that of the surrounding NS ideology of the "alien", suggesting that discourse on translation may indeed act as a focal point of such debates. Within them, the position of the translator as mediator between source and target cultures is highly charged, and the demands made by the ideological and regulatory environment are clamorous: the importer's responsibility is to screen, slant and present the imported elements in such a way as to reduce their danger and provide succour to the regime.

Bibliography

Abbott, C. C. (ed) (1955) *The Letters of Gerard Manley Hopkins to Robert Bridges,* 2nd ed., Oxford: Oxford University Press.

Adams, M. (1968) *Censorship: The Irish Experience,* University, Alabama: University of Alabama Press.

Aigner, Dietrich. (1971) *Die Indizierung 'schädlichen und unerwünschten Schrifttums' im Dritten Reich,* Frankfurt/Main: Buchhändler-Vereinigung GmbH.

Alexandrov, Vladimir E. (ed) (1995) *The Garland Companion to Vladimir Nabokov,* New York: Garland.

Ali, Yusuf (1982) *The Holy Qur'an Translation and Commentary,* Jeddah: Dar Al-kitab.

Aliaga, J. V. and J. M. G. Cortés (1997) *Identidad y diferencia. Sobre la cultura gay en España,* Barcelona: Egales.

Álvarez, R. and M. C.-A. Vidal (1996) 'Translating: A Political Act', in Álvarez and Vidal (eds), 1-9.

Álvarez, R. and M. C.-A. Vidal (eds) (1996) *Translation, Power, Subversion,* Clevedon: Multilingual Matters.

Arndt, Walter (1963) trans. *Eugene Onegin,* New York: Dutton.

Audigier, Gallet (1989) *De l'origine de la beauté suivi de Poèmes et d'Écrits, traduction de Jean-Pierre Audigier et René Gallet,* Seyssel: Comp'act.

Bair, Deirdre (1990) *Samuel Beckett: A Biography,* London: Jonathan Cape.

Baker, Mona (1992) *In Other Words,* London: *Routledge.*

Bandy, W.T. (ed) (1973) Charles Baudelaire, *Edgar Allan Poe, sa vie et ses ouvrages,* Toronto: University of Toronto Press.

Barbian, Jan-Pieta (1995) *Literaturpolitik im 'Dritten Reich'. Institutionen, Kompetenzen, Betätigungsfelder,* Munich: Deutscher Taschenbuch.

Barnstone, W. (1993) *The Poetics of Translation,* New Haven: Yale University Press.

Barrett, Elizabeth (1844) *To George Sand;* trans. A. Pichot as *Traduction Libre in Revue Britannique,* Dec. 1884:717.

Barton Johnson, D. (1985) *Worlds In Regression.* Ann Arbor: Ardis.

Bassnett, Susan (1996) 'The Meek or the Mighty: Reappraising the Role of the Translator', in R. Álvarez and M. C.-A. Vidal (eds) *Translation, Power, Subversion,* Clevedon: Multilingual Matters, 10-24.

Baudelaire, C. (1976) *Sur mes contemporains: Victor Hugo, Œuvres Complètes II,* Paris: Gallimard (article first published in 1861).

Beaton, R. (1994) *An Introduction to Modern Greek Literature,* Oxford: Clarendon Press.

Beaujour, E. (1995) 'Translation and Self-Translation' in V. Alexandrov (ed) *The Garland Companion to Vladimir Nabokov,* New York: Garland, 714-725.

Beckett, Samuel (1929) 'Che Sciagura', *TCD: A College Miscellany* 36:42.

Beckett, Samuel (1976) 'Dante ... Bruno. Vico ... Joyce', in *I can't go on, I'll go on,* New York: Grove Weidenfeld, 105-126.

Bely, Andrei (Boris Bugaev) (1979) *Petersburg* (trans) R. Maguire and J. Malmstad, Bloomington: Indiana University Press.

Benjamin, W. (1972) 'Die Aufgabe des Übersetzers' in T. Rexroth (ed) *Gesammelte*

Schriften, Frankfurt: Suhrkamp, 9-21.

Bergman, D. (ed) (1993) *Camp Grounds,* Amherst, Massachusetts: University of Massachusetts Press.

Berman, Antoine (1984) *L'Épreuve de l'Étranger, Culture et tradition dans l'Allemagne romantique,* Paris: Gallimard.

Boase-Beier, Jean (1987) *Poetic Compounds: The Principles of Poetic Language in Modern English Poetry,* Tübingen: Niemeyer.

Boccaccio, Giovanni (1893) T*he Decameron of Boccaccio,* trans. John Payne, ill. Louis Chalon, 2 vols, London: Lawrence and Bullen.

Bollmus, Reinhard (1970) *Das Amt Rosenberg und seine Gegner. Studien zum Machtkampf im nationalsozialistischen Herrschaftssystem,* Stuttgart: Deutsche Verlagsanstalt.

Börsenblatt für den deutschen Buchhandel (1933), Volume 100, No 112, Leipzig: Börsenverein der Deutschen Buchhändler.

Boswell, J. (1981) *Christianity, Social Tolerance and Homosexuality. Gay People in Western Europe from the Beginning of the Christian Era to the Fourteenth Century,* Chicago: University of Chicago Press.

Boyd, Brian (1990) *Vladimir Nabokov. The Russian Years,* London: Chatto and Windus.

------ (1992) *Vladimir Nabokov. The American Years,* London: Chatto and Windus.

Bray, A. (1982) *Homosexuality in Renaissance England,* London: Gay Men's Press.

Brion, M. (1958) review of Leyris, *Reliquiae,* Seuil, 1958, in *Le Monde* 19 February 1958.

Brower, R. A. (1959) 'Seven Agamemnons' in R.A. Brower (ed), *On Translation,* Cambridge, Mass.: Harvard University Press, 173-195.

Brown, R. (1993) 'Textuality, Social Science and Society' in A. Pertti, (ed) *Tracing the Semiotic Boundaries of Politics,* Berlin: Mouton de Gruyfer.

Bücherkunde. Amtliches Organ der Dienststelle des Beauftragten des Führers für die gesamte geistige und weltanschauliche Erziehung der NSDAP, und der Reichsstelle zur Förderung des deutschen Schrifttums (1934-1944), Volumes 1-11, Bayreuth: Gauverlag Bayerische Ostmark.

Butler, J. (1990) *Gender Trouble,* London: Routledge.

Butt, J. (trans) (1947) *Candide, or Optimism,* West Drayton: Penguin Books.

Castille, H. (1852) 'De la Propriété Intellectuelle', *Revue de Paris,* Part I, December 1852, 71-95, Part II, January 1853, 33-60.

Cattaui, G. (1947) *Trois poètes: Hopkins, Yeats, Eliot,* Paris: Egloff.

Cavafy, K. P. (1984) *Apanta poiimata* 1896-1933 (Complete Poems 1896-1933), Athens: Stroubouki.

Celenio, I. (1798) *Hamlet. Tragedia de Guillermo Shakespeare. Traducida e ilustrada con la vida del autor y notas críticas (Hamlet.* Tragedy by William Shakespeare. Translated and illustrated with the life of the author and critical notes), Madrid: Oficina de Villalpando.

Chateaubriand, F.R. (nd) 'Le Paradis Perdu', in M. Sainte-Beuve (ed) *Oeuvres Complètes,* Vol XI, Paris: Garnier Frères.

Chateaubriand, F.R. de (1990) Introduction to *Paradis Perdu,* Paris: Berlin (first publication 1830).

Cladera, C (1800) *Examen de la tragedia intitulada Hamlet,* (study of the tragedy *Hamlet*), Madrid: Imprenta de la viuda de Ibarra.

Clum, J. M. (1991) *Acting Out,* New York: Columbia University Press.

Conejero, Manuel and Jenaro Talens (1992) 'Introducción', in W. Shakespeare, *Hamlet,* Madrid: Cátedra, 7-64.

Core, P. (1984) *Camp: The Lie That Tells the Truth,* New York. Delilah Books.

Craft, C. (1990) 'Alias Bunbury: Desire and Transgression in *The Importance of Being Earnest', Representations* 31:107-133.

Cronin, Michael (1996) *Translating Ireland: Translation, Languages, Cultures,* Cork: Cork University Press.

Crowley, M. (1968) *The Boys in the Band,* New York: Dramatists' Play Service.

------ (1975) *Los chicos de la banda,* trans Ignacio Artime and Jaime Azpilicueta, Madrid.

Davydov, Sergej (1995) 'Nabokov and Pushkin', in V. Alexandrov (ed) *The Garland Companion to Vladimir Nabokov,* New York: Garland.

Day-Lewis, C. (1970) *On Translating Poetry,* Abingdon-on-Thames: The Abbey Press.

de Grunne, D. (1953) 'Technique du poète: Gerard Manley Hopkins', *Critique* 9: 579-600.

de Jongh, N. (1993) *Not in Front of the Audience,* London: Routledge.

de Magny, O. (1958) 'Gerard Manley Hopkins', *Les lettres nouvelles* 6:248-56.

de Moratín, L. F. (1812) *Comentario a un auto de fe celebrado en la ciudad de Logroño en los días 6 y 7 noviembre de 1610,* (Commentary on an auto-da-fé carried out in the city of Logrono on the 6th and 7th of November 1610), Cádiz, Imprenta Tormentaria.

------ (1867-1868) *Obras póstumas* (Complete works), Madrid: R.A.E., republished by Bruguera, Barcelona, 1984.

------ (1944) 'Discurso preliminar a las comedias', *Obras completas* (Complete works), Madrid: R.A.E., 307-25.

------ (1944) 'Hamlet', *Obras completas* (Complete works), Madrid: R.A.E., 473-554.

------ (1973) *Epistolario* (Letters), edited by René Andioc, Madrid: Castalia.

de Staël, Madame (1838) 'De l'esprit des traductions', in *Œuvres,* tome 3, Paris: Lefèvre (article first published in 1816).

Deacon, Philip (1996) 'La traducción de *Hamlet* de Leandro Fernández de Moratín', in Ángel Luis Pujante and Keith Gregor (eds) *Teatro clásico en traducción. Texto, representación, recepción,* Murcia: Universidad de Murcia, 299-309.

Delabastita, Dirk and Lieven D'hulst (1992) *European Shakespeares,* Amsterdam: John Benjamins.

Deutsch, Babette (1936) (trans) with Avrahm Yarmolinsky (ed) of *Eugene Onegin,* Harmondsworth: Penguin.

Deutche Nationalbibliographie (Series A), Leipzig: Börsenveven Deutscher Buchhändler.

Die Bücherei. Zeitschrift der Reichsstelle für das Volksbüchereiwesen (1939) Volume 6, Leipzig: Einkaufshaus für Büchereien.

Die Werkbücherei. Mitteilungsblatt der Reichsarbeitsgemeinschaft deutscher Werkbüchereien in der Reichsschrifttumskammer (1939, 1940), Berlin.

Dolinin, Alexander (1995) 'Eugene Onegin', in Alexandrov (ed), 117-130.

Dollimore, J. (1991) *Sexual Dissidence,* London: Oxford University Press.

Dürrenmatt, F. (1985) *Der Besuch der alten Dame. Tragische Komödie,* Zürich: Diogenes.

------ (1990) *Poseštenieto na starata dama (The visit of the old lady),* Trans Sophia Totzeva, produced in Dăr žaven Satiričen teatăr, Sofia, director P. Markov.

------ (1990) *The Visit: Plays and Essays* (The German Library 89), Trans Patrick Bowles, New York: Grove Press.

Edelman, L. (1994) *Homographesis. Essays in Gay Literary and Cultural Theory,* London: Routledge.

Effross, S. H. (1965) 'Leandro Fernández de Moratín in England', *Hispania,* 48: 43-50.

Eliot, T. S. (1971) *The Waste Land,* London: Faber & Faber.

Elton, Oliver (trans) (1937) *Evgeny Onegin,* London: Pushkin Press.

Even-Zohar, Itamar (1978) 'The Position of Translated Literature within the Literary Polysystem', in J.S. Holmes, et al. (eds) *Literature and Translation: New Perspectives in Literary Studies* Leuven: Acco, 117-127.

Fairclough, Norman (1989) *Language and Power,* London: Longman.

Farinelli, A. (1924) *Guillaume de Humbolt et l'Espagne: avec une esquisse sur Goethe et l'Espagne,* Turin: Fratelli Bocca.

Fast, Adela Alfonso (1975) 'Two Spanish Translations of Hamlet's Soliloquies', *Shakespeare Translation* 2:74-8.

Faulkner, W. (1930) *As I Lay Dying,* London: Chatto & Windus.

Fitzgerald, E. (nd) *The Rubáiyát of Omar Khayyám,* London: Collins.

Friedberg, M. (1997) *Literary Translation in Russia: A Cultural History,* Pennsylvania: Pennsylvania State University Press.

Gaddis Rose, Marilyn (1997) *Translation and Literary Criticism. Translation as Analysis,* Manchester: St Jerome.

Galanaki, R. (1980) *To keïk* (The Cake), Athens: Kedros.

------ (1983a) 'I diadromi mias apantisis' (The Way towards an Answer), *I Lexi* 23:405-07.

------ (1983b) 'Rethra Roon Pighnisi Reontes: sholia stin tehniki poiisis tis Mantos Aravantinou' (Notes of the Technique of Mantos Aravantinou's Poetry), *O Politis* 64:118-19.

------ (1983c) 'Interviews', *Diavazo* 69:21.

------ (1989) *O vios tou Ismaïl Ferik Pasa* (The Life of Ismaïl Ferik Pasha), Athens: Agra.

------ (1993) *Tha ypografo Loui* (I Shall Sign Louis), Athens: Agra.

------ (1994) *Plin efharis; Ta orykta* (Albeit Pleasing; The Minerals), Athens: Agra.

Gallet, R. (1980) 'Hopkins en France', in L.M. van Noppen (ed) *The Critical Reception of Gerard Manley Hopkins in the Netherlands and Flanders, 1908-1979,* Waterloo, Ontario: International Hopkins Association, 52-68.

------ (1993) 'Hopkins: introductions, traductions, reflets (1889-1989)', in *Traductions passages: le domaine anglais. Essais dédiés à Pierre Leyris,* Tours: Groupes de Recherches Anglo-Americaines de l'Université François Rabelais de Tours, 77-92.

Garvin, P. (ed) (1964) *A Prague School Reader on Esthetics, Literary Structure, and Style,* Washington: Georgetown University Press.

Gautier, T. (1884) *Émaux et camées,* Paris: Charpentier.

Genette, Gérard (1962) *Palimpsestes,* Paris: Editions du Seuil.

------ (1982) *Palimpsestes, la littérature au second degré,* Paris: Seuil.

Gerschenkron, Alexander (1966) 'A Manufactured Monument?', *Modern Philology* 63:336-347.

Gibbs, R. (1994) *The Poetics of Mind: Figurative Thought, Language and Understanding,* Cambridge: Cambridge University Press.

Goddard, B. (1990) 'Theorizing Feminist Theory/Translation', in S. Bassnett and A. Lefevere (eds) *Translation: History and Culture,* London: Frances Pinter.

------ (1991) 'Translating (with) the Speculum', TTR (*Traduction, Terminologie, Rédaction*) 4(2):85-121.

Golding, William (1962) *Lord of the Flies,* London: Faber & Faber.

Goldman, L. (1964) *The Hidden God,* London: Routledge & Kegan Paul.

Grayson, J. (1977) *Nabokov Translated,* Oxford: Oxford University Press.

Gumperz, J. (1982) *Discourse Strategies,* Cambridge: Cambridge University Press.

Halperin, D. M. (1990) *One Hundred Years of Homosexuality and Other Essays on Greek Love,* London: Routledge.

Hewson, Lance (1997) *Redefining Translation,* London: Routledge.

Hodge, R. and G. Kress (1993) *Language as Ideology,* 2nd ed., London: Routledge.

Hofstadter, Douglas (1997) *Le Ton beau de Marot,* New York: Basic Books.

Hölderlin, F. (1998) *Selected Poems and Fragments,* trans. M. Hamburger, Harmondsworth: Penguin.

Holman, Michael (1997) 'The Sanification of Tolstoy's *Resurrection*', in Karl Simms (ed) *Translating Sensitive Texts: Linguistic Aspects,* Amsterdam: Rodopi, 273-81.

Hooker, J. (1983) T.S. *Eliot's Poems in French Translation: Pierre Leyris and Others,* Epping: Bowker.

Hopkins, Gerard Manley (1963) *Poems and Prose,* edited by W. H. Gardner, Harmondsworth: Penguin.

Hudson, M. (1977) *Arab Politics, The Search for Legitimacy,* New York: Vail-Ballou Press.

Hughes, Ted (1983) *River,* London: Faber & Faber.

------ (1997) *Tales from Ovid,* London: Faber & Faber.

Jacquin, Danielle (1994) 'L'un et l'autre: Hopkins en français', *Cahiers Charles V* 17:79-94.

Jakobson, Roman (1959) 'On linguistic aspects of translation', in R. A. Brewer (ed) *On Translation,* Cambridge, Mass.: Harvard University Press, 232-39.

Johnson, R. (1970) 'Moratín's Diary', *Bulletin of Hispanic Studies* 47, 24-36.

Joyce, James (1960) *Ulysses,* Harmondsworth: Penguin.

Karama, A. (1996) *News Discourse, Ideology and the Translator: A Critical Perspective,* unpublished M. A. Dissertation, University of Salford.

Karlinsky, Simon (ed) (1979) *The Nabokov-Wilson Letters 1940-1971,* London: Chatto & Windus.

Katamba, F. (1994) *English Words,* London: Routledge.

Knowlson, J. (1996) *Damned to Fame: The Life of Samuel Beckett,* London: Bloomsbury.

Lefevere, A. (ed) (1992a) *Translation History Culture: A Sourcebook,* London: Routledge.

------ (1992b) *Translation, Rewriting and the Manipulation of Literary Fame,* London: Routledge.

Levin, S. (1971) 'The Analysis of Compression in Poetry', *Foundations of Language* 7:38-55.

------ (1977) *The Semantics of Metaphor,* Baltimore: Johns Hopkins University Press.

Levine, Suzanne Jill (1991) *The Subversive Scribe,* St Paul: Graywolf.

Leyris, Pierre (1948) 'A Propos de G. M. Hopkins', *Esprit et Vie,* October 1948, 548-555.

------ (1980) *Poèmes accompangnés de proses et de dessins: Choix et traduction de Pierre Leyris,* 3me ed., Paris: Seuil.

Liste der für Jugendliche und Büchereien ungeeigneten (1943) For the Reichsministerium für Volksaufklärung und Propaganda, Abteilung Schrifttum, Leipzig: Börsenverein der Deutschen Buchhändler, Schriften Second revised edition.

Littré, Emile (1971) *Dictionnaire de la langue française: édition intégrale du dictionnaire de Littré conçue pas J.-J. Pauvert et réalisée d'après les maquettes de Jacques Darche,* Paris: Gallimard/Hachette.

Lodge, David (1984) *Small World: An Academic Romance,* London: Secker & Warburg.

Longfellow, H.W. (1980) *The Poetical Works,* London: Oxford University Press.

Lonsdale, R. (ed) (1969) *The Poems of Thomas Gray, William Collins, Oliver Goldsmith*, London & New York: Longman.

Magnusson, M. and H. Pálsson (trans) (1960) *Njal's Saga,* Harmondsworth: Penguin.

Maier, Carol (1994) 'Carol Maier Discusses Women in Translation: Current Intersections, Theory and Practice', *Delos*, 5(2):29-39.

Mambrino, J (1958) 'Review of Leyris, *Reliquiae*, Seuil, 1958', *Etudes* 297:136-7.

------ (trans) (1980) *Grandeur de Dieu et autres poèmes 1876-1889* (Gerard Manley Hopkins), Paris: Granit.

Mancini, Guido (1969) *Dos estudios de literatura española* (Two studies of Spanish literature), Barcelona: Planeta.

Marteau, R. (1990) 'G.M. Hopkins, *Henry Purcell*', *Recueil* 15:47-49.

Mastoraki, J. (1972) *Diodia* (Tolls), Athens: Kedros.

McWilliam, G. H. (trans) (1972) *The Decameron,* Harmondsworth: Penguin Books.

Merriman, B. (1949) *Cúirt an Mheadhón Oidhche,* new edition by Risteárd [*sic*] Ó Foghludha, Dublin: Hodges, Figgis & Co.

------ (1971) *Cúirt an Mheadhón Oidhche / The Midnight Court,* text and translation by Patrick C. Power, Cork: Mercier.

Merryman, Bryan [*sic*] (1912) *Cúirt an Mheadhón Oidhche,* Riseárd Ó Foghludha I. Fiachra Éilgeach (ed), with an essay by Piaras Béaslaí, Dublin: Hodges, Figgis.

Meyer, M. (ed) (1994) *The Politics and Poetics of Camp,* London: Routledge.

Meyer, Priscilla (1987) *Find What the Sailor Has Hidden,* Middletown, Conn.: Wesleyan University Press.

Milton, J. (1961) *The Poems*, edited by H. Darbishire, Oxford: Oxford University Press.

Montesinos, José F. (1960) *Introducción a una historia de la novela en España en el siglo XIX* (Introduction to a history of the novel in Spain in the 19th century), Madrid: Castalia.

Mortier, R. (1982) *L'Originalité, une nouvelle catégorie esthétique au siècle des lumières*, Paris: Droz.

Mukařovský, J. (1964) 'Standard Language and Poetic Language', in P. Garvin (ed), 17-30.

Nabokov, D. and M. Bruccoli (eds) (1989) *Selected Letters 1941-1977*, New York: Harcourt Brace Jovanovich.

Nabokov, Vladimir (1941) *The Real Life of Sebastian Knight*, Norfolk, Conn.: New Directions.

------ (1947) *Bend Sinister*, Reprinted 1964, New York: Time.

------ (1955) *Lolita*, New York: McGraw-Hill.

------ (1957) *Pnin*, New York: Doubleday.

------ (1962) *Pale Fire*, New York: Putnam's.

------ (1966) *Despair*, trans. by author, New York: Putnam's.

------ (1966) *Speak Memory: An Autobiography Revisited*, New York: Putnam's.

------ (1969) *Ada or Ardor: A Family Chronicle*, New York: McGraw-Hill.

------ (1970) *Mary*, trans. M. Glenny and V. Nabokov, New York: McGraw-Hill.

------ (1973) *Strong Opinions*, New York: McGraw-Hill.

------ (1981) *Lectures on Russian Literature*, edited by F. Bowers, London: Weidenfeld, Nicholson.

------ (1984) *'Signs and Symbols', in Nabokov's Dozen*, New York: Archer Press.

------ (1986) *The Enchanter*, trans. Dmitri Nabokov, New York: Putnam's.

Nabokov, V. (trans) (1922) *Nikolka Persik* (Colas Breugnon) by Romain Rolland, Berlin: Slovo.

------ (trans) (1923) *Ania v strane chudes* (Alice in Wonderland) by Lewis Carroll, Berlin: Gamayun.

------ (trans) (1947) *Pushkin, Lermontov, Tyutchev*, London: Lindsay Drummond.

------ (trans) (1960) *The Song of Igor's Campaign: an Epic of the Twelfth Century* (anonymous), New York: Vintage.

------ (1964) *Eugene Onegin* by Aleksandr Pushkin, Princeton: Princeton University Press.

Nida, E. and J. de Waard (1986) *From One Language to Another: Functional Equivalence in Bible Tanslating*, New York: Thomas Nelson.

O'Faolain, J. (1970) *Godded and Codded*, London: Faber & Faber.

Ortiz Armengol, Pedro (1985) *El año que vivió Moratín en Inglaterra, 1792-1793* (The year Moratín lived in England, 1792-1793), Madrid: Castalia.

Par, Alfonso (1936) *Representaciones shakespearianas en España*, (Performances of Shakepeare in Spain) vol. I, Madrid: Libería general de Victoriano Suárez.

Perrin, N. (1971) *Dr Bowdler's Legacy: A History of expurgated books in England and America*, New York: Doubleday Anchor (originally published New York, Atheneum 1969).

Pichois, C. (1967) 'Baudelaire ou l'incapacité créatrice' in *Baudelaire, études et témoignages,* Neuchâtel, Le Baconnière, 242-261.

Pinker, S. (1997) *How the Mind Works,* London: TSP.

Pit-Corder, S. (1973) *Introducing Applied Linguistics,* Harmondsworth: Penguin Books (reprinted 1979).

Poe, Edgar Allan, (1951) *Oeuvres en prose d'Edgar Allan Poe,* trans. Charles Baudelaire, Paris: Gallimard.

------ (1989) *The Complete Tales and Poems,* London: Dorset.

Pound, E. (1934) *The ABC of Reading.* Cited in *The Penguin International Thesaurus of Quotations,* ed. Rhoda Thomas Tripp, 521:19.

Regalado Kerson, Pilar (1989a) 'Leandro Fernández de Moratín, primer traductor de Shakespeare al castellano. Antecedentes y preliminares a su versión de *Hamlet'* (Leandro Fernández de Moratín, first translator of Shakespeare into Castilian. Precursors and forerunners to his version of *Hamlet*), *Dieciocho* 12:45-65.

------ (1989b) 'Moratín y Shakespeare: un ilustrado español ante el dramaturgo inglés' (Moratín and Shakespeare: a Spaniard of the Enlightenment confronts an English dramatist), *Actas del IX Congreso de la Asociación Internacional de Hispanistas,* vol II, Frankfurt am Main: Vervuert Verlag, 75-83

Rey, Alain, Marianne Tomi, Tristan Hordé, Chantal Tanet et al (eds) (1993) *Le Robert: Dictionnaire Historique de la langue française,* 2nd ed, Paris & Montreal: Dictionnaires Le Robert.

Ritz, J.-G. (1980) 'Gerard Manley Hopkins, Poèmes 1862-1868, 1876-1889', in *Traduction, introduction et notes par Jean-Georges Ritz,* Paris: Aubier Montaigne.

Robinson, Douglas (1991) *The Translator's Turn,* Baltimore: The John Hopkins University Press.

Robyns, Clem (1994) 'Translation and discursive identity', in *Translation and the (Re)production of Culture,* Leuven: The CERA Chair for Translation, Communication and Cultures, 57-81.

Rodari, G. (1960) *Filastrocche in cielo e in terra,* Turin: Einaudi.

Roditi, E. (1935) 'Poèmes de Gerard Manley Hopkins', *Mesures* 1:91-102.

Rodríguez, Juan Carlos (1991) *Moratín o el arte nuevo de hacer teatro,* Moratín and the new art of creating theatre), Madrid: Cátedra.

Ross, J. (1980) 'Ikonismus in der Phraseologie: Der Ton macht die Bedeutung', *Zeitschrift für Semiotik* 2:39-56.

Ruiz Morcuende, Francisco (1933) 'Prólogo', in L.F. de Moratín (ed) *Teatro,* Madrid: Espasa-Calpe, 7-57.

Salines, E. (1996) 'The Opium Landscape in Translation: Baudelaire's *Un Mangeur d'opium* and De Quincey's Autobiographical Writings', *New Comparison* 21:22-39.

Sand, G. (1856) Preface to *Comme il vous plaira,* Paris: Librairie Nouvelle.

Saussure, F. de (1916) *Cours de linguistique générale,* Paris: Payot.

Scarfe, F. (1986) *Baudelaire, The Complete Verse,* London: Anvil Press.

Schnitzler, A. (1978a) *Anatol,* Stuttgart: Reclam.

------ (1978b) *Reigen,* Frankfurt a. M.: Fischer.

------ (1982a) *Anatol,* trans. Frank Marcus, London: Methuen.

------ (1982b) *La Ronde,* in E. Schwarz (ed) *Arthur Schnitzler, Plays and Stories,* trans Eric Bentley, New York: Continuum, 53-116.

Schulte, R. and J. Biguenet (1992) *Theories of Translation: An Anthology of Essays from Dryden to Derrida,* Chicago: University of Chicago Press.

Sedgwick, E. K. (1991) *Epistemology of the Closet,* Berkeley: University of California Press.

Shakespeare, William (1818) *Hamlet, Prince of Denmark,* in *The Family Shakespeare* by Thomas Bowdler Esq., F.R.S. and S.A. London: reprinted by Longman, Brown, Green and Longmans, 1953.

------ (1948) *Hamlet, Prince of Denmark,* edited by J.J. Hogan, Dublin: Browne & Nolan Limited.

------ (1959a) *King Henry VI Parts 1, 2 and 3,* Cambridge: Cambridge University Press.

------ (1959b) *King Henry VI Part 1,* (trans) Fathi Muhammad, Cairo: Dar El-Ma'arif.

Shorter Oxford English Dictionary (1996) Oxford: Clarendon Press.

Silverman, K. (1983) *The Subject of Semiotics,* New York: Oxford University Press.

Simon, Simon (1996) *Gender in Translation. Cultural Identity and the Politics of Transmission,* London: Routledge.

Simpson, M. (ed) (1997) *Anti-Gay,* London: Cassell.

Sinfield, A. (1994) *The Wilde Century,* London: Cassell.

Sontag, Susan (1983) 'Notes on Camp', in *A Susan Sontag Reader,* Harmondsworth: Penguin.

Steiner, George (1992) *After Babel: Aspects of Language and Translation,* 2nd ed., Oxford: Oxford University Press.

Sternberg, M. (1981) 'Polylingualism as Reality and Translation as Mimesis', *Poetics Today* 2:221-239.

Strothmann, Dietrich (1963) *Nationalsozialistische Literaturpolitik. Ein Beitrag zur Publizistik,* Bonn: H. Bouvier & Co.

Sullivan, A. (1996) *Virtually Normal,* London: Picador.

Swift, G. (1996) *Last Orders,* London: Picador.

Thomas, H. (1958) 'Gerard Manley Hopkins', *Nouvelle Revue Française* 6:122-25.

Tierney, W. (1997) *Academic Outlaws: Queer Theory and Cultural Studies in the Academy,* Thousand Oaks, California: Sage.

TLS (1958) 'Hopkins in French' (Review of Leyris' *Reliquiae*), *The Times Literary Supplement,* April 4, p. 184.

Tolstoy, Leo (1900) *Resurrection,* London: F. R. Henderson.

Totzeva, S. (1995) *Das theatrale Potential des dramatischen Textes. Ein Beitrag zur Theorie von Drama und Dramaübersetzung* (Forum Modernes Theater, Schriftenreihe 19), Tübingen: Narr.

Tourniaire, C. (1996) *'Albeit Pleasing* by Rea Galanaki: A Bilingual Translation into English and French with Commentary', MA Dissertation, University of East Anglia.

Toury, Gideon (1995) *Descriptive Translation Studies and Beyond,* Amsterdam & Philadelphia: John Benjamins.

Valéry, Paul (1957) 'Discours sur l'esthétique', *Oeuvres,* vol I, Paris: Gallimard.

------ (1959) 'Translation from St. John of the Cross', in R. Brower (ed) *On Translation.*

------ (1974) *Cahiers,* II, edited by Judith Robinson, Paris: Gallimard.

Van Dyck, K.R. (1990) *The Poetics of Censorship in Greek Poetry since 1967*, D.Phil. Thesis, Oxford: University of Oxford Press.

------ (1996) *Kassandra and the Censor: Greek Poetry since 1967*, New York: Cornell University Press.

Venuti, Lawrence (ed) (1992) *Rethinking Translation: Discourse, Subjectivity, Ideology*, London: Routledge.

------ (1995) *The Translator's Invisibility: A History of Translation*, London & New York: Routledge.

Verzeichnis englischer und nordamerikanischer Schriftsteller (1942) For the Reichsministerium für Volksaufklärung und Propaganda, Abteilung Schrifttum, Leipzig: Börsenverein der Deutschen Buchhändler.

Villena, L. (1995) *La importancia de llamarse Ernesto (siendo formal y moderadamente ambiguo)*, Madrid: Visor.

Vizinczey, S. (1965) *In Praise of Older Women: The Amorous Recollections of András Vajda*, London: Barrie & Rockcliff.

Voltaire (1942) *Candide*, edited by O.R. Taylor, Oxford: Basil Blackwell.

von Flotow, Luise (1991) 'Feminist Translation: Contexts, Practices and Theories', TTR *(Traduction, Terminologie, Rédaction)* 4(2):69-81.

Vondung, Klaus (1973) *Völkisch-nationale und nationalsozialistische Literaturtheorie*, Munich: List-Verlag.

Wilson, E. (1971) *Upstate*, New York: Farrar, Straus & Giroux.

Wolff, H. (1959) 'Intelligibility and interethnic attitudes', in D. Hymes (ed) *Language in Culture and Society: A Reader in Linguistics and Anthropology*, New York: Harper & Row, 440-449.

Yingling, Thomas E. (1990) *Hart Crane and the Homosexual Text*, New Thresholds, New Anatomies, Chicago: University of Chicago Press.

Zukofsky, C. and L. Zukofsky (trans) (1969) *Catullus*, London: Gape Goliard Press.

Index of Names

Index of Subjects